Seven Myths of the Crusades

Seven Myths of the Crusades

Edited, with an Introduction and Epilogue, by
Alfred J. Andrea and Andrew Holt

Hackett Publishing Company, Inc.
Indianapolis/Cambridge

18 17 16 15   1 2 3 4 5 6 7

For further information, please address
  Hackett Publishing Company, Inc.
  P.O. Box 44937
  Indianapolis, Indiana 46244-0937

  www.hackettpublishing.com

Cover design by Rick Todhunter and Brian Rak
Interior design by Elizabeth L. Wilson
Composition by Aptara, Inc.

Cover image: Westminster Psalter (ca. 1250), British Library Royal MS 2A XXII, fol. 220.

Library of Congress Cataloging-in-Publication Data
Seven myths of the Crusades / edited, with an introduction, by Alfred J. Andrea and
Andrew Holt.
    pages cm. — (Myths of History: A Hackett Series)
    Includes bibliographical references and index.
  ISBN 978-1-62466-403-8 (paper) — ISBN 978-1-62466-404-5 (cloth)
1. Crusades. 2. History—Errors, inventions, etc. 3. Crusades—Public opinion. 4.
Crusades in literature. 5. Crusades in motion pictures. I. Andrea, Alfred J., 1941– II.
Holt, Andrew (Andrew P.)
  D160.S38 2015
  909.07—dc23   2015008080

The paper used in this publication meets the minimum requirements of American
National Standard for Information Sciences—Permanence of Paper for Printed Library
Materials, ANSI Z39.48–1984.

∞

Contents

Dedicated with Love to
Peter Damian Andrea, Kristina Ladas Andrea,
Isabella Penelope Holt, Claire Marie Holt,
and Jack Bernard Holt.

PREFACE

In 2003, Matthew Restall published with Oxford University Press *Seven Myths of the Spanish Conquest,* in which he single-handedly refuted what he perceived to be seven myths, or fictions, regarding the Spanish conquest of the Americas that were generated both by the participants in that conquest and by latter-day historians. His daring critique of some long-held "truths" and his equally audacious positing of counternarratives inspired one of the editors of this book, Andrew Holt, to propose to the other that we engage colleagues in a similar effort to explode (or at least modify) seven popular myths or misconceptions of the crusades. Our choice of seven myths is a homage to Restall's book, but seven chapters also make for a manageable book that will not overwhelm readers.

Despite the seemingly ever-expanding outpouring of first-rate books on the crusades over the past half century, including some fine surveys intended for general audiences, distortions of the crusades seem to be proliferating in all the popular media. These include pseudo-documentaries for TV, big and small budget movies, novels, mainstream news reporting, editorials, political speeches by highly visible and influential politicians, the sermons and writings of radical clerics and zealous laity of all three Abrahamic religions (Judaism, Christianity, and Islam), and textbooks prepared for collegiate and high school students enrolled in Western civilization and world history courses. This has particularly been the case since the events of September 11, 2001, as cultural and political commentators have sought to find historical rationales to explain the supposed clash of civilizations in the modern world. Whatever its impetus, we have chosen to term "mythic history" this outpouring of exaggerations, misperceptions, errors, misrepresentations, and fabrications.

Certainly none of the ten historians involved in producing this book claims to know the full, absolutely true, and immutable history of the crusades. We acknowledge and celebrate the debates that enliven and push forward the frontiers of historical research and understanding. Historians, quite simply, bring to their work different perspectives and questions and quite often arrive at different interpretations as they wrestle with ambiguous and fragmentary evidence. No advancement in our understanding of the past is achieved without a lively exchange of insights. And when the dust has settled, questions and uncertainties almost always remain. In light of that method of inquiry, we fully appreciate the limitations of historical knowledge and, for that matter, the imperfection of all human understanding. Yet good history, carefully arrived at through the winnowing process of research and professional discourse, is so much more than just anyone's opinion of what happened and what it means. In the context of this book, we use the term "myth" to delineate notions and views of the crusades that run counter to the mainstream of today's scholarly interpretation—a general consensus built upon decades of research, reflection, and debate. The crucible of academic discourse is fairly efficient in separating the precious elements of reasonable interpretation from the dross of myth. It is not infallible, however, and insights gained through this process are subject to constant revision and refinement, but it is far more valid than mythic history, which is not based on a critical analysis of the available evidence, has not undergone the process of peer review, and has not been refined through the process of scholarly debate.

Much of mythic history is the product of a society that seeks simple explanations of complex phenomena and comforting certitudes in the face of an uncertain world. The unwillingness or inability to see nuances and ambiguities in the complex patterns of human history leads one to search for clear, irrefutable facts, and those supposed facts are, more often than not, wrong or, at least, so incomplete as to be misleading. Closely allied to this is the assumption that we know much more than we do about the past and that all major issues are settled. Every historian has been told at some point in her or his career, "Well, your job is easy. All you have to do is tell us what happened." Such certainty, which proceeds from a total misunderstanding of the interpretive nature of historical scholarship, inevitably results in poor history. In the case of the crusades, it has led to unreflective acceptance of some bizarre views of the crusades that are accepted as unimpeachable truth simply because they have entered into the canon of popular history and been repeated almost endlessly.

Likewise, the notion that medieval people (or people of any long-past era or alien culture) were "just like us" and acted out of motives very much like our own and within the context of a mindset, worldview, and set of ethical standards that we share has led to some basic misunderstandings of the crusades and the people involved in them. This misguided equivalency has tempted many to offer moral judgments based on a set of assumptions that have little or no historical validity. In the case of the crusades, it has led to a failure to understand medieval Christian and Islamic belief systems on their own terms. It has also resulted in an inability to understand the values and perspectives of medieval authors and the genres in which they were writing. This in turn has led the unwary to read crusade accounts uncritically.

Another erroneous way of viewing the past is to approach it with the idea that history is a straight line without dead ends and side channels, so that there is an inevitable and clear development from some event in the past to a contemporary situation. In the case of the crusades, it has led to an erroneous explanation of the roots of the contemporary anti-Westernism held by some radical Islamic elements.

This little book is an attempt to counter some of the myths engendered by simplistic and, in some cases, perversely distorted narratives that purport to tell, in whole or part, the story of the crusades. Yet, in taking on this task, we proceed with a good deal of humility. The story of the crusades is far from fixed for all time, and it never will be, given the nature of human inquiry. In trying to lay bare and to correct some of the prevailing myths that surround the crusades, we must be aware of the limitations of our evidence, our knowledge, and our perspectives. That reality admitted, we can still say that the historians studying the crusades today are highly trained professionals who go about their craft with great care and are able to build upon the work and insights of numerous predecessors and contemporaries. Moreover, they are now exploring elements of crusade history that were beyond the ken and interests of their nineteenth- and early twentieth-century forebears, who were primarily interested in the crusades as political and military adventures.

This widening of historical horizons has greatly expanded our understanding of the manifold aspects of the crusades. As commendable as this is, it has had one unhappy consequence insofar as it has led to an ever-widening gap between popular images of the crusades and the ways in which professional crusade historians today interpret these holy wars. We hope that this book will contribute toward closing that gulf.

The study of history is a continuous dialogue between the present and the past. When the historian carefully listens to the past, he or she is able to fashion a nuanced, albeit never complete, understanding of that past. When anyone conducts a monologue and is deaf to voices from the past, the result is mythic history, and such history begs for correction.

Let us now proceed to turn monologues into dialogues by looking at the evidence and questioning seven myths of the crusades.

Alfred J. Andrea

Andrew Holt

Introduction

Once More into the Breach: The Continuing War against Crusade Myths

> As compared with many fields of medieval history, the crusades have been overworked. One of the real problems in the historical study of the crusades is the amount of remarkably bad history that they have called forth. The romantic allure of the crusades has always been so great that, with the possible exception of Renaissance Florence, probably no field has been the subject of so much worthless pseudo-historical trash.[1]

Those words, written almost seventy-five years ago by the eminent crusade historian John L. La Monte, were aimed at judgments and views of the crusades presented by historians and non-historian popularizers alike. La Monte did not condemn as "pseudo-historical trash" all histories of the crusades written by earlier generations of historians, although he judged even the best of them to be at most "adequately accurate" in their day and now obsolete because they had been written "at a time when modern historical criteria and technique had not yet been established."[2] At their worst, crusade histories composed in previous eras reflected the perspectives of "medieval piety, Renaissance chivalry, Reformation fanaticism, eighteenth-century skepticism, [and] nineteenth-century romanticism"—ideologies that were not in accord with the spirit of critical scholarship.[3] Added to that were nationalistic sentiments and concerns from which proceeded much that was "pure junk."[4]

In contrast to what he judged to be flawed histories and worse, La Monte offered his readers the vision and promise of an English-language, multi-volume history of the crusades produced by the cooperative efforts of the world's leading historians in the field and reflecting the highest standards of contemporary critical scholarship. This venture, which several American crusade historians had been promoting since the 1920s, finally resulted, almost twenty years after La Monte wrote those words, in the first volume of what would become a six-volume *History of the Crusades*.[5] Despite its

---

1. John L. La Monte, "Some Problems in Crusading Historiography," *Speculum* 15 (1940): 57–75 at 58.

2. Ibid.

3. Ibid., 59.

4. Ibid., 66.

5. Kenneth M. Setton et al., eds., *History of the Crusades*, 2nd. ed., 6 vols. (Madison: U of Wisconsin P, 1969–1989). The series is available at: http://digital.library.wisc.edu/1711.dl/History.HistCrusades (accessed February 20, 2014).

inevitable flaws and the fact that several of its chapters were already behind the curve of crusade scholarship by the time they appeared in print, this multi-authored work is a fitting symbol and product of a dramatic upsurge in crusade research and studies in the years following World War II.

La Monte, however, was wrong when he stated that the crusades were overworked. Scholars in his day could not even dream of some of the questions that their students, their students' students, and all who followed would ask and of the many new areas of crusade research into which they would delve. The development over the past several generations of an international community of crusade historians dedicated to exacting standards of scholarly inquiry and engaged in an ever-expanding vision of what are legitimate and potentially fruitful avenues of inquiry has resulted in highly nuanced interpretations of the crusades based on the unearthing of new evidence and a careful analysis of all available evidence—old and new.[6]

This is not to say that today's crusade historians have achieved a final, absolutely correct and complete understanding of the crusades. Crusade historians, as is true of historians in all other areas of inquiry, disagree among themselves over many points and passionately debate issues.[7] Disagreement and debate are the lifeblood of historical scholarship and a sure sign of its vitality. Differences of interpretation and insight and the academic dialogues engendered by those disagreements are major forces in pushing forward our widening and deepening historical insight. For that reason, the discipline of history does not allow for orthodoxy or conformity to a single-party line. Indeed, crusade historians do not even agree on a single definition of "crusade."

What Were the Crusades?

Crusade historians disagree over the definition of crusade? How can that be? Most of the Western reading public would reply if asked to define the crusades: "They were medieval wars that Christian Europeans waged against Muslims." Islamic extremists would add that they continue today in the assaults of Americans and Zionists on Islam.[8] Crusade historians, however, as is true of all historians, are not content to keep

---

6. An example of this international cooperation and professionalization of crusades studies is the Society for the Study of the Crusades and the Latin East (SSCLE), which was founded in 1980. The SSCLE, which at latest count has 467 members from forty-one nations, sponsors quadrennial international conferences and the journal *Crusades* (2002–). Its web page is at sscle.slu.edu.

7. Christopher Tyerman, *The Debate on the Crusades* (Manchester: Manchester University Press, 2011), presents a comprehensive survey of the history of historians' debates on crusades issues. See also Peter Lock, *The Routledge Companion to the Crusades* (London: Routledge, 2006), "Historiography, or What Historians Have Said about the Crusades," 255–72, and "Brief Biographies of Crusade Historians," 273–86.

8. See Osama bin Laden's 1998 declaration, "World Islamic Front for Jihad against the Jews and Crusaders," which is discussed in Ahmed S. Hashim, "The World according to Usama bin Laden," an

matters simple and unambiguous. Consequently, for the past eighty or so years, they have waged a friendly battle over the definition of a crusade, a definition that depends on one's perception of the origins, participants, and spatial and temporal limits of the crusades.

Because it persisted over a long period, the crusade was an ever-evolving entity. It took on a definitive organizational form, so far as the Roman Church was concerned, only in the pontificate of Innocent III (r. 1198–1216), but even thereafter it continued to evolve in response to circumstances.[9] It is safe to say that the crusades of the thirteenth century differed in degree and kind from the First Crusade (1096–1099), from twelfth-century crusades, and from the fourteenth-century crusades that followed.

From beginning to end, contemporaries had many different terms for this special type of holy war, such as *peregrinatio* (pilgrimage), *passagium generale* (general passage), *iter crucis* (the way of the cross), and *negotium Jhesu Christi* (the business of Jesus Christ). Words that we recognize as the source of "crusade," such as the southern French and Spanish *crozada/cruzada* (taking the cross), only emerged in the early thirteenth century.

The earliest known appearance in an English text of the word "crusade" dates to 1577, and "crusader" only appears in the mid-eighteenth century.[10] Samuel Johnson's *A Dictionary of the English Language* of 1755 listed four variants for "a war carried on against infidels under the banner of the cross": *croisade, croisado, crusade,* and *crusado,* with the French *croisade* Johnson's apparent first choice.[11] Likewise, crusade participants were known variously to their medieval contemporaries as *peregrini* (pilgrims), *Hierosolymitani* (Jerusalemites), *milites Dei* (soldiers of God) and by a wide variety of other appellations. It was not until the late twelfth century that *crucesignati* (persons signed with a cross) and *cruciferi* (bearers of the cross) became common but far from universally applied terms for the men and women who undertook this "affair of the cross" (another term for a crusade).[12]

This multiplicity of terms suggests a level of ambiguity in the medieval West as to what the crusade was, and it likewise suggests a process of evolution. That noted, it is possible to delineate the distinguishing characteristics of the classic crusade as it had

---

article prepared for the U.S. Naval War College at http://www.usnwc.edu/getattachment/4f6818d4-232f-4ce5-a2c0-fb9fe9dd2493/World-According-to-Usama-Bin-Laden,-The---Hashim,- (accessed February 26, 2014).

9. Christopher Tyerman, *The Invention of the Crusades* (Toronto: University of Toronto Press, 1998), argues that the crusade as a recognizable institution of Western Christendom developed over a long period, roughly a century from 1095 to the end of the twelfth century.

10. *Oxford English Dictionary*, 2nd ed., s.v. "crusade" and "crusader."

11. http://johnsonsdictionaryonline.com/?page_id=7070&i=508 (accessed March 3, 2014) and ibid., 513.

12. Tyerman, *Invention*, 49–55, provides an excellent survey of the many terms used for crusade.

developed by the early thirteenth century and as it was understood by the leaders of the Roman Church.

In the eyes of the popes, cardinals, bishops, theologians, canon lawyers, preachers, and polemicists of the thirteenth-century Church, a legitimate crusade was a just and holy war called by the Roman papacy and fought in defense of Christendom against an "unbelieving" aggressor, be that person a Muslim, a heretic, or a pagan.[13] Those who were engaged in this war, as either soldiers or accompanying supporters of the military, had publicly sworn a sacred vow to engage in this enterprise, and failure to fulfill that vow or to be relieved of it for a valid reason would incur eternal damnation in Hell if this grave sin were not absolved by a duly authorized cleric.[14]

This threat of potential sin and punishment was balanced by the assurance that fulfillment of the vow merited a heavenly reward. The duty that crusaders had freely taken upon themselves was an act of penance for their sins, and in recognition of the sacrifices incurred, the papacy bestowed upon them a plenary indulgence, which was full remission of the penance owed the Divine Judge for all sins for which they were contrite and that they had confessed to a priest. In addition, as penitent pilgrims traveling to war for God and the Church and engaged in an act of supreme love,[15] crusaders enjoyed a special status. Their persons, families, and properties were inviolate (at least in theory) and came under the protection of the Church. Payment of their debts was also suspended as long as they were engaged in this "holy undertaking" (another term for a crusade). As a token of their commitment and special status, persons who had vowed to "take up their cross and follow [in the service of] Jesus" (Matthew 16:24–26; Luke 9:23) wore a cross on their outer garments.[16]

There was an inevitable discrepancy between theory and reality and also a discrepancy between what church leaders, theoreticians, and authorized preachers believed

---

13. One dissonant voice among crusade historians regarding the defensive nature of the First Crusade is that of Jay Rubenstein, who wrote in a 2011 blog, "The First Crusade, then, was not about turning back centuries of Muslim expansion. It was about seizing control of sacred landscapes. It was, in modern parlance, 'a war of choice' or 'an act of aggression.'" He further characterizes it as a "war of vengeance." This view can be read in its entirety at http://www.huffingtonpost.com/jay-rubenstein/myths-about-crusade-myths_b_1031722.html (accessed August 12, 2014). Paul Crawford offers a counterview to Rubenstein's position in this book's initial chapter.

14. More detailed definitions of the crusade and the duties and privileges of crusaders can be found in Jonathan Riley-Smith, *What Were the Crusades?* 3rd ed. (San Francisco: Ignatius Press, 2002); Christopher Tyerman, *The Crusades: A Very Short Introduction* (Oxford: Oxford University Press, 2004), especially 12–18; and Lock, *Routledge Companion*, 289–98.

15. Jonathan Riley-Smith, "Crusading as an Act of Love," *History* 65 (1980): 177–92. Without denying the motivational role of love, Susanna Throop offers a view of an equally powerful motive, which to modern sensibilities would seem to be diametrically opposed to love but was not seen as such by medieval Latin Christians: *Crusading as an Act of Vengeance, 1095–1216* (Farnham, UK: Ashgate, 2011). See Brett Edward Whalen's review of Throop's book at http://www.history.ac.uk/reviews/review/1118 (accessed February, 28, 2014).

16. Riley-Smith, *What Were the Crusades?* provides an overview of crusade ideology and institutions.

and taught and how the other orders of society, including the lower clerical ranks, viewed crusading and acted accordingly.[17] We can therefore say, and this is myth buster number one, that medieval Christian Europe did not have an ideologically coherent and consistent view of crusading from start to finish or across all levels of society at any time. The crusade was many things to many different people and, as already noted, it was an entity that was constantly evolving as circumstances changed. These multiple medieval views and realities are reflected today in four different schools of interpretation regarding what exactly crusades were, who participated in them, where and when they were waged and against whom, and when they began and ended.[18]

By way of placing those four schools into context, let us consider the most common of crusade myths. History textbooks of every sort and level as well as popular accounts identify the crusades by number: The First Crusade of 1096–1099 that captured Jerusalem; the ill-fated Second Crusade of 1147–1149 that unsuccessfully attacked Damascus;[19] the Third Crusade of 1188–1192, known as the Crusade of Kings, which pitted Richard the Lionheart against Saladin; the Fourth Crusade of 1202–1204 that captured Constantinople; the Fifth Crusade of 1217–1221 to Damietta that ended in disaster in the Egyptian Delta; and the Sixth Crusade of Emperor Frederick II, 1227–1229, but many do not accord this expedition its own number because they see it as an extension of the Fifth Crusade[20] or because they do not consider it a crusade given that Frederick had been excommunicated by the pope before embarking on it (horrors!) and (double horrors!) he negotiated the peaceful return of Jerusalem to Christian hands; the Seventh (or Sixth) Crusade of Louis IX of France, 1248–1254, which also experienced a disaster in the Nile Delta;[21] the Eighth (or Seventh) Crusade of Louis IX and Prince Edward of England, 1270–1272, on which

17. Norman Housley, *Contesting the Crusades* (London: Blackwell Publishing, 2006), 75–98, devotes a chapter to "The Intentions and Motivations of Crusaders."

18. The four categories that are enumerated and explained below were initially articulated by Giles Constable, "The Historiography of the Crusades," in *The Crusades from the Perspective of Byzantium and the Muslim World*, ed. Angeliki E. Laiou and Roy Parviz Mottahedeh (Washington, D.C.: Dumbarton Oaks Research Library and Collection, 2001), 12–15. A revised and expanded version of that essay appears in Giles Constable, *Crusaders and Crusading in the Twelfth Century* (Burlington, VT: Ashgate, 2008), 18–22. Housley, *Contesting*, 1–23, covers these schools in depth in the chapter "Defining the Crusade." Riley-Smith, *What Were the Crusades?*, 101–102, lists leading proponents of each school and their most significant works.

19. Giles Constable, "The Second Crusade as Seen by Contemporaries," in *Crusaders*, 229–300, has shown that contemporaries did not see this crusade as the single-theater disaster that textbook authors usually claim it to have been.

20. James M. Powell, *Anatomy of a Crusade, 1213–1221* (Philadelphia: University of Pennsylvania Press, 1986), 200, notes that the "Fifth Crusade actually ended in Jerusalem [in 1229]" although "tradition has maintained the separate character of these two crusades."

21. Peter Jackson, ed. and trans., *The Seventh Crusade, 1244–1254: Sources and Documents* (Aldershot, UK: Ashgate, 2007), counts Louis IX's initial crusade as the seventh.

one king (Louis) died and another (Edward) became king without knowing it until he returned to Europe.

So we have eight or seven or maybe nine crusades because King Louis and Prince Edward proceeded by separate routes to two different regions, respectively, Tunis and Syria-Palestine.[22] Right? Wrong! Medieval crusaders did not say, "Okay, let's join the Fifth Crusade." Twelfth- and thirteenth-century Europeans did not assign numbers to crusades.[23] In fact, because the crusade was such a personal experience and because crusaders were constantly coming and going to various frontiers and theaters in small and large groups throughout the Age of the Crusades (however long that was), we can say with only a bit of exaggeration that there were thousands, maybe tens of thousands of crusades.

But it is silly to say that. So maybe these numbers, which historians have affixed to certain crusades since at least the sixteenth century,[24] indicate the major crusades with the largest armies. Even that criterion does not hold up under examination. The Crusade of Pope Calixtus II of 1122–1126 was fought on two fronts by large armies and navies and with some success. Likewise, the Crusade of 1239–1241, termed the Barons' Crusade, was waged on two fronts with sizeable forces.[25] This list could be substantially expanded, but the point has been made. However, the numbers have been fixed (more or less) to a handful of major crusades by tradition, and they will stay stuck on, probably forever—at least for the first four so-numbered crusades.[26] As for the rest, we should not lose any sleep, our minds, or ourselves in what is largely a quibble proceeding from an over-scrupulous desire to count and categorize.

Beyond not agreeing on their numbering (or whether they should be numbered at all), modern historians of the crusades also disagree on what constituted a "true crusade." Currently there are four major schools of opinion on the issue, but we should take to heart Norman Housley's double warning to anyone who would draw

---

22. As Giles Constable, "Historiography," [2001], 16–17; [2008], 24, points out, the numbering of the crusades to Jerusalem that stretched from the late eleventh to the late thirteenth century is far more complex, problematic, and confused than suggested here. See also his "The Numbering of the Crusades," *Crusaders*, 353–56.

23. The sole exception was Odericus Vitalis, a twelfth-century writer, who referred to the crusade of 1107 (not one of the crusades that today receives a number) as "the third expedition of Westerners to Jerusalem." Cited by Constable, "Numbering," 354.

24. In the 1560s, Etienne Pasquier counted six crusades, possibly mirroring an established tradition, and in 1709 Georg Christoph Müller counted five (1096, 1147, 1190, 1217–1229, and 1248) but acknowledged that others counted eight crusades. Tyerman, *Debate*, 47–48 and *Invention*, 111.

25. Michael Lower, *The Barons' Crusade: A Call to Arms and Its Consequences* (Philadelphia: University of Pennsylvania Press, 2005).

26. Even this enumeration did not receive near universal acceptance before the twentieth century. In the mid nineteenth century, Charles Mackay, who figures prominently in James Muldoon's chapter, counted the German Crusade of 1197-1198 as the Fourth Crusade and applied the number five to the crusade of 1202–1204: http://www.econlib.org/library/Mackay/macEx9.html#Ch.9, The Crusades (accessed March 10, 2014).

strict boundaries around these categories: "The very nature of crusading means that any definition is fragile" and "historians are usually far too individual to be readily sorted into schools of thought."[27] This is good advice, the wisdom of which was brought home to the ten historians associated with this little book when we decided, for reasons of transparency, to identify for our readers the school with which each of us most closely identifies. As you can see in note 32, it is not that simple. But first, let us identify those four schools.

One group, known as the Traditionalists or the Minimalists, limits the Age of the Crusades to the period 1096–1291—from the start of the First Crusade to the fall of Acre, the last significant outpost of crusader Europe on the continental shores of the Middle East—and further limits crusades to those that were aimed, in one way or another, at recovering or defending Jerusalem from the armies of Islam. For them, without Jerusalem and without an Islamic enemy there was no crusade. Although they might quibble about the number of major crusades that occurred during those two centuries, they agree with the overall picture of a fairly small number of major crusades waged over the period of just under two hundred years.[28]

A second school, termed the Pluralists, argues that limiting the crusades to those holy wars directed solely or mainly at Jerusalem and restricting our study of crusading to just two centuries of holy warfare against a single foe is plain wrong and is based on a misunderstanding of the ways crusading evolved over many centuries, was manifested in many theaters of operation, and was directed against many perceived enemies of Christendom—not just Muslims. The Pluralist School, which today is the most widely accepted of the four schools, defines a crusade as any holy war against enemies of the Faith that was authorized by the pope. As such, crusading had many theaters: North Africa, Spain, southern France and Italy, the Baltic region, Central and Eastern Europe, the Balkans, and the Mediterranean and Aegean seas, as well as the Middle East. And crusades were launched against multiple enemies: pagans, heretics, schismatic Christians, and political opponents of the Roman papacy as well as Muslims. Moreover, crusading extended at least to the end of the seventeenth century and possibly into the eighteenth century.[29]

---

27. Housley, *Contesting*, 2.

28. The leading exponent of this position has been Hans Eberhard Mayer, *The Crusades*, 2nd English ed., trans. John Gillingham (Oxford: Oxford University Press, 1988).

29. Riley-Smith, *What Were the Crusades?*, 89, maintains that these later crusades might have even extended into the eighteenth century but admits that more research is needed on this issue. On pages 91–100, he provides a chronological list of all wars that he considers to have been crusades. A slightly modified and expanded version of that chronology appears in his *The Crusades, A History*, 3rd ed. (London: Bloomsbury, 2014), 369–76, in which he lists a crusading venture as late as 1890–1892 (described in some detail on pages 336–40). Riley-Smith and his former student Norman Housley are two of the leading proponents of Pluralism. Other leading exponents of this school are John France, Peter Lock, Helen Nicholson, Thomas F. Madden, Alan V. Murray, and Christopher Tyerman.

A third school of interpretation is known as the Popularists or the Internalists. The Popularists essentially see crusading as a mass, enthusiastic movement driven by apocalyptic hopes and fears. It was essentially a collective act by the *populares* (the lower orders of society), the *humiles* (the lowly), and the *pauperes* (the poor/the weak)—the true inheritors of the Kingdom of God and those who would cleanse Christendom and the world. For the Popularists, who emphasize the "inner spirit" of the crusaders, the First Crusade was a true crusade, but thereafter the institutional Church and secular authorities largely tamed and transformed the crusade as they institutionalized it. On occasion, however, this eschatological vision reemerged as a driving force in such movements of religious fervor as the Children's Crusade of 1212, which is the subject of one of this book's chapters; various attacks on Jewish communities that accompanied or preceded a significant number of crusades (and the subject of another chapter in this book); the Ribauds of the Albigensian Crusade (1209–1229); and the Shepherds' Crusades of 1251 and 1320.[30]

Whereas the Popularist School is the most restrictive in its vision of crusading, the fourth school, termed the Generalists, is the most expansive. Generalists broadly define crusading as holy war whose combatants believe they are fighting on the direct authority of God (and not necessarily the pope) in either defense of the Faith or to expand its reach. In this view of the crusades, a crusader earns heavenly merit by engaging as God's agent in such a war. Carried to its logical conclusion, the holy war launched by Urban II in 1095 was not the first crusade nor were the many clashes between Christians and Muslims and Christians and pagans prior to 1095/1096 proto-crusades or preliminaries to the crusades. They were crusades. Moreover, rather than being waged on three continents, as the Pluralists contend, crusades were fought not only in Asia, Africa, and Europe but also in the Americas by the conquistadors of the sixteenth and seventeenth centuries.[31]

---

30. Gary Dickson's studies of medieval religious enthusiasm have undergirded the Popularist School: *Religious Enthusiasm in the Medieval West: Revivals, Crusades, Saints* (Aldershot, UK: Ashgate Variorum, 2000); *The Children's Crusade: Medieval History, Modern Mythistory* (New York: Palgrave Macmillan, 2008). See also his articles "Shepherds' Crusade, First (1251)" and "Shepherds' Crusade, Second (1320)" in Murray, *Encyclopedia*, 4:1093–95. The work of Jay Rubenstein has also contributed to the Popularist School: *Armies of Heaven: The First Crusade and the Quest for Apocalypse* (New York: Basic Books, 2011). Malcolm Barber, *Crusaders and Heretics, 12th–14th Centuries* (Aldershot, UK: Variorum, 1995) should also be consulted for the Shepherds' Crusades. On the Ribauds, see A. J. Andrea, *Encyclopedia of the Crusades* (Westport, CT: Greenwood Press, 2003), 265.

31. The modern progenitor of this school might be said to be Carl Erdmann, *The Origins of the Idea of Crusading*, trans. M. W. Baldwin and W. Goffart (1935; Princeton, NJ: Princeton University Press, 1977). James A. Brundage, "Holy War and the Medieval Lawyers," in *The Holy War*, ed. Thomas Patrick Murphy (Columbus, OH: Ohio State University Press, 1976), 99–140, at 124–25, notes that the crusade expanded as time went on to include holy war against all enemies of Christendom and as a model for the expansion of European Christendom. Paul E. Chevedden is a strong voice for the position that the crusades preceded Urban II's call for holy war at Clermont in 1095. See his "The Islamic View and the Christian View of the Crusades: A New Synthesis," *History* 93

These definitions drawn by the four schools of crusade studies are not empty theories or exercises in semantic hairsplitting. Rather, they go to the heart of what a crusade was or was not, and they also fuel continued research and dialogue in what is today one of the most dynamic areas of medieval historical scholarship. Regardless of which school a crusade historian belongs to (and many find themselves sympathetic to several of them),[32] all are united in the battle to correct the oversimplifications, misstatements, errors, and downright bizarre theories and beliefs that pervade popular perceptions and depictions of the crusades. For lack of a better term, crusade historians refer to these inaccuracies as "crusade myths."

Crusade Myths: Defenders and Opponents

Myths surrounding today's views of the crusades come in many different forms and hues, as the seven chapters of this book illustrate. Probably the most pervasive of all is the Grand Myth that the crusades were an assault on a peaceful, sophisticated, cosmopolitan, and tolerant Eastern world by fanatical barbarians from the West who managed to deal a mortal blow to Byzantine civilization and taught the Islamic world to fight savage assailants in a like manner—giving no quarter. In the end, the crusades produced nothing but failure and hate.

The Counter Grand Myth is that the crusades were noble and righteous ventures fought by heroic and selfless Latin Christians against a rising tide of Eastern aggression and the threat of submersion by Islamic forces. Rather than being failures, they prepared the way for modernity and the triumph of the Christian West. This latter notion of the crusaders' inherent nobility and lack of self-interest was inspiration for the transformation of the word "crusade" into a generic term that today is used

---

(2008): 181–200 and "The View of the Crusades from Rome and Damascus: The Geo-Strategic and Historical Perspectives of Pope Urban II and ʿAlī ibn Ṭāhir al-Sulamī," *Oriens* 39 (2011): 257–329. Regarding the transfer of a crusading ethos to the Americas, see Max Harris, *Aztecs, Moors, and Christians: Festivals of Reconquest in Mexico and Spain* (Austin: University of Texas Press, 2000).

32. When the authors of this book were polled as to where they stood, their responses were revealing. Andrea identifies himself as a Pluralist with strong Generalist leanings, who also acknowledges that Jerusalem was the ultimate crusade goal. Crawford identifies himself as "a Pluralist who thinks the crusades to the Holy Land held a higher place in people's 'hierarchy of importance' than did other crusades (which were, nonetheless, crusades)." Franke and Hammad define their position as Pluralists with Generalist leanings, whereas Holt, Muldoon, and Peters see themselves as Pluralists with Traditionalist leanings, and Holt especially likes the way that Crawford and other Pluralists stress the primacy of Jerusalem. Sheffler is a Pluralist with some Generalist tendencies, and Stuckey notes, "Put me down as a Pluralist." The editors deviated from a strict alphabetic sequence in listing these positions because Slack's insightful comments deserve lengthy quotation and should be the last word: "Well, I think this debate is a bit silly, which I guess puts me in the Pluralist camp. I read with great attention Norman Housley's *Contesting the Crusades* [in which he warned of the pitfalls of such categories (see above at note 27)]."

to designate any idealistic enterprise that aims to achieve a social good. [33] It is also employed as a metaphor for a struggle against evil, and it was in this sense that General Dwight D. Eisenhower assured the soldiers, sailors, and airmen on the eve of D-Day in 1944 that they were "about to embark upon a great crusade."[34]

The Grand Myth of crusader barbarism, fanatical superstition, and total failure was politically correct long before "PC" became part of our vernacular vocabulary. Some eighteenth-century writers such as Voltaire, David Hume, and Edward Gibbon, drawing upon the anti-Catholicism of earlier Protestant critics of the crusades and the skepticism of some seventeenth-century commentators as well as upon the secularism and perceived rule of reason of their own age of "enlightenment," saw the crusades as, in Hume's words, "the most durable folly that has yet appeared in any age or nation."[35] For Edward Gibbon (1737–1794), "the principle of the crusades was a savage fanaticism" and "the final progress of idolatry flowed from the baleful fountain of the holy war." Indeed, "the lives and labors of millions which were buried in the East would have been more profitably employed in the improvement of their native country."[36]

Beginning in the sixteenth century, but picking up momentum in the seventeenth century and growing stronger in the course of the following two centuries, a counter myth took shape from the convergence of three elements: a Catholic reaction to both Protestant polemics and extreme secularism; French nationalism that gloried in its crusader past and perceived the crusades as a prelude to its colonial efforts in North Africa and the Middle East; and Romanticism. François-René de Chateaubriand (1768–1848), the literary father of Romanticism, depicted the crusades as a war against "a system of ignorance, despotism, and slavery." This war, defensive in nature, saved the world from "an invasion of new barbarism." What is more, the crusades presaged the future and necessary conquest of these decadent Muslim states by the West.[37]

The six-volume *Histoire des croisades* (History of the Crusades) of Joseph François Michaud (1767–1839)—which was published in its final form in 1841 and was, by the end of the century, translated into four European languages, including English—had

---

33. Elizabeth Siberry, *The New Crusaders: Images of the Crusades in the Nineteenth and Early Twentieth Centuries* (Aldershot, UK: Ashgate, 2000), 104–11, outlines the use of crusade imagery and language for religious and social reform campaigns in nineteenth- and early twentieth-century Great Britain.

34. For the text of his message, see http://www.kansasheritage.org/abilene/ikespeech.html (accessed March 26, 2015). See also his war memoirs, *Crusade in Europe* (Garden City, NY: Doubleday, 1948). For further treatment of this use of "crusade," see the chapter by Mona Hammad and Edward Peters, "Islam and the Crusades: A Nine-Hundred-Year-Long Grievance?" especially note 9.

35. Cited by Tyerman, *Debate*, 81.

36. Edward Gibbon, *The History of the Decline and Fall of the Roman Empire*, 6 vols. (New York: The Nottingham Society, n.d.), 6:228–30, passim.

37. Tyerman, *Debate*, 102–3. Throughout his book, Tyerman deals with the origins and manifestations of these two Grand Myths in far greater detail and with far more nuance than is possible here. Our debt to him is considerable.

an even more profound impact on the popular vision of the crusades than did Chateaubriand's writings. A royalist and journalist, and by no means a serious scholar, Michaud saw the crusades as a necessary step in the march toward civilization, as the crusaders battled a stagnant and barbaric Islam. And in that battle, the French had assumed the leading role from beginning to end. Like Chateaubriand, he viewed the crusades as a prelude to his own day—a day that witnessed the French invasion of Algeria and the beginning of a long and bloody war of conquest (1830–1847).[38] The brilliant engraved images by Gustave Doré that illustrated the 1871 edition of Michaud's popular history underscored the presumed heroism, nobility, and piety of the crusaders and the perfidy of the Muslims and fixed in French eyes the story told by Michaud.[39]

Gustave Doré, *King Louis IX in Captivity in Egypt.* The artist favorably compares the saintly Louis IX, stolidly enduring the taunts of his Egyptian Mamluk captors, with Jesus, crowned with thorns and being mocked by his captors. Photo source: Wikimedia.

Michaud's narrative had far less impact on the English-speaking world for several reasons. Michaud largely played to French cultural and national pride, which found little sympathy among Anglophones for whom Francophobia, or at least a distrust of things French, has long been a predilection. Moreover, England produced its own widely popular narratives of the crusades. In addition to the sonorous eighteenth-century voice of Edward Gibbon, which mesmerizes with its rhetoric and amuses with its irony, there was the romantic nineteenth-century storytelling of Sir Walter Scott (1771–1832), which gained an international readership.

Scott was an innovator of the historical novel, several of which centered on crusade themes. Noted for his religious and cultural tolerance, Scott had no stomach for what he perceived was the fanaticism of the crusades and the greed and hubris of so many crusaders.[40] His novel of 1825, *The Talisman*, portrayed many of the leaders of the Third Crusade as scheming, dishonest, and profligate and held up Saladin

---

38. Ibid., 105–16.

39. These engravings have been reproduced in *Doré's Illustrations of the Crusades* (Mineola, NY: Dover Publications, 1997).

40. See the excellent study of Scott in Siberry, *New Crusaders*, chapter 7, "Scott and the crusades," 112–30.

as a paragon of knightly chivalry, decency, generosity, and prudence. Indeed, Scott favorably contrasted Saladin with King Richard the Lionheart, whose courage he recognized but whom he faulted for cruelty and a propensity for violence. If there is a single hero of the novel, it is Saladin. *The Talisman* was avidly read in its original English and in numerous translations across the world, and it was adapted for a variety of musical and dramatic performances from grand opera to comedy. As a result, this single novel was a major factor in creating the popular view of Saladin in the West that has persisted down to today, as exemplified by the 2005 film *The Kingdom of Heaven*.[41]

English Romanticism cut both ways, as does almost every literary and artistic movement, and English children, too young to read Walter Scott, were regaled with a number of edifying books on the crusades, such as Barbara Hutton's *Heroes of the Crusades* and Henry Firth's *In the Brave Days of Old: The Story of the Crusades*. As the titles indicate, they and similar rip-roaring children's books presented the crusades as heroic adventures and the crusaders as exemplars of muscular Christianity. Naturally, the Third Crusade, in which the English and their king figured so prominently, was the single most popular setting for these books, although they did range over the entire two centuries of crusading in the Holy Land. As with Scott and so many other popular writers of the nineteenth and early twentieth centuries, the authors of these romanticized books for youths generally presented Saladin in a highly favorable light.[42]

Images of the crusades by authors expounding one or the other of these two Grand Myths have proved to be powerful rhetorical weapons in the hands of polemicists.[43] In the mid-twentieth century, Sir Steven Runciman, who described himself as "not a historian, but a writer of literature,"[44] composed a three-volume history of the crusades, which has had a profound impact on popular perceptions of crusading.[45] In the words of one

41. Ridley Scott's film has been universally pointed to by crusade historians as cinematographically interesting but anachronistic in spirit and often erroneous in detail. Tyerman, *Debate*, 235, characterizes this movie as containing "fundamental, meretricious historical errors." Whatever its failings and virtues, it presents Saladin in a highly favorable light. Among the many reviews of the film, see http://3brothersfilm.com/2012/02/medieval-as-modern-the-historical-accuracy-of-kingdom-of-heaven/ (accessed March 4, 2014). See also Charlotte Edwardes' 2004 article in *The Telegraph*, "Ridley Scott's New Crusades Film 'Panders to Osama bin Laden,'" in which she quotes several British experts on the crusades who savage the film. At http://www.telegraph.co.uk/news/worldnews/northamerica/usa/1452000/Ridley-Scotts-new-Crusades-film-panders-to-Osama-bin-Laden.html (accessed March 11, 2014).

42. Siberry, *New Crusaders*, 150–60.

43. On this point, see Jonathan Riley-Smith, *The Crusades, Christianity, and Islam* (New York: Columbia University Press, 2008).

44. Cited by Jonathan Riley-Smith recollecting an on-camera interview he had with Steven Runciman shortly before Runciman's death: Jonathan Riley-Smith, review of *The First Crusade*, by Steven Runciman, *Crusades* 6 (2007): 217.

45. Steven Runciman, *A History of the Crusades*, 3 vols. (Cambridge: Cambridge University Press, 1951–1954).

crusade historian, Sir Steven crafted a work that "across the Anglophone world . . . continues as a base reference for popular attitudes, evident in print, film, television and on the internet."[46] This is not an exaggeration. *The Kingdom of Heaven* mentioned above might well be termed Runciman-lite, as is Terry Jones' four-part series *The Crusades*, which we will look at shortly. The popularity and wide acclaim in non-professional circles for Runciman's history of the crusades is as deep and loud today as it was sixty years ago.

A brief survey of the more than sixty reviews by readers of this work on Amazon.com reveals the three-volume set and each of the individual books equally receiving four and a half stars out of five. A sample of the reviews of just volume I, *The First Crusade and the Foundation of the Kingdom of Jerusalem*, yields statements such as "the book of requirement for anyone with serious devotion to study it [The First Crusade]," "widely recognized as one of the greatest works of history written in the English language in the twentieth century," and "Runciman was a genius."[47] Comments of a similar tone abound. Moreover, many of today's older generation of crusade historians, who came of age in the 1950s, 1960s, and 1970s, admit to having thrilled to Runciman's history of the crusades, for he was a brilliant storyteller and a master prose stylist, and being initially drawn to crusade history by this work. Yet, for all of this feeling of filial piety toward Runciman that so many of us share, crusade historians are today, and have been for several generations, agreed that *A History of the Crusades* is "a polemic masquerading as epic"[48] and a morality play pretending to be serious history.

Runciman's sympathies lay with the Byzantine Empire, and he viewed the crusaders as intolerant barbarians who destroyed the foundations of this ancient and brilliant civilization, thereby making it mortally vulnerable to the Ottoman Turks who eventually conquered Constantinople and the last remnants of Byzantium in 1453. Runciman is eminently quotable, and two of his statements, which every crusade historian knows by heart, deserve quotation, for combined they sum up the essence of his work. In his chapter on the Fourth Crusade, which captured and sacked Constantinople in April 1204, thereby establishing the Latin Empire of Constantinople (1204–1261), Runciman exclaimed:

> There was never a greater crime against humanity than the Fourth Crusade. Not only did it cause the destruction or dispersal of all the treasures of the past that Byzantium had devotedly stored, and the mortal wounding of a civilization that was still active and great; but it was also an act of gigantic political folly.[49]

---

46. Tyerman, *Debate*, 192.

47. http://www.amazon.com/History-Crusades-Vol-Foundations-Jerusalem/product-reviews/ 052134770X/ref=sr_1_1_cm_cr_acr_img?ie=UTF8&showViewpoints=1 (accessed March 4, 2014).

48. Tyerman, *Debate*, 192.

49. Runciman, *Crusades*, 3:130.

As many commentators have noted, these words were published less than a decade after the Second World War had ended and the world had learned in brutal detail of the Holocaust. Never a greater crime against humanity? As terrible as it was, the capture and sack of Constantinople does not make the top twenty list of all-time crimes against humanity. But judicious analysis and nuance were not Runciman's strong suits. In like manner, he ended his work with the following pronouncement from on high:

> The triumphs of the Crusades were the triumphs of faith. But faith without wisdom is a dangerous thing. By the inexorable laws of history the whole world pays for the crimes and follies of each of its citizens. In the long sequence of interaction and fusion between Orient and Occident out of which our civilization has grown, the Crusades were a tragic and destructive episode. . . . There was so much courage and so little honour, so much devotion and so little understanding. High ideals were besmirched by cruelty and greed, enterprise and endurance by a blind and narrow self-righteousness; and the Holy War itself was nothing more than a long act of intolerance in the name of God, which is the sin against the Holy Ghost.[50]

Such stirring sentences are as immortal as any can be. Runciman was channeling the ghost of Gibbon, and like Gibbon he will be read for centuries after his death and long after his detractors—we evidence-obsessed, footnote-addicted historians—have been forgotten. But his vision of the crusades was mythic, as was the case with his most well-known British acolyte, Terry Jones.

Terry Jones, a former member of Monty Python, a British troupe of surreal and outrageously funny comic actors that was popular in the 1970s and early 1980s, co-wrote, narrated, and acted in a four-part video series titled *The Crusades* that appeared in 1995 on BBC and was later picked up in the United States by the History Channel. Jones read medieval English literature and history at Oxford, achieving upper second class honours. His continuing interest in these two areas of medieval studies resulted in his eventual publication of a book on Chaucer's Knight that calls into question, and somewhat reasonably so, the general view of a worthy man who "loved chivalrie, trouthe, and honour, fredom and curteisie."[51] His venture into crusade history was far less sure-footed and, at least in an academic sense, unsuccessful. Unfortunately, it has been responsible for disseminating quite a bit of misinformation and myth to millions of viewers.

---

50. Ibid., 480.

51. From the description of the "Knyght" in the General Prologue of *The Canterbury Tales*. Terry Jones, *Chaucer's Knight: The Portrait of a Medieval Mercenary* (Baton Rouge: Louisiana State University Press, 1980). John H. Pratt, "Was Chaucer's Knight Really a Mercenary?" *The Chaucer Review* 22 (1987): 8–27, offers a corrective to Jones's overstated thesis.

The tone and enduring theme of the series is set dramatically in the opening scene of "Pilgrims in Arms," the first of the four parts of this supposed documentary. Funereal music plays, the ruins of a hilltop castle appear amid a desolate landscape, and flames begin to engulf it. Jones, speaking off camera, says, "Three hundred miles north of Jerusalem, the pilgrim road runs through Ma`arrat an-Nu'man. In midwinter of the year 1098, this small town was invaded by cannibals, men who had marched two thousand miles to do good in the name of Christ." Then a solitary Norman warrior appears, standing stock-still and holding a white banner on which is emblazoned a red cross. A voice-over, quoting the twelfth-century Norman chronicler Ralph of Caen, intones, "Our troops boiled pagan adults in cooking pots; they impaled children on spits and devoured them grilled." Jones continues: "This was the First Crusade."[52]

European and Muslim chronicles leave no doubt that horrific acts of cannibalism took place at Ma`arrat an-Nu'man, although there is some ambiguity as to their extent and nature, but clearly impoverished and desperately hungry crusaders did eat human flesh there and earlier at Antioch.[53] Clearly also, the two key Western sources reporting this cannibalism showed revulsion for it and indicated that the crusaders had stepped over a line.[54] Given the reality of the incident, Jones had every right to begin the series in this manner. Artistically it is brilliant, and so far as history is concerned, he provides an important detail often left out or treated cursorily by modern crusade historians.[55] Only one modern crusade historian, Jay Rubenstein, has made much of this incident.[56] Where Jones goes wrong, at least in our eyes, is when he asks the question "What made the crusaders into monsters?"

He answers that question almost immediately by stating that they came from a society totally based on fighting and continues throughout his video "documentary" to characterize crusaders as brutes and barbarians, who, "if safety pins had been invented [then] . . . would have worn them through their noses." These "barbarous warlords [who] emerged from the German forests" stand in stark contrast to the urbane,

---

52. http://www.dailymotion.com/video/x1kntw5_crusades-1-pilgrims-in-arms_shortfilms (accessed April 3, 2015).

53. Andrea, *Encyclopedia*, "Cannibalism," 51–52.

54. Thomas Asbridge, *The First Crusade, A New History* (Oxford: Oxford University Press, 2001), 274.

55. For example, the best and most detailed history to date of the First Crusade fails to mention cannibalism at either Ma`arrat an-Nu`man or (earlier) at Antioch. John France, *Victory in the East: A Military History of the First Crusade* (Cambridge: Cambridge University Press, 1994). France does later mention in passing and without context the cannibalism of the Tafurs (a band of Flemish and northern French infantry from the lowest classes), whose eating of human flesh repelled friend and foe alike, 287. Peter Frankopan, *The First Crusade: The Call from the East* (Cambridge, MA: Belknap, 2012), 172, mentions but does not focus on this cannibalism.

56. Jay Rubenstein, "Cannibals and Crusaders," *French Historical Studies* 31 (2008): 525–52, and *Armies of Heaven*, 240–41, interprets the cannibalism as both effective psychological warfare and an act consonant with the apocalyptic frenzy of the crusaders.

tolerant, and far less militant Byzantines and Muslims. As for the pope, Urban II was nothing more than an ambitious politician who used Emperor Alexius I's request for military help in stopping the Turkish advance as an excuse to conquer the East. The characterizations of crusader perfidy and brutality are piled one on top of the other. Throughout the four segments Jones introduces occasional "talking heads." Some are eminent crusade historians, such as Jonathan Riley-Smith, John France, Benjamin Kedar, and Norman Housley, whose words, as several of them subsequently lamented privately and publicly, were carefully edited into the program to make them appear in total agreement with Jones' pronouncements.

Several others are not crusade scholars. One member of this latter group, Karen Armstrong, whose foray into crusade history writing was less than well received by experts in the field,[57] overstates her case. Speaking of the very real anti-Judaism that was an integral part of the cultural fabric of Christian Europe in the Age of the Crusades, she incorrectly claims that "every time a crusade to the Holy Land was called there were pogroms against Jews back home" and that crusading institutionalized anti-Semitism in Europe, making it "an incurable disease in Christendom."

Jones, referring to the undeniably horrific Rhineland massacres of Jews of 1096, agrees with Armstrong and states that the process begun in the eleventh century was completed in the twentieth. Not to be outdone, Sir Steven Runciman states that the crusaders were "utterly boorish" (perhaps the worst charge that a British gentleman can lay against anyone) and that "their idea of God's work was not civilized." Added to this are numerous jokes and scenes enacted for comic effect that make the crusaders look like the bloodthirsty progenitors of the Keystone Cops of American silent films. But one must admit that some of Jones' lines are uproariously funny, even as they are wildly wrongheaded. Persons from the lower social orders who went crusading early in 1096 were "fanatical peasants armed with only bad breath." Comedy militates against complexity, whereas historical scholarship embraces it. Unfortunately, Jones opted for comic effect.

Less obviously funny are a number of myths or, at least, highly questionable statements that would make only a pedantic crusade historian chuckle—or throw up hands in exasperation. One such myth is "Chivalry was learned in *Outremer* [the crusader states "across the sea"], where once-barbaric knights learned to enjoy life." This is blatantly false. Twelfth-century French chivalry was possibly influenced by cultural elements from Muslim Spain, but there is absolutely no evidence of its having originated or flourished in the Latin states of the East.

Another myth is that the Muslims whom the crusaders initially encountered and fought were unaccustomed to the sheer brutality of the "Franks" (a generic term

---

57. Karen Armstrong, *Holy War: The Crusades and Their Impact on Today's World* (New York: Doubleday, 1991). See the scathing assessment of this book by James M. Powell, "Rereading the Crusades: An Introduction," *The International History Review* 17 (1995): 663–69 at 663–64, note 4.

applied to all Westerners by Easterners) and only eventually learned from them how to reply in kind. According to Jones, "It took two hundred years for the crusaders to create this Muslim intolerance" as manifested by Baybars, the Mamluk sultan of Egypt and Syria (r. 1260–1277), whose conquests of crusader state fortifications and cities were often accompanied by the cold-blooded slaughter of captives. He also claims, in reporting Richard I's massacre of some reported 2,600 Muslim captives at Acre in August 1191, that "no Muslim army had ever treated a Christian army with this mechanical brutality." Jones is wrong on several levels.

First, war was, is, and always will be a brutal affair, and added to this was the fact that accepted protocols for the treatment of captives taken in battle were far crueler in the Middle Ages than they are today. The great Islamic jurists of the eighth and ninth centuries, whose commentaries on the Qur'an and Hadith (tradition) defined Shari'a (religious law), were agreed that a Muslim leader could licitly kill all adult male captives, except the elderly and holy men, and could also kill those women, children, old men, and holy men who had fought against the Muslim forces.[58] Generally, captives who could not be safely enslaved or advantageously ransomed off were killed by Muslims and Christians alike. Thus, following the Battle of the Field of Blood of 1119, the numerous Christian warriors taken captive were butchered in especially brutal ways both on the battlefield and later in Aleppo. Four years before Richard's execution of Muslim captives, Saladin had purchased from their captors a hundred or more Templars and Hospitalers captured at the Battle of Hattin and then ordered their beheading. To add to the captives' agony and to provide some amusement, he gave the task to the Sufi holy men and scholars who accompanied his army, knowing that most of these unwarlike men could not kill their victims cleanly. As for the rank-and-file captives, a Muslim source notes that all were either killed or enslaved.[59]

Jones also asserts that jihad was a specific reaction to the crusades. He is partially correct. There was an upsurge in calls for jihad around 1144, when finally Zengi was able to create something of a united front against the crusader states. Prior to Zengi, calls by religious authorities for jihad against the Franks largely fell on deaf secular ears due to Muslim disunity, and it was only during the reign of Zengi's son and successor, Nur ad-Din (r. 1146–1174), that "jihad as a rallying cry for the Muslims gathered real momentum."[60] However, as Carole Hillenbrand has also pointed out, in the era preceding the crusades, "there were very few stages, if any at all, during the medieval period when there were not some manifestations of jihad on one of the many borders of the

---

58. James Turner Johnson, *The Holy War Idea in Western and Islamic Traditions* (University Park: Pennsylvania State University Press, 1997), 115–27.

59. From the account by Saladin's secretary, an eyewitness to the event, 'Imād ad-Din: Francesco Gabrieli, ed. and trans., *Arab Historians of the Crusades*, trans. E. J. Costello (Berkeley: University of California Press, 1957), 138–39.

60. Carole Hillenbrand, *The Crusades: Islamic Perspectives* (New York: Routledge, 2000), 131.

'House of Islam.'"[61] Such jihads included holy wars against not only non-Muslims but also dissident Muslims. When the Shi'a population of Jerusalem rebelled against Sunni Seljuk control of the city in 1077, Emir Atsiz ibn Uwaq retook the city in a bloodbath, in which he massacred a significant percentage of the population—twenty-two years before the crusaders' bloody taking of the city, which Jones finds so extraordinary in its brutality and bloodletting.[62] Indeed, the number of dead in 1077 according to a Muslim source was 3,000, a figure that was strangely mirrored in another Muslim source's report of the number of slain in Jerusalem in 1099.[63] In that same year, Atsiz carried on a campaign of annihilation throughout portions of Syria-Palestine as he waged war against Shi'a enemies.[64] The point is that Muslim warriors needed no lessons from the Western crusaders when it came to a warrior ethic, brutality, or the calling of holy war.

Numerous other myths run throughout this video series, but to list and refute each would result in a book-length Introduction. Yet, a few of the more egregious ones deserve quick mention: prior to the crusades the Turks had only massacred Arabs and

---

61. Ibid., 100. Hillenbrand studies the complexities and evolution of the concept of jihad before and during the Age of the Crusades: 89–167. Overall, this book, by a leading Islamicist, is an excellent corrective to Jones' stereotypical portrayal of the Muslim world at the time of the crusades. More recently, Paul M. Cobb, *The Race for Paradise. An Islamic History of the Crusades* (Oxford: Oxford University Press, 2014), offers a history of the crusades from a Muslim perspective. The best and most recent book on jihad in the Age of the Crusades is Suleiman A. Mourad and James E. Lindsay, *The Intensification and Reorientation of Sunni Jihad Ideology in the Crusader Period: Ibn 'Asakir of Damascus (1105–1176) and His Age, with an Edition and Translation of Ibn 'Asakir's The' Forty Hadiths for Inciting Jihad* (Leiden, Netherlands: Brill, 2013). On jihad as a general phenomenon, see Michael Bonner, *Jihad in Islamic History: Doctrines and Practice* (Princeton: Princeton University Press, 2006) and Chapter 1 by Paul Crawford, "The First Crusade: Unprovoked Offense or Overdue Defense?" See also note 14 of Chapter 7, "Islam and the Crusades: A Nine-Hundred-Year-Long Grievance?" for further bibliography on the issue of jihad.

62. The best recent study of the level of blood spilled in Jerusalem in 1099 is Thomas F. Madden, "Rivers of Blood: An Analysis of One Aspect of the Crusader Conquest of Jerusalem in 1099," *Revista Chilena de Estudios Medievales* 1 (2012): 25–37; http://www.academia.edu/4081837/Rivers_of_ Blood_An_Analysis_of_One_Aspect_of_the_Crusader_Conquest_of_Jerusalem?login=&email_ was_taken=true (accessed July 8, 2014). Madden has built upon the seminal article by Benjamin Z. Kedar, "The Jerusalem Massacre of July 1099 in the Western Historiography of the Crusades," *Crusades* 3 (2004): 15–75. A forthcoming study in *Crusades* (volume 14) by Konrad Hirschler, "The Jerusalem Conquest of 492/1099 in the Medieval Arabic Historiography of the Crusades: From Regional Plurality to Islamic Narrative," will offer some additional perspectives and arguments, including his argument that the Jewish population of the city was especially marked out for slaughter by the crusaders: http://www.academia.edu/3522981/The_Jerusalem_Conquest_ of_492_1099_in_the_Medieval_Arabic_Historiography_of_the_Crusades_From_Regional_ Plurality_to_Islamic_Narrative?login=&email_was_taken=true (accessed July 8, 2014)

63. Kedar, "Jerusalem Massacre," 70 and 73, note 190. Hirschler's forthcoming article will argue that the number 3,000 is highly problematical because it appears in a number of Muslim accounts of various events such as this.

64. Moshe Gil, *A History of Palestine, 634–1099*, trans. Ethel Broido (Cambridge: Cambridge University Press, 1992), 412.

not Christians; the only women to go on crusade were washerwomen and prostitutes;[65] the crusaders decided they could not trust Emperor Alexius when he refused to torture prisoners taken at Nicaea; Reynald of Châtillon attacked and pillaged a caravan carrying Saladin's sister (Ridley Scott goes Jones one better by having Reynald kill the hapless sister); following the expulsion of the crusaders from Syria-Palestine "civilized life could go on as it had before the invasion"; and a Venetian treaty with the sultan of Egypt to keep the Fourth Crusade from attacking Alexandria was the reason that Doge Dandolo took over control of the Fourth Crusade and diverted it to Constantinople.

In addition, Jones reports as established fact a number of items and supposed incidents whose historicity is, at best, highly doubtful. The best example of this is the legend of the Assassin death leap, in which followers of the Old Man of the Mountain demonstrated to visitors their loyalty to their leader by willingly leaping to their deaths at his command. The validity of the testimony upon which this legend is based is questionable,[66] but Jones' insouciantly presenting it as unalloyed truth allows him to insert into the video a Monty Python skit of the Queen's Own McKamikaze Highlanders, Britain's first suicide regiment.

The supposed Venetian treaty with the Mamluk sultan of Egypt, listed above as an outright myth with no factual basis whatsoever, leads us to the Fourth Crusade (1202–1204), which Jones gets totally wrong,[67] despite the fact that an excellent study of the Fourth Crusade, which disputes almost every statement that Jones makes about that crusade, was available to him, had he looked for it.[68] But Jones

65. See Lock, "Women and the Crusades," in *Routledge Companion*, 343–47; Natasha Hodgson, "Women," in Murray, *Encyclopedia*, 4:1285–91; and Andrea, "Women," *Encyclopedia*, 332–34. In addition to the many studies they list, add Natasha R. Hodgson, *Women, Crusading and the Holy Land in Historical Narrative* (Woodbridge, UK: Boydell, 2007).

66. Farhad Daftary, *The Assassin Legends: Myths of the Isma`ilis* (London: I. B. Tauris & Co., 1994), 104–7, demonstrates the weakness of the testimony upon which this legend was based and consequently rejects it, but Moojan Momen, in his review of Daftary's book, states that the legend cannot be rejected out of hand: *Iranian Studies* 32 (1999): 427–29 at 429.

67. Jones deals with this crusade in part 4, "Destruction," at http://www.dailymotion.com/video/x1kq8wt_crusades-4-destruction_shortfilms (accessed April 3, 2015).

68. Donald E. Queller, *The Fourth Crusade: The Conquest of Constantinople* (Philadelphia: University of Pennsylvania Press, 1978). A second edition of this book, co-authored with Thomas F. Madden and with an essay on the crusade's primary sources by Alfred J. Andrea, appeared in 1997. For an overview of the crusade that reflects contemporary scholarship, see Alfred J. Andrea and Thomas F. Madden, "The Fourth Crusade," in Murray, *Encyclopedia*, 2:449–57. Giles Constable, "The Fourth Crusade," *Crusaders*, 321–47. Benjamin Z. Kedar, "The Fourth Crusade's Second Front," in *Urbs Capta: The Fourth Crusade and Its Consequences*, ed. Angeliki Laiou (Paris: Lethielleux, 2005), 89–110, traces the actions of Fourth Crusade participants who managed to get to the Latin Kingdom of Jerusalem, thereby putting the lie to Jones' statement that this crusade did nothing in the way of fighting Muslims in the Holy Land and no Muslim was killed in the course of the crusade. Other books worth consulting are Michael Angold, *The Fourth Crusade: Event and Context* (Harlow, UK: Pearson, 2003), which gives greater attention than Queller/Madden and Andrea/Madden to the Byzantine perspective, and Jonathan Phillips, *The Fourth Crusade and the Sack of Constantinople* (New York: Viking, 2004).

was following his own artistic muse. According to Jones, who echoes Runciman,[69] the crusader sack of Constantinople was a grotesque act by "barbarians with theology," whatever that means. Without going further, it suffices to note that Jones claims, without any evidence whatsoever, that Enrico Dandolo, doge of Venice and a "savage enemy of the Church," planned from the start to seduce the gullible Frankish crusaders into bankruptcy and then to take over the crusade and lead it to Constantinople.[70] Although Jones' depiction of the crusade is completely wrong, his storyline allows for one memorable cinematic moment when he intrudes himself into a Venetian *carnivale* party that is staged to illustrate how "the Venetians drew the crusaders into a fantasy world." A fantasy world, indeed, is Jones' depiction of this and the other crusades.[71]

Our focus on Jones' video series might seem excessive and an example of disgruntled historians venting their anger at the effrontery of someone who is not a professional academic venturing into our sacred space. We disagree that either is the case. As we see it, three factors impel us to single out this supposed documentary: its more than average number of distortions of the crusades; an incorrect story line that feeds into a number of contemporary charges against Western civilization by extremist elements whose knowledge of the past is equally skewed and dangerously so; and its ability to disseminate its errors far and wide—much further than any single book—by virtue of the medium Jones employs, his inconsistent but still often engaging humor, and the high quality of its cinematography.

The study of our past is too important not to get it right or at least as right as the limitations of our intellects and our evidence allow. No reconstruction of the past is perfect or complete, and the same is true of the histories that we construct from the remnants of the past. But it is our duty as historians to try to get it as right as possible, and when we see obvious distortions of the past, what we call myths, it is also our duty to challenge them.

Some of our colleagues have entered the lists to take on, refute, and correct a number of what they perceive to be crusade myths. They include Jonathan Riley-Smith,[72]

---

69. Runciman, *History*, 3:107–31, sees Venetian perfidy as the cause for the crusade's going astray.

70. For a corrective, see Thomas F. Madden, *Enrico Dandolo and the Rise of Venice* (Baltimore: Johns Hopkins University Press, 2003).

71. Terry Jones and Alan Ereira, who produced, directed, and co-authored the script of *The Crusades*, co-wrote an illustrated book based on their video script: *Crusades* (New York: Facts on File, 1995). The book tones down or eliminates some of the more extreme pronouncements that Jones makes in the video, eliminates a few myths and dubious "facts" (the Assassin death leap, the attack on Saladin's sister, and the Venetian treaty with Egypt), adds some material (such as the Albigensian Crusade and the Children's Crusade), but it creates or presents new myths (such as its portrayal of Pope Innocent III) and largely hews to the basic thesis of the video.

72. http://www.firstthings.com/article/2007/01/rethinking-the-crusades (accessed March 7, 2014).

William Urban,[73] Thomas F. Madden,[74] Jessalynn Bird,[75] and Paul Crawford,[76] who has contributed a chapter in this book. Yet, despite crusade historians' best attempts, crusade myths continue to live on, repeated endlessly as fact.

In addition to ones already mentioned or ones that will be dealt with in these seven chapters, a few of the more popular myths are: the People's Crusade of 1096 consisted solely of peasants;[77] the European settlers in the so-called crusader states of the Latin East were crusaders by virtue of living there;[78] the crusades were the necessary prelude to Western Europe's economic, intellectual, and artistic revival in the twelfth century;[79] the crusades were a disaster and total dead end with no gains whatsoever for the West;[80] no contemporary voices were raised against the crusades in the West;[81] the

---

73. http://www.historians.org/publications-and-directories/perspectives-on-history/october-1998/rethinking-the-crusades (accessed March 7, 2014).

74. See the following Websites: http://www.ignatiusinsight.com/features2005/tmadden_crusademyths_feb05.asp (accessed January 30, 2014); http://www.tfp.org/current-campaigns/2006/an-interview-with-professor-thomas-madden-dispelling-myths-about-the-crusades.html (accessed January 30, 2014).

75. Jessalynn Bird, "The Crusades: Eschatological Lemmings, Younger Sons, Papal Hegemony, and Colonialism," in Stephen J. Harris and Bryon L. Grigsby, *Misconceptions about the Middle Ages* (New York: Routledge, 2008), 85–89.

76. Paul F. Crawford, "Four Myths about the Crusades," *Intercollegiate Review* 46:1 (Spring 2011), 13–22.

77. Tyerman, *God's War*, 80, is one of numerous studies that debunks that myth.

78. In order to be a crusader, one had to swear the crusade vow. The fact that crusades were preached in these states and some colonists living there, but surely a small minority from that cohort, enlisted in the crusades shows the falsity of this myth.

79. Although the crusades certainly stimulated trade and travel between East and West, Western Europe's economic, intellectual, and artistic upswing was already well underway before the First Crusade, and arguably the First Crusade would not have been possible without such an upsurge. See Robert S. Lopez and Irving W. Raymond, eds., *Medieval Trade in the Mediterranean World* (New York: Columbia University Press, 1995, 1990, 2001); David Abulafia, "Trade and Crusade, 1050–1250," in *Cross Cultural Convergences in the Crusader Period*, ed. Michael Goodich, Sophia Menache, and Sylvia Schein (New York: Peter Lang, 1995), 1–20; Charles Homer Haskins, *The Renaissance of the Twelfth Century* (Cambridge, MA: Harvard University Press, 1927); Christopher Brooke, *The Twelfth Century Renaissance* (Norwich, UK: Harcourt Brace Jovanovich, 1969).

80. John France, *The Crusades and the Expansion of Catholic Christendom, 1000–1714* (London: Routledge, 2005), puts the lie to this notion. See also the books on the Baltic and Iberian crusades listed in Suggested Reading.

81. Palmer A. Throop, *Criticism of the Crusade: A Study of Public Opinion and Crusade Propaganda* (Amsterdam: N. v. Swets & Zeitlinger, 1940). Subsequent research has resulted in a general rejection of many of Throop's core arguments, but it remains valuable as a starting point. For correctives, see Elizabeth Siberry, *Criticism of Crusading, 1095–1274* (Oxford: Clarendon Press, 1985), and Norman Housley, *Later Crusades*, 377.

Franciscans were pacifistic anti-crusaders;[82] Saladin unified Islam and was admired by all Muslims;[83] Saladin was universally regarded as a paragon of chivalry by his Western enemies;[84] the Iberian crusade against the Moors was the starting point of Western racism;[85] the crusaders' belief in miracles, apparitions, and a coming apocalypse sprang from medieval superstitions that were effectively put to rest by modernity's appeal to reason,[86] the crusades were righteous wars;[87] and the Catholic Church was guilty of crimes against humanity for which it should make reparations.[88]

---

82. Both the Franciscans and Dominicans were enthusiastic supporters of crusading from the early thirteenth century onward: Christoph T. Maier, *Preaching the Crusades: Mendicant Friars and the Cross in the Thirteenth Century* (Cambridge: Cambridge University Press, 1994).

83. Mohamed el-Moctar, "Saladin in Sunni and Shi'a Memorials," in *Remembering the Crusades: Myth, Image, and Identity*, ed. Nicholas Paul and Suzanne Yeagar (Baltimore: Johns Hopkins University Press, 2012), 197–214, lays to rest this myth.

84. Archbishop William of Tyre, the most notable churchman and historian of the late twelfth-century Latin Kingdom of Jerusalem, was no admirer of the sultan. Among other charges, he accused Saladin of treachery and avarice in regard to his imprisonment of shipwrecked Christians. William of Tyre, *A History of Deeds Done beyond the Sea*, 2 vols., trans. Emily Atwater Babcock and A. C. Krey (New York: Octagon Books, 1976), 2:467–68. He was not alone in his hostility toward Saladin. At the same time, Archbishop William characterized Nur ad-Din, Saladin's Syrian master, as "a mighty persecutor of the Christian name and faith" but also saw in him "a just prince, valiant and wise, and, according to the traditions of his race, a religious man," 2:394.

85. Anouar Majid, *We Are All Moors: Ending Centuries of Crusades against Muslims and Other Minorities* (Minnesota: University of Minneapolis Press, 2009). See Sarah Gualtieri's review in the *Journal of American Ethnic History* 31 (2012): 152–53, in which she finds Majid guilty of a "cavalier treatment of historical causality" in a work that is a "fragile scholarly edifice."

86. Philip Jenkins, *The Great and Holy War: How World War I Became a Religious Crusade* (New York: HarperOne, 2014), demonstrates how World War I had many of the faith-based, supernatural trappings of the Age of the Crusades, including the three elements mentioned here.

87. Steve Weidenkopf, *The Glory of the Crusades* (El Cajon, CA: Catholic Answers Press, 2014), has produced a history of the crusades based totally on his use of selective secondary sources, whose avowed purpose is "to present a restored narrative of the Crusades . . . to give Catholics today the tools to answer the critics and defend the Church and its history" (27). Although he assails a number of "main myths" that are likewise scrutinized in our book (listed at ibid., 19) and raises some valid points, his use of only secondary works, many of them of dubious merit, his apologetic design, and the book's significant number of errors and oversights render his work less than reliable.

88. The Vatican recently found itself on both sides of this issue, although it did not use the term "righteous" in conjunction with the crusades or even hint at reparations. In 2000, Pope John Paul II expressed sorrow over the Church's sins of violence and persecution: Rory Carroll, "Pope says sorry for sins of Church," *The Guardian*, March 13, 2000, http://www.theguardian.com/world/2000/mar/13/catholicism.religion (accessed April 30, 2014). Carroll notes, "The Pope did not identify guilty individuals or name the crusades, the Inquisition or the Holocaust, but the references were clear." Weidenkopf, *Glory*, 25–26; 160–61, argues that, despite popular opinion to the contrary, Pope John Paul II did not apologize for the crusades in 2000 or in 2004, when Ecumenical Patriarch Bartholomew visited Rome, "because an apology is not necessary" (26). In March 2006, the papacy under Benedict XVI reopened the crusade debate by sponsoring a conference that characterized

These are just some of the more popular myths that circulate but that we cannot address in this book in any way that rebuts them in detail. But that last charge, "crimes against humanity" (touched on briefly above when discussing Runciman's indictment of the crusaders' sack of Constantinople), deserves a few additional words.

The notion of a crime against humanity springs from a post-World War II sensitivity (and a long-overdue sensitivity at that) to the special crime of genocide, which has fouled the history of the twentieth and early twenty-first centuries.[89] Over the past seven decades, the term "genocide," which was coined in 1944, has occasionally been used to characterize the crusades.[90] The question is Were the crusades genocidal crimes against humanity? Taking the United Nations' 1948 "Convention on the Prevention and Punishment of the Crime of Genocide" as our starting point, we define genocide as a series of systematic acts committed with the intent to eradicate, in whole or substantial part, an ethnic, racial, cultural, religious, or political group.[91] By that definition, the crusades to Syria-Palestine and North Africa were not genocidal.

Although massacres of European Jews preceded many (but not all) of the crusades, and though crusaders fighting in "the lands across the sea" at times massacred soldiers and non-combatants alike, there is no evidence whatsoever that either the crusaders or the Latin inhabitants of the so-called crusader states ever envisioned, much less attempted, the eradication through murder of any entire population group in these regions. Not only was it never an articulated or even implied goal, but such an

---

the crusades as defensive reactions to Muslim aggression. Richard Owen, "Vatican Change of Heart over 'Barbaric' Crusades," *UKTimes online*, March 20, 2006, http://www.freerepublic.com/focus/religion/1599391/posts (accessed April 30, 2014). Pope Francis has not addressed the issue of the crusades, although his proclamation of support for the Christians of Iraq who are being massacred by ISIL/ISIS forces has been misunderstood in some circles as a call for a new crusade. Elizabeth Stoker Bruenig, "On ISIS, Pope Francis Is No Crusader," http://www.thedailybeast.com/articles/2014/08/19/on-isis-pope-francis-is-no-crusader.html (accessed December 29, 2014).

89. See the forthcoming book by John Cox, *To Kill a People: Genocide in the Twentieth Century* (New York: Oxford University Press, 2015).

90. For example, Kurt Jonassohn and Karin Solveig Björnson, "Genocides during the Middle Ages," in *Encyclopedia of Genocide*, 2 vols., ed. Israel W. Charney, et al. (Santa Barbara, CA: ABC-Clio, 1999), 1:275–77. https://books.google.com/books?id=8Q30HcvCVuIC&pg=PA275&lpg=PA275&dq=genocide+Middle+Ages&source=bl&ots=jZczMucQkk&sig=YhhwBHlive4d8EWWg1kpNf6WWQk&hl=en&sa=X&ei=tUQbVZmNN4XCggTT4YGgBg&ved=0CEcQ6AEwBg#v=onepage&q=genocide%20Middle%20Ages&f=false (accessed April 2, 2015). The authors claim "[t]he period of the Crusades represents the beginning of the transition from utilitarian to ideological genocide" (276). Factual errors abound in this article, rendering it less than useful. One of the more egregious errors is their statement that when crusaders captured Constantinople in April 1204, "rivers of blood flowed down the city's streets for days . . . few survived the slaughter. The city and its population were almost completely destroyed" (277).

91. The text of Article II of United Nations Resolution 260, adopted December 9, 1948, is available in the original French and English at http://www.un.org/documents/ga/res/3/ares3.htm (accessed October 16, 2014).

action was beyond the capabilities of the relatively small numbers of crusaders and Latin settlers. Moreover, it would have been self-defeating. The Latins who resided in *Outremer* depended on the vast numbers of native peasants and urban dwellers for their very existence.

What about the charge of cultural genocide in the East? There is evidence of an incident in the course of the First Crusade in which a captive Muslim garrison was given the choice of baptism or summary execution.[92] This act of forced baptism, which flew in the face of established Latin Christian theology and canon law, appears to have been a relatively rare phenomenon perpetrated in the midst of desperate times following the crusaders' capture and defense of Antioch in 1098. We know from overwhelming evidence that, once the crusader states were established, native communities residing within them continued their customs, including their religions, and normally retained their local leaders.[93] Indeed, a Muslim from Al-Andalus who passed through the Latin Kingdom of Jerusalem in 1184 remarked that Muslim peasants were better treated by their Frankish lords than by their Muslim masters.[94] It is true that Latin missionaries worked in the Frankish states of *Outremer* during the thirteenth century, but their attempts to convert Muslims, Jews, and Eastern Christians were minimal and the results even slighter.[95]

A far better case for cultural-religious genocide (a notion that would have been alien to any Christian or Muslim during the Age of the Crusades) can be made for the Baltic Crusades (1147–1525) and the Albigensian Crusade in Languedoc (1209–1229), in which the crusaders' avowed aims were the eradication, respectively, of paganism and heresy through violence and more peaceful means.[96] That noted, the

---

92. According to the chronicler Peter of Tudebode, when the stronghold of Tell-Mannas surrendered to Raymond Pilet, a knight in the army of Count Raymond of Toulouse, the "pagans . . . who accepted Christ as their Saviour and desired holy baptism" were spared. The rest were immediately killed. Peter Tudebode, *Historia de Hierosolymitano Itinere*, trans. John Hugh Hill and Laurita L. Hill (Philadelphia: The American Philosophical Society, 1974), 92.

93. See Jean Richard, *The Latin Kingdom of Jerusalem*, trans. Janet Shirley (Amsterdam: North-Holland, 1979); Joshua Prawer, *The History of the Jews in the Latin Kingdom of Jerusalem* (Oxford: Clarendon Press, 1988); Christopher MacEvitt, *The Crusades and the Christian World of the East: Rough Tolerance* (Philadelphia: University of Pennsylvania Press, 2008).

94. Ibn Jubayr, a native of Valencia, spent a total of thirty-two days in the kingdom. A translation of relevant passages from his account is in A. J. Andrea and J. H. Overfield, *The Human Record: Sources of Global History*, 2 vols. (Boston, MA: Cengage, 2015), 1:275–80.

95. Benjamin Z. Kedar, *Crusade and Mission: European Approaches toward the Muslims* (Princeton: Princeton University Press, 1984), demonstrates that the appearance of European Christian missionaries to the Muslims in conjunction with the crusades was belated and limited, becoming a reality only in the thirteenth century. Paul Cobb, *Race for Paradise*, 175, notes, "The few outbursts of actual Christian missionary activity directed at Muslims (principally in Spain) were aberrations—and, it bears noting, dismal failures."

96. One of the most notorious examples of the articulation of a program for the eradication of "paganism" through either conversion or the sword was Abbot Bernard of Clairvaux's call in 1147

judgment by a respected scholar, Mark Gregory Pegg, that "the Albigensian Crusade ushered genocide into the West by linking divine salvation to mass murder. . . ." has not gained general acceptance in the ranks of crusade scholarship.[97] Unfortunately space precludes our examining in the depth they deserve these two crusades and the other holy wars that were waged in Europe from the mid-twelfth century onward. The crusades in Europe are largely unknown to the average educated American and reside, therefore, in the region of historical exotica as far as popular perceptions are concerned.

The seven myths addressed in this present book are fairly common ones and are all connected, in one way or another, with the crusades to the Holy Land. Paul Crawford confronts Terry Jones' core thesis as he explores the degree of historical reality in the claim that the First Crusade was nothing more than an unprovoked attack on a peaceful and tolerant Islamic world.[98] Also in that vein of evaluating the validity of Jones' vision of the First Crusade and its participants,

The coat of arms of the Order of the Holy Sepulcher on the Porta Sancta (Holy Door) of the papal basilica of Santa Maria Maggiore, Rome. The Templars are not the only myth-enveloped order associated with the crusades. The Order of the Holy Sepulcher is a lay religious and charitable confraternity with origins in the fourteenth century, but it claims a foundation by Godfrey of Bouillon in 1099. The phrase "Deus Lo Vult" (God Wills It), the rallying cry of the First Crusade, serves as the Order's motto. The five-fold cross, known as the Jerusalem Cross (or the Crusaders' Cross), has origins extending back to the eleventh century. Photo: Courtesy of Alfred J. Andrea. All rights reserved.

for holy war against the Wends of the Baltic, in which he advocated no truce with them until, "by God's help, they shall either be converted or wiped out." *The Letters of St. Bernard of Clairvaux*, trans. Bruno Scott James (Kalamazoo, MI: Cistercian Publications, 1998), 467.

97. Mark Gregory Pegg, *A Most Holy War: The Albigensian Crusade and the Battle for Christendom* (Oxford: Oxford University Press, 2008). See Alan Friedlander's respectful but critical review of the book in *Speculum* 84 (2009): 763–65. Another historian who rejects Pegg's indictment of this crusade as genocidal in the sense of an attempt to eradicate through mass murder is Lawrence W. Marvin, *The Occitan War: A Military and Political History of the Albigensian Crusade, 1209–1218* (Cambridge: Cambridge University Press, 2008). See Pegg's generous but critical review of Marvin's book in *Speculum* 85 (2010): 167–69. An interview with Marvin, in which he addresses the issue of the presumed special brutality of this crusade, is at: http://www.medievalists.net/2010/01/20/interview-with-laurence-marvin/ (accessed October 16, 2014).

98. See also his recent critique of Terry Jones' video at http://www.the-orb.net/non_spec/bbcx.html (accessed March 9, 2014).

James M. Muldoon looks at the role that presumed crusader religious madness played in the origins of that enterprise. Even before the crusaders left Europe in 1096, vicious attacks were carried out against Jewish communities in the Rhineland and elsewhere. Daniel P. Franke studies the relationship between the crusades and the Jews and asks, Were the crusades directed against the Jews?

The First Crusade resulted in the creation of four "crusader states" in the Middle East. In light of the "Latin East" that the crusaders carved out, Corliss Slack evaluates the validity of the charge of selfish greed and colonial ambitions that many commentators, especially since the early twentieth century, have laid against the first crusaders. One of the most myth-laden moments in crusade history is the so-called Children's Crusade of 1212, and David Sheffler offers guidance on how we might navigate the myths that surround this movement from its inception to today. Another issue surrounded by the mists of myth is the origin of the Freemasons, who claim direct descent from the crusade military order known as the Knights of the Temple. Are Masons latter-day Templars? Jace Stuckey helps us to separate fact from fiction in our search for an answer to this question. Finally, Mona Hammad and Edward Peters address what is probably the most oft-repeated myth of our day and one that we have heard repeated endlessly, especially since 9/11: The Muslim memory of the crusades has burned hot throughout the past seven centuries and lies at the core of radical Islam's hatred for the West. In investigating these seven issues, our contributors will strip away some of the myths, fabrications, exaggerations, and over-simplifications that have become embedded in the story of the crusades.

Alfred J. Andrea

Andrew Holt

1. The First Crusade: Unprovoked Offense or Overdue Defense?

Paul F. Crawford

The Muslim nation has never attacked a neighboring nation.[1]
—*Abd al-Sabour Shahin, professor of Arabic, faculty of Dar al-Ulum at Al-Azhar University*

It was not by force of arms that islamisme established itself over more than half of our hemisphere. It was by enthusiasm and persuasion.[2]
—*Voltaire*

[The First Crusade was the] starting point of a millennial hostility between Islam and the West.[3]
—*Amin Maalouf, Lebanese writer and journalist*

Five centuries of peaceful coexistence elapsed before political events and an imperial-papal power play led to [a] centuries-long series of so-called holy wars that pitted Christendom against Islam and left an enduring legacy of misunderstanding and distrust.[4]
—*John Esposito, professor of religion, international affairs, and Islamic studies at Georgetown University*

As this brief set of quotations shows, there has been a working consensus among a wide variety of intellectuals, across some centuries, that a historically peaceful Islamic world was only provoked to conflict with the West as a result of Western Christian aggression and that this aggression began with the First Crusade. All the elements of this claim are demonstrably false, yet the influence of the argument, and of those

---

1. Abd al-Sabour Shahin, *MEMRI Special Dispatch*, no. 296 (Nov. 1, 2001).

2. Voltaire, qtd. in Martin Kramer, "Coming to Terms: Fundamentalists or Islamists?" *Middle East Quarterly* 10 (2003): 65–77; http://www.meforum.org/541/coming-to-terms-fundamentalists-or-islamists (accessed June 4, 2014), citing André Versaille, *Dictionnaire de la pensée de Voltaire par lui-même* (Brussels: Complexe, 1994).

3. Amin Maalouf, *The Crusades through Arab Eyes*, trans. Jon Rothschild (New York: Schocken Books, 1984), xvi. This is a volume widely used in university and collegiate crusade courses.

4. John Esposito, *Islam: The Straight Path*, 3rd ed. (Oxford: Oxford University Press, 1998), 58.

who promote it, is commonly found in the statements of textbook authors, leading politicians and media personalities, and in popular film, television "documentaries," and literature. To take just one example, on April 8, 2002, in an apparent attempt to explain the horrifying attacks by Muslim terrorists on the Twin Towers the previous September, *US News & World Report* published a feature article on the crusades under the title "The First Holy War," implying that conflict between Muslims and Christians began with the crusades.

The article's subtitle went further and was more explicit: "During the Crusades, East and West first met—on the battlefield," and the text characterizes the crusades as "the first major clash between Islam and Western Christendom, which lasted more than three centuries."[5] The magazine's cover is striking, portraying a crowned crusader with upraised sword astride a rearing horse that looms over a barefoot corpse. In bold letters the words "The Crusades: The Truth about the Epic Clash between Christianity and Islam" lure the reader on. The interior, two-page centerfold is even more graphic, depicting triumphant, European-looking crusaders led by a bearded, pale-skinned hermit, with the bodies of fallen, dark-skinned Muslims at their feet and the still-living inhabitants of Jerusalem pleading for mercy. The juxtaposition of aggressors and victims is unmistakable, and the racial subtext is none too subtle.

The notion that the crusades, which began in the late eleventh century, represent the "first major clash between Islam and Western Christendom," and therefore something attributable solely to unprovoked Western aggression, is a rather sweeping, not to say striking, claim. In making such a claim in one of its feature articles, *U.S. News & World Report* was echoing former president Bill Clinton, who had delivered a speech the previous November at Georgetown University claiming that Americans of European descent had somehow at least partially brought the September 11 attacks on the United States because "those of us who come from European lineages are not blameless," implying, again, that the First Crusade had been an unprovoked atrocity.[6] The *U.S. News* article, though containing a number of factual inaccuracies, was widely read and accepted by a general public.[7]

---

5. Andrew Curry, "The First Holy War," *U.S. News & World Report*, April 8, 2002, 36–42.

6. William Jefferson Clinton, "A Struggle for the Soul of the 21st Century," speech at Georgetown University, November 7, 2001. Available mainly on journalistic sites such as http://www.salon.com/2001/11/10/speech_9/ (accessed February 9, 2014). The relevant passage reads, "Those of us who come from various European lineages are not blameless. Indeed, in the first Crusade, when the Christian soldiers took Jerusalem, they first burned a synagogue with three hundred Jews in it, and proceeded to kill every woman and child who was Muslim on the Temple Mount. The contemporaneous descriptions of the event describe soldiers walking on the Temple Mount, a holy place to Christians, with blood running up to their knees. I can tell you that that story is still being told today in the Middle East, and we are still paying for it."

7. Andrew Curry, "The First Holy War," http://www.andrewcurry.com/portfolio/TheFirstHolyWar.html (accessed February 9, 2014). Two persons who joined forces to point out some of the more egregious errors of fact and emphasis in Curry's article were Vincent Carroll, *"U.S. News Gets*

One could cite many more examples of this view that the crusades were some-how an entirely unprovoked and irrational outbreak of evil on the part of Western Christians. To pick another, almost at random, the History Channel aired a program called "Inside Islam" in summer 2002, which as of March 2015 was still available on YouTube[8]; in it, viewers are informed that it was not until "the end of the eleventh century [that] the Islamic East and Christian West were on a collision course."[9] The program goes on to offer the opinions of Khalid Yahya Blankinship, chair of the department of religion at Temple University.[10] In one clip, Blankinship offers the opinion that "the actual crusades were an attempt to *colonize* the Middle East by Western Europeans" (emphasis added).

It is impossible to know what support Blankinship might have offered for this statement had he been asked about his sources, but as it stands, this is a value-laden statement that anachronistically brings to mind modern colonialism, which was based on a sense of racial superiority, national pride, a search for military advantage over potential and real foes, and a desire for enrichment of a mother country through economic exploitation—all factors that were conspicuously missing from the settlements of the so-called crusader states of Syria-Palestine. The majority of crusade historians are not comfortable with the term "colonization" when referring to the crusader states of the Latin East, and, as Corliss Slack points out in her chapter of this book, scholars who use the term clearly define the special characteristics that set these settlements apart from modern colonies.[11] What is more, as Slack forcefully demonstrates, the initial motive that drove the First Crusade was not a desire to colonize the East. Godfrey of Bouillon and Raymond of Toulouse had nothing in common with Robert Clive of India.

"It," says the narrator then (referring to the "collision" between "the Islamic East and the Christian West") "began when the Seljuk Turks took Anatolia, cutting off

---

History Wrong," and Thomas F. Madden, "The Crusades in the Checkout Aisle: Crusade Nonsense from the *U.S. News & World Report*," which are combined in the online posting of December 19, 2009 (edited by Crethi Plethi): http://www.crethiplethi.com/the-crusades-and-islam/global-islam/2009/ (accessed August 11, 2014).

8. History Channel, "Inside Islam," part 4 of 9 (accessed February 9, 2014).

9. http://www.youtube.com/watch?v=MvSszGfTNQw (accessed May 16, 2014).

10. Khalid Yahya Blankinship was still Religion Department chair as of March 2015, according to Temple University's website http://www.cla.temple.edu/religion/faculty/dr-khalid-a-y-blankinship/ (accessed May 16, 2014).

11. Joshua Prawer and a few other crusade historians explored the idea of crusaders as colonialists in the 1970s and 1980s in books such as Prawer's *The Crusaders' Kingdom: European Colonialism in the Middle Ages* (New York: Praeger, 1972), but the comparison does not, in the end, work, not least because modern European colonialism kept the mother country in firm, exploitative control of its colonies, which was not the way medieval Western Europe related to the crusader states. See Riley-Smith, *The Crusades: a History*, 3rd ed. (London: Bloomsbury, 2014), 6–9, and Ronnie Ellenblum, *Crusader Castles and Modern Histories* (Cambridge: Cambridge University Press, 2007), 43–61.

the overland routes used by European pilgrims to visit Christian shrines in the Holy Land. The Catholic Church was quick to respond." It is true that the Turks defeated the Byzantines in 1071 at the Battle of Manzikert. That defeat led to the near-complete loss of Anatolia (the Asian portion of present-day Turkey, also referred to as Asia Minor) over the next two decades, which in turn resulted in the calling of the First Crusade in 1095. But though twenty-four years might seem "quick" to a television producer gazing across a millennium, it probably didn't feel very rapid to the Byzantine Christians who were waiting for help from the Latin Church.[12]

In any event, Blankinship then continues: "Pope Urban II in 1095 preached the First Crusade, and that was because Jerusalem, he said, was held by the infidels. Well, Jerusalem had been held by the Muslims for hundreds of years and there had never been that thought before." There is no mention here of the Byzantines' desperate pleas for military aid, sent to leading members of the Western nobility as well as popes Gregory VII and Urban II between about 1073 and 1095, which we will examine later. Nor is there any suggestion that Muslim armies had been assaulting Western Christians as well for many centuries. In fact, the loss and recovery of Jerusalem had very much "been [a] thought" before; indeed, Christians had been bewailing the loss of Jerusalem since its fall in 637, and at least one Byzantine campaign had come close to recovering it in the tenth century.[13] On these important issues, at least as the History Channel producers depicted him, Professor Blankinship is silent.

The statements made in the *U.S. News & World Report* article and during the History Channel program on Islam are excellent starting points for examining relations between Muslims and Christians from the foundation of the Islamic *umma* (community) at Medina in 622 to the calling of the First Crusade in 1095. They are also useful for investigating whether the prevailing popular view that the crusades were unprovoked, and the concomitant notion that the crusades represented the "first major clash" between Islam and Western Christendom, are accurate.

The Rise of Islam

The origins of Islam date to 622, with the Prophet Muhammad's migration from Mecca to Medina. According to the usually accepted narrative, after leaving Mecca for the more welcoming environment of Yathrib (which became known thereafter as al-Medina, "the city") in this year, Muhammad and his followers grew stronger. This enabled them to spend much of the next eight years waging war against both their

---

12. See the chapter in this book by James M. Muldoon, "Mad Men on Crusade: Religious Madness and the Origins of the First Crusade."

13. John V. Tolan, *Saracens: Islam in the Medieval Imagination* (New York: Columbia University Press, 2002), 43. The date has been traditionally given as 638, but there is disagreement in the Muslim sources, and many scholars now prefer 637.

perceived internal enemies in or near Medina and their external enemies, their former fellow citizens of Mecca. The internal enemies were mostly Jewish, as initially friendly relations between Muhammad and the Jews of Medina had soured not long after his arrival in the city.

In 624 and 625, concerned over Jewish loyalties as he sought the conquest of pagan Mecca, Muhammad expelled two Jewish tribes from Medina, and in 627, he destroyed the last Jewish tribe at Medina, ordering the death of all the men and enslaving all the women and children.[14] Soon afterward, the Meccans negotiated a truce in 628 and then agreed to surrender to Muhammad in 630, allowing him to take possession of the city.[15] Two and a half years later he was dead, but his followers took up his cause and, with the Arab tribes increasingly united behind them politically and militarily, if perhaps not yet entirely religiously, they began to raid their Christian Byzantine and Zoroastrian Persian neighbors.

Much has been said about Islam being a "religion of peace," with world leaders as disparate as President George W. Bush and Pope Francis supporting this description. Indeed, the very word "Islam," which means "submission" [to Allah, or God], derives from the root of the Arabic word *salam*, "peace." By extension, then, submission to Allah via Islam results in peace and security, with resistance to Islam naturally and unavoidably yielding violence and insecurity. Despite the argument that Islam has historically been a religion of peace, warfare was central to the spread of Islam in the Middle East and Mediterranean, conceptually as well as historically. Pre-Islamic Arab culture was predicated to a significant degree on raiding (known as razzias) and warfare, in ways similar to that of pre-Christian Viking culture; Islam emerged in a violent context and expanded with even more violence. In many ways Muhammad appears as a warrior chieftain, despite his religious message.[16] Indeed, as Rice University religion scholar David Cook has pointed out, Muhammad personally participated in or sanctioned no fewer than eighty-six military campaigns or raids against various

---

14. Patricia Crone, "The Rise of Islam in the World," in *The Cambridge Illustrated History of the Islamic World*, ed. Francis Robinson (Cambridge: Cambridge University Press, 1996), 8.

15. On the circumstances leading to the surrender of Mecca, see Crone, "Rise of Islam," 7–8. On the heightened use of violence by Muhammad and his followers after they moved from Mecca to Medina, Michael Bonner, professor of medieval Islamic history at the University of Michigan, has explained it as follows: "At first Muhammad and his community in Mecca, in a position of weakness, avoid the use of violence, though they do not 'turn the other cheek.' With the *hijra*, or Emigration to Medina, in 1/622 and the founding of a new state there, organized violence becomes an option, but practiced sparingly and within traditional restraints. In time, as Muhammad gains in strength and his conflict with Mecca grows more bitter, these restrictions are cast away." See Michael Bonner, *Jihad in Islamic History: Doctrines and Practice* (Princeton, NJ: Princeton University Press, 2006), 26. See also Bernard Lewis, who echoes Bonner's analysis in *The Crisis of Islam: Holy War and Unholy Terror* (New York: Random, 2003), 30.

16. On Muhammad's role as a military leader, see chapter one of Efraim Karsh, *Islamic Imperialism: A History* (New Haven, CT: Yale University Press, 2006).

opponents, including Jews, pagans, and Byzantine Christians, as he and his early followers established political control over the Arabian Peninsula.[17] Because Islam theo-
retically forbids warfare between Muslims, for the deeply entrenched razzia tradition
of Arabia to continue, raiding activity had to be turned against non-Muslims.

Jihad, "struggle in the way of God," is a core principle of Islam. Jihad has different
meanings within Islamic society and, in one of its manifestations, has been interpreted as
an internal, spiritual struggle against sinfulness. This is usually referred to as the "greater
jihad."[18] There are, however, other manifestations of jihad, including the "lesser jihad,"
or jihad of the sword, which is violent in nature. As Cook has further pointed out, the
Qur'an contains a well-developed doctrine of military jihad (jihad of the sword), with
one of its primary goals the conquest and subjugation of non-Muslims, and Hadith (the
collection of sayings and actions ascribed to the Prophet and his companions) established holy war as a tradition within Islam from a very early date.[19]

Qur'an 9:29 states, "Fight those who believe not in Allah nor the Last Day . . .
until they pay the jizya [the poll tax paid by non-Muslims] with willing submission,
and feel themselves subdued"; this principle was re-affirmed by Caliph Umar I, as
quoted by the early Muslim historian al-Tabari: "Summon the people to God . . .
those who refuse must pay the poll tax out of humiliation and lowliness. If they
refuse this, it is the sword without leniency."[20] In any case, from the origins of Islam
onward, jihad was primarily understood as armed conflict, at least in the form that
non-Muslims encountered it.[21]

The principal purpose of jihad was, and still is, to induce non-Muslims and hetero-
dox Muslims alike to submit to Islamic law[22] (though it was not and is not the only
method employed for doing that; for example, Islam was spread principally by merchants, Sufi holy men, and other non-military agents in sub-Saharan Africa, Southeast
Asia, and other areas outside the core of the Middle East and Mediterranean). Brief
truces could be made with non-Muslims if such were deemed expedient by the Muslim

---

17. David Cook, *Understanding Jihad* (Berkeley: University of California Press, 2005), 6.

18. For a consideration of the meaning of jihad, in both its internal and external forms, see Bonner, *Jihad in Islamic History*, 1–14. See also Reuven Firestone, *Jihad: The Origin of Holy War in Islam* (New York: Oxford University Press, 1999), 16–18.

19. Cook, *Understanding Jihad*, 5–19.

20. *The History of al-Tabari*, trans. Yohanan Friedmann, vol. XII, (Albany, NY: State University of New York Press, 1992), 167.

21. Cook, *Understanding Jihad*, 35–44. See especially pp. 39–44.

22. "The physical jihad was aimed at unbelievers outside the Muslim community, as well as 'hyp-ocrites and troublemakers' within the Muslim ranks. Its goal was to establish the supremacy of divine law and thereby to promote justice and social welfare according to Islamic values." Sohail H. Hashmi, "Jihad," *Encyclopedia of Islam and the Muslim World*, ed. Richard C. Martin. 2 vols. (New York: Macmillan Reference USA, 2004), 1: 377–79, at 377. *Gale Virtual Reference Library* http://go.galegroup.com/ps/i.do?id=GALE%7CCX3403500244&v=2.1&u=vol_b92b&it=r&p=GVRL&sw=w&asid=98a625b439999ed5ddea18ad542b8a89 (accessed July 8, 2014).

side, but such truces were generally limited to approximately ten years in duration, and even then could be broken at the convenience and desire of the Islamic partner.[23]

As recorded in the Qur'an (the eternal word of God, which Muslims believe was dictated to the Prophet by the angel Gabriel), Muhammad declared that non-Muslims were to be attacked "until . . . religion becomes Allah's in its entirety."[24] As Carole Hillenbrand, an authority on Islam and the crusades, has pointed out:

> Jihad is generally considered to be a collective, not individual, duty to all Muslims and it is perpetual. . . . It is the duty of Muslims to strive perpetually in the path of God, in other words, to wage jihad. According to Islamic law there is an obligatory state of hostilities between the "House of Islam" and the "House of War" until the conversion or subjugation of all mankind has been achieved. Legally, a peace treaty between the Muslims and non-Muslims is impossible. Jihad may not be terminated; it can only be suspended by a truce which should not exceed ten years.[25]

What does Hillenbrand mean when she refers to a "House of Islam" or "House of War?" Classical Islam teaches that the world is divided into three elements, two major and one minor: (1) the *Dar al-Islam* (the House of Islam), the region that has submitted to the rule of shari'a (Islamic law), thereby placing itself under the "will and peace of Allah"; (2) the *Dar al-Harb* (the House of War or Confusion), against which it is permissible (though not mandatory) to fight either because it has not submitted to Islam or is at war against it, and which must be brought under shari'a, by persuasion if possible but by force if necessary; and (3) the *Dar al-Sulh* (the House of Truce), a non-Muslim entity with which Islam has a temporary treaty or cease-fire truce, which, as already noted, is not supposed to exceed about ten years.[26]

Conquered Jews and Christians (and occasionally other groups included for pragmatic reasons) were known as "dhimmis" (people of the compact, or treaty) and were placed in a subject and inferior status. The term "dhimmi," and the practice of conferring this status on subject non-Muslims, may be traced to a treaty (*dhimma*) given by Muhammad to the conquered Jews of the Khaybar Oasis in 628. The surviving community was allowed to remain on the land in peace in return for an annual tribute of one-half of their produce and by submitting to various other restrictions. Subsequently, Caliph Umar (r. 634–644) resettled the Jews of Khaybar and nearby Christian communities in newly conquered lands in Syria and Iraq in his drive to rid the holy Hejaz (western Arabia) of all non-Muslim residents.

---

23. Carole Hillenbrand, *The Crusades: Islamic Perspectives* (New York: Routledge, 2000), 97, and Bat Ye'or, *The Dhimmi,* rev. and enlarged ed. (Rutherford, NJ: Fairleigh Dickinson, 1985), 45–46.

24. Qur'an 8:39; see also 2:193 (Medina: Custodian of the Two Holy Mosques King Fahd Complex for the Printing of the Holy Qur'an, ca. 1992).

25. Hillenbrand, *Crusades,* 97.

26. Cook, *Understanding Jihad,* 19–21.

As this resettlement suggests, although dhimmi status is often celebrated as a type of advancement in the treatment of religious minorities, the status has always been precarious and second class; from the beginning, it could be revoked or changed at will by a Muslim overlord.[27] Moreover, it involved numerous restrictions on the civil and religious liberties and practices of the conquered, and such restrictions became increasingly substantial after the mid-eighth century. As Carole Hillenbrand has noted, significant "discriminatory measures" against Christians and Jews had become "enshrined" in Islamic legal books by the later eleventh century, on the eve of the First Crusade no less, although the degree to which these discriminatory measures were enforced by Islamic authorities varied from place to place.[28]

Though dhimmi status was flexible and often tailored to the situation as perceived by the Muslim conquerors or rulers, central to the status was the payment of the jizya, an annual head tax placed on all non-Muslim adult men that is mentioned above. Combined, the jizya and the *kharaj*—the levy on dhimmi-held land—usually exceeded twenty percent of a person's wealth; this was very high for a pre-modern tax, but they could be set at much higher levels if the Muslim authorities chose to do so. Muslim women were not allowed to marry non-Muslim men, but the reverse was encouraged, for obvious reasons.

New churches and synagogues generally could not be built; conversion to another religion—such as Christianity—from Islam was (and in many parts of the world, still is) punishable by death; physical postures assumed by dhimmis before Muslims had to be subservient and humiliating to the dhimmi; dhimmis were not to ride horses (noble and militarily useful animals) or bear arms, display their religious symbols (such as crosses on churches), or celebrate religious ceremonies in public; and a host of other restrictions on dress, comportment, marriage, and the economic, social, and religious life of the dhimmi were imposed, varying somewhat by time and place. One of the most critical restrictions was a ban on proselytization; dhimmis were forbidden to try to influence those about them to convert to their religion. This stricture meant that Christians, who were commanded by Christ to "go into all the world and preach the gospel,"[29] were required to violate one of the prime directives of their faith.[30] Conversion to Islam was

---

27. Ye'or, *Dhimmi*, 44.

28. Hillenbrand, *Crusades*, 408–10. Hillenbrand points out that an important legal work composed in the second half of the eleventh century in Baghdad by the legal scholar al-Shirazi reflected heightened discriminatory rules for dhimmis but that the treatment of dhimmis during the same period in the Fatimid Empire appears to have been marked by greater tolerance.

29. Mark 16:156.

30. There are many examples of a *dhimma* between Islamic conquerors and Jews or Christians. See, for example, the translated collection in *Islam from the Prophet Muhammad to the Capture of Constantinople*, ed. and trans. Bernard Lewis, Vol. II: *Religion and Society* (New York: Harper, 1975), 217–35, which includes the famous "Pact of Umar" (217–19) that purports to be from the seventh century, though it probably dates from the ninth in its current form.

not supposed to be forced (though at times it was), but in all cases the dhimmi was inferior to, and at the mercy of, his Islamic rulers.[31]

Initial Conquests

Raids into Byzantine and Persian territory by Arab tribesmen had long been a feature of life in the region, but it had been sporadic and usually desultory and had not previously been conducted by a unified Arab power. Moreover, by 633 the Byzantine and Persian empires were at a moment of unique weakness; having engaged from 602 to 628 in a mortal struggle that left Persia defeated and both empires thoroughly exhausted, neither was in good condition to recognize, react to, or cope with a serious invasion from another quarter. Yet that is exactly what confronted both powers.

Zoroastrian Persia, which Christian optimists had once hoped would become a Christian state due to the growing popularity of the faith in the region, was overrun and conquered in a series of campaigns carried out by Muslim Arabs between about 633 and 651 but it does not particularly concern us here.[32] Christian Byzantium, exhausted though it was, had considerably more resilience, and a titanic struggle commenced between Muslims and Eastern Christians that would last from the 630s to May 29, 1453 (when Constantinople finally fell to the Ottoman Turks) and even beyond. This long history of attacks against Byzantine Christian territories by varying Muslim armies over the course of several centuries, which would ultimately result in the complete conquest of the Byzantine Empire, began only about fifteen months after the Prophet Muhammad's death.

Indeed, Muhammad had envisioned Syria as the primary objective of Islamic expansion and had made provision for its invasion. Caliph Abu Bakr (r. 632–634) was left to carry out the project, launching a moderately successful raid in depth on southern Syria by an army of about 24,000 in the autumn of 633. A full invasion of this key province began in 634 under the leadership of Caliph Umar (r. 634–644).[33] In 634 or 635 (sources differ), Damascus fell, and the Byzantine emperor Heraclius realized

---

31. It is not the purpose of this essay to document the dhimmi condition, but in addition to Hamilton, *Religion*, see also Bat Ye'or, *Dhimmi*, and *The Decline of Eastern Christianity under Islam: From Jihad to Dhimmitude, Seventh-Twentieth Century* (Rutherford, NJ: Fairleigh Dickinson, 1996), for extensive translations of primary sources and, in the latter case, a discussion of the condition of Christian dhimmis. See also "Islam and Unbelievers" in Alfred J. Andrea and James H. Overfield, *The Human Record: Sources of Global History*, 2 vols., 8th ed. (Boston: Cengage, 2015), 1: 234–41, for representative texts of Muslim-dhimmi relations in various lands and times before 1500.

32. On the hope of Sassanian Christians that Zoroastrian Persia could become a Christian state before its conquest by the Muslims in 651, see Crone, "Rise of Islam," 2.

33. Warren Treadgold, *A History of the Byzantine State and Society* (Stanford, CA: Stanford University Press, 1997), 301; Hugh Kennedy, *The Prophet and the Age of the Caliphates*, 2nd ed. (London: Pearson, 2004), 52–53 and 58–60.

he had a serious situation on his hands. Scraping together all available troops, many of whom were Christian Arab auxiliaries, he sent out an army against the Muslim invaders. At the River Yarmuk, Heraclius' army was decisively defeated and destroyed, leaving him with no choice but to cede Syria and withdraw. In 637 Antioch, in northern Syria, fell. The Muslims then turned their attention south, taking Byzantine-controlled Christian Jerusalem in 637 (or 638). Moving into Egypt, they occupied Alexandria in 642. The Byzantines counterattacked and recaptured Alexandria, but it fell again, and definitively, in 646.[34]

Thus, in less than a decade, some of the most important cities of the Christian world—including three of its five great patriarchates (Jerusalem, Alexandria, and Antioch; Rome and Constantinople being the other two)—had fallen to Islamic conquerors, causing acute alarm among contemporary Christian authors.[35] These were all important centers of the early Christian world. Saul of Tarsus had formalized his conversion to Christianity as Saint Paul in Damascus, and he had been let down over the wall in a basket to escape his enemies there; it was also the site of the magnificent Basilica of Saint John the Baptist (which would be converted into a mosque in the early eighth century).

Antioch was the place where Christians had first been given the very name "Christian" and the city where Peter, according to church tradition, had first served as bishop before moving to Rome. Saint Mark the Evangelist was associated with Alexandria, as were the later, influential Christian writers Origen and Saint Clement of Alexandria, and it was here that Patriarch Athanasius had, almost alone, withstood the heresy of Arius in the fourth century. And the loss of Jerusalem—the site of many of the most important events of the New Testament, including Christ's crucifixion and resurrection, and the most important locus of Christian pilgrimage in Late Antiquity, the Middle Ages, and beyond—was particularly painful, not only spiritually but also emotionally. The reaction of Patriarch Sophronius of Jerusalem, upon seeing the Muslim leader Umar preparing a shrine on the Temple Mount, was typical: he is reported to have cried out, in anguish, "Truly this is the Abomination of Desolation spoken of by Daniel the Prophet, and it now stands in the Holy Place," and to have burst into tears.[36]

The loss of Syria, Palestine, and Egypt was crippling to Byzantium economically, politically, and militarily, but more blows to Christan lands were to come. Christian

---

34. One theory offered to explain the rapid Arab conquest of Egypt is that it was due, at least in part, to Coptic antipathy toward Byzantium as a consequence of imperial religious policies that treated the Coptic Church as heretical and heavy taxes imposed by Constantinople. In other words, many Christian Copts probably initially welcomed the invaders.

35. Walter Emil Kaegi, Jr., "Initial Byzantine Reactions to the Arab Conquest," *Church History* 38 (1969): 139–49.

36. F. E. Peters, *Jerusalem* (Princeton, NJ: Princeton University Press, 1985), 190–91, citing Theophanes in Guy Le Strange, *Palestine under the Moslems* (Boston: Houghton Mifflin, 1890, reprinted 1965), 140n.

The Stone of the Anointing. Among the many sites within Jerusalem's Church of the Holy Sepulcher that are sacred to the Christian memory of Jesus' crucifixion and resurrection is the Stone of the Anointing, which Christians venerate as the place where they believe Jesus' body was prepared for burial. Photo courtesy of A. J. Andrea. All rights reserved.

Axum (Ethiopia) and Nubia (Sudan), in northeast Africa, managed to beat off the first waves of Muslim attacks, which began as early as 640. Muslim advances against Nubia would recommence in the late thirteenth century, turning Nubia into a vassal state of Mamluk Egypt. The Christians of the Ethiopian highlands managed to hold out against Islam, although significant Muslim enclaves were established in the lowlands and along the coast during this later period. Muslim armies entered the Christian kingdoms of Armenia and Georgia in 642–643 and were in Cappadocia in

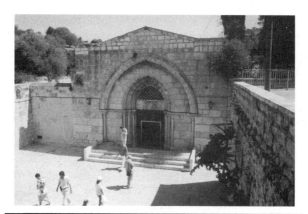

Outside the walls of Jerusalem lies the grotto containing what Christians believe to be the empty tomb of the Virgin Mary, a tomb made empty when she was assumed bodily into Heaven. Photo courtesy of A. J. Andrea. All rights reserved.

central Anatolia by 647. Cappadocia was the region where, in the first century, Saint Paul had lavished a great deal of missionary energy; later on, in the fourth century the important Eastern Christian fathers Saint Basil the Great, Saint Gregory of Nyssa, and Saint Gregory of Nazianzus had lived and written there, and Saint Macrina (older sister of Saints Basil and Gregory of Nyssa) had founded an influential convent of nuns there.[37]

Between 649 and 655, the formerly land-bound Arabs learned to use the resources of Alexandria to launch naval attacks on the Byzantines that progressively challenged the latter's fleet, and in the Battle of the Masts off the southwestern coast of Anatolia (Asia Minor) in 655, the Muslim fleet decisively defeated the Byzantines and destroyed Byzantine naval superiority in the eastern Mediterranean.[38] Nor were the central and western Mediterranean regions immune. With lightning speed, the Muslims exploited their position; they began to raid Byzantine Sicily as early as 652.

From the 640s on, it becomes difficult to detail Muslim conquests in a strict chronological sequence, as multiple campaigns were usually under way at once, so let us examine various theaters of war in turn.

North Africa

In 647, Muslims who were advancing west from Egypt took Sufetula (modern Sbeitla in Tunisia) and put Carthage—the ancient city that had been home to two influential Christian writers, Tertullian and Saint Cyprian—in jeopardy; that city and its port fell in 698, and with it went Byzantine naval control of the western Mediterranean.[39]

Here Muslims encountered a short-lived, but surprising, resistance from a shadowy figure: a Berber princess known as "the Kahina." Whether she was pagan, Jewish, or (most probably) Christian is not entirely clear from the sources, but she rallied her people and managed what the imperial Byzantines seemed frequently incapable of in the seventh century—she rebuffed the Islamic armies, at least for a time. But the Muslim juggernaut was not to be delayed for long; by 702 or 703 the Kahina was dead, apparently killed in battle, as she herself took part in the fighting. According to an Islamic legend, in a gesture of despair, she sent her sons to join the enemy before her death at her last stand.[40] In any case, the Muslims had already bypassed her and, as early as 670, had reached the Atlantic Ocean. When their commander, Uqba ibn Naf'i, reached the

---

37. A. A. Vasiliev, *History of the Byzantine Empire*, 2. vols. (Madison: University of Wisconsin Press, 1952), 1:115–16.

38. Treadgold, *Byzantine State*, 314.

39. Michael Brett and Elizabeth Fentress, *The Berbers* (Oxford: Blackwell, 1996), 84, 86.

40. The Kahina, whose name is sometimes given as "Dihya," did not enjoy the luxury of survivors of her own people and faith to write her story, and as a result it is hard to obtain a clear outline of her activities. See Brett and Fentress, *Berbers*, 85–87.

Atlantic, reflecting the intertwined nature of the Islamic faith with the goals of the conquerors, he was said to have ridden exultantly out into the waves, shouting, "Oh Allah! If the sea had not prevented me, I would have coursed on forever like Alexander the Great, upholding your faith and fighting all who disbelieved!"[41]

Less than a generation after the Prophet's death, Christian North Africa—home of theologians such as Saint Augustine and martyrs like Saints Felicity and Perpetua, who were central to the development of Christian tradition and thought, and rich with Christian history—had fallen to Islam. Along with Syria-Palestine and Anatolia, it had been the site of desert hermits and one of the birthplaces of Christian monasticism, home to the great and ancient patriarchate of Alexandria with its vast heritage of ancient learning, and the stage for the conflict between Catholic orthodoxy and two major heretical movements known as Arianism and Donatism, with all the theological developments that sprang from those conflicts.

The final version of the New Testament's canon (the books approved as genuine) had been sent to the pope in Rome for confirmation by the Council of Carthage in 397. And the list goes on. In short, North Africa, from Egypt to present-day Morocco, was a vibrant and vital part of the pre-Islamic Christian world. Not all of its population was immediately converted to Islam—far from it. Large enclaves of Christians endured till the turn of the millennium or later, especially in Egypt, where perhaps 10 percent of the population remains Christian even today.[42] Nevertheless, for all intents and purposes the deeply rooted public Christian culture of North Africa had been abruptly and violently suppressed by 700—by the armies of Islam.

Anatolia (Asia Minor) and the Aegean

Back in the eastern Mediterranean, Constantinople, the capital of the Eastern Roman (Byzantine) Empire and the most important Christian city in the world at the time, was fighting for its life. After 663, Muslim armies made near-annual raids into Anatolia, encroaching ever farther over the next fifteen years, soon reaching the Christian city of Chalcedon, situated across the Bosporus from Constantinople and the site of the historic Fourth Ecumenical Council in 451.[43] The Muslims had been working toward controlling the islands of the Mediterranean and Aegean seas, and they established a base on the southern shore of the Sea of Marmara. Smyrna, farther south on

---

41. Ibid., 82.

42. Richard W. Bulliet, *Conversion to Islam in the Medieval Period: An Essay in Quantitative History* (Cambridge, MA: Harvard University Press, 1979), 102, concludes that the conversion process in Egypt passed the halfway point just before the year 900, with the ninth century being the tipping point.

43. George Ostrogorsky, *History of the Byzantine State*, trans. Joan Hussey (New Brunswick, NJ: Rutgers University Press, 1969, original German text, 1952), 123. The Council of Chalcedon (451) was perhaps the most significant Christian council after Nicaea (325).

the coast of Anatolia, fell in 672, leaving Islamic forces in control of most of the vast peninsula.[44] By 674, a Muslim fleet was cruising outside Constantinople.

In following years their fleets returned, attempting to besiege and capture the city. In 678, the Byzantines, using their famous "Greek fire" apparently for the first time, drove the Islamic invaders off with heavy losses. A thirty-year truce was concluded, in theory at least, between the Muslim Arabs and the Christian Byzantines, which specified a heavy annual tribute to be paid by the Arabs to the emperor.[45] For the first time, the tide had been stemmed and an important victory won. The Byzantine historian George Ostrogorsky saw it as critical:

> The Arab attack . . . was the fiercest which had ever been launched by the infidels against a Christian stronghold, and the Byzantine capital was the last dam left to withstand the rising Muslim tide. The fact that it held saved not only the Byzantine Empire, but the whole of European civilization.[46]

Alexander Vasiliev, another great Byzantine historian of the twentieth century, was of the same opinion: "By the successful repulse of the Arabs from Constantinople and by the advantageous peace treaty, [the Byzantines] performed a great service, not only for [the] Empire, but also for western Europe, which was thus shielded from the serious Muslim menace."[47] A number of historians have questioned whether the achievement was quite that far-reaching, but there is no question that the gateway to what we would call Eastern Europe and beyond had been held closed. For the moment.

But only for the moment, which was brief. Clashes resumed in 691,[48] and in 709 the Muslims took an important fortress in Cappadocia, the heartland of Anatolia. During the next two years they made significant advances into Cilicia, the southeastern coastal region of Anatolia, bordering Syria.[49] Tarsus, Cilicia's capital city, was the birthplace of Saint Paul and home to a large number of early Christian martyrs. But worse was yet to come; in August 717, a great Muslim army and fleet appeared at Constantinople and settled down to besiege the city in earnest again, this time for an entire year.

Once again the Byzantines, fighting desperately, drove off their attackers, and once again passage to the rest of continental Europe was blocked, with great effort. The Muslim threat was still by no means neutralized, however. For some time after 726, Muslim forces invaded Anatolia annually, besieging important and historic Christian

---

44. Ibid., 124.

45. Ibid.; Treadgold, *Byzantine State*, 327. Note that the length of this truce exceeds that which Muslims were supposed to accept; the rules were not always followed.

46. Ostrogorsky, *Byzantine State*, 125.

47. Vasiliev, *History*, 1:215.

48. Ostrogorsky, *Byzantine State*, 131.

49. Ibid., 143.

cities such as Nicaea, the site in 325 of perhaps the most important of all the ecclesiastical councils in Christian history. In 740, however, the Byzantines won another battle, at Acroinon, and suppressed the attacks on their heartland for the time being.

By now, the Umayyad dynasty was losing its hold over the Muslim world (and the *Dar al-Islam* was about to meet a long-term check in Central Asia by a Chinese army at Talas in 751), and the Byzantines were allowed a respite and a chance to rebuild and even counterattack. In 746 they reoccupied part of Syria and in 747 destroyed a Muslim fleet. And they temporarily reoccupied areas of Armenia and Mesopotamia, though these were quickly lost to powerful Muslim counter-thrusts.[50] In 781, Arabs inflicted a sharp defeat on the Byzantines in western Anatolia. For more than half a century thereafter, the line between the two faiths settled into inconclusive, if bloody, border war. Life was more or less difficult for Christians in the area, depending on the whim and resources of local Muslim rulers. Christian writers recount a tale of repeated harassment and outright persecution, from the seventh century to the eleventh, with occasional respites.[51]

When matters heated up again, it was because the Byzantines had gotten their feet under them sufficiently to mount significant campaigns with a real chance of success. In 843 the Byzantines recovered Crete, though only for about a year, and this brief advance was answered by a Muslim victory in Anatolia in 844. But in 853, the Byzantines sent a great fleet to the south, taking and sacking Damietta in the Nile Delta in the first Byzantine counter-thrust against Egypt since the 640s. Unfortunately for them, the principal long-term result of this action was to inspire the Muslim rulers of Egypt to concentrate more intently on their own naval power, which would cause the Byzantines a great deal of trouble in the next century.[52] But at the moment, it was a great achievement, and Christian arms began to advance steadily.

In 853, Emperor Michael III sent his general Petronas to campaign against the Muslims in Anatolia, and the military momentum began to shift back toward the Byzantines. When the emir of Melitene in northern Mesopotamia, who had been raiding and harassing Anatolia since the 850s, penetrated as far as Amisos on the Black Sea, they caught him on his way home in 863, encircled his army, and killed him. Following up this victory with a counterattack into Muslim lands, the Byzantines thereby eliminated the immediate threat to their frontiers and took the fight back to the enemy.

The mid-tenth century saw a great wave of Byzantine victories. In 943 and 944, they retook the northern end of Mesopotamia, besieging Edessa, which had fallen to Muslim forces in 638 but still had a majority Christian Armenian population.[53]

---

50. Ibid., 167.

51. Moshe Gil, *A History of Palestine, 634–1099* (Cambridge: Cambridge University Press, 1992), 469–78 (see p. 475 regarding a respite in the later ninth and early tenth centuries).

52. Ibid., 221–22.

53. Edessa would become the first area to be recovered and administered by the crusaders, as the "County of Edessa" in 1098.

Edessa famously possessed the relic known as the "Mandylion," believed to be an imprint of the face of Jesus Christ and thought by some to be the "Veil of Veronica" or even what is now called the "Shroud of Turin." The emir of Edessa handed over this relic to the Byzantines in exchange for some two hundred Muslim prisoners.[54] In 960 and 961, the Byzantines finally retook Crete, which would remain in Christian hands till 1669. The island had been a major staging ground for Islamic campaigns in the Mediterranean, so this was an important victory. It was followed up by the reconquest of Cilicia and the island of Cyprus in 965 and of Antioch in 969. In the next year Aleppo was captured and its emir made a tributary of Byzantium, though the city was not formally re-incorporated into the empire.

The next decade—the 970s—saw the high point of the Byzantine counterattack. It would not be correct to call these campaigns actual "crusades," as some writers have attempted to do,[55] but in the words of George Ostrogorsky, they "breathed the veritable crusading spirit."[56] The idea that Jerusalem was a Christian city that ought to belong to Christians, not Muslims, was not, as Khalid Yahya Blankinship claims, original to Pope Urban II, nor was it at all unheard of before 1095; rather, everyone knew that Jerusalem, for reasons including those given above, was *central* to the Christian faith, and the Byzantines were demonstrably trying very hard to recover it more than a century before the First Crusade.

In pursuit of this goal, Emperor John Tzimiskes mounted a series of major, and mostly successful, campaigns against the Muslims. He pressed farther into Mesopotamia, placed Damascus under tribute, and retook Lebanon (including Beirut and Sidon), Tiberias, Nazareth (Christ's home town), the area around the Sea of Galilee (where Christ had carried out much of his ministry, including, it was believed, delivering the Sermon on the Mount), Acre, and even Caesarea (one of several centers of apostolic activity in the first century). He lacked the resources to reach Jerusalem, however, and some of his conquests were short lived, though he wrote rather optimistically to his Armenian allies that "all Phoenicia, Palestine and Syria are freed from the yoke of the Saracens [Muslims] and recognize the rule of the Romans [Byzantines]." Unfortunately for the Byzantines, this energetic and capable ruler died in early 976,

---

54. Holger Klein, "Sacred Relics and Imperial Ceremonies at the Great Palace of Constantinople," *Byzas* 5 (2006): 79–99 at 91–92 and n80, http://www.columbia.edu/cu/arthistory/faculty/Klein/Sacred-Relics-and-Imperial-Ceremonies.pdf (accessed August 11, 2014).

55. For example, Geoffrey Regan, *First Crusader: Byzantium's Holy Wars* (New York: Palgrave Macmillan, 2003). Even Vasiliev, *History*, 1:310, using the term loosely, writes that in his campaigns, which aimed to free Jerusalem from Muslim occupation, Emperor John Tzimiskes "undertook a real crusade." Indeed, the idea of Byzantine proto-crusades goes back at least to the late twelfth century: William of Tyre (ca. 1130–1186) began his history of the First Crusade and the subsequent fortunes of the kingdom of Jerusalem down to 1184 with Heraclius' recovery of Jerusalem from the Persians in 630, as did the thirteenth-century Old French continuation of William's history known as *Eracles* (Heraclius).

56. Ostrogorsky, *Byzantine State*, 297.

and the program of reconquest slowed.[57] But the Byzantines retained Antioch and were able to use it as an operational base for the next several decades.[58]

The Muslims promptly contested this; in the mid-990s, the Fatimid Egyptians mounted serious attacks on both Antioch and Aleppo and were barely fought off. Within the Shi'a Fatimid Empire, which was often more tolerant than the Sunni caliphate toward Christians and Jews, the period of the late tenth to early eleventh centuries proved difficult for dhimmis. The "mad" Fatimid caliph al-Hakim (996–1021) persecuted Christians and Jews with unusual vigor. He outlawed wine (which had the practical and probably intended effect of interdicting not only the Christian Eucharist but also some Jewish rituals, such as the Passover seder meal), forced conversions, forbade the celebration of Epiphany and Easter, required them to wear identification of their subject status in public, and, in 1009, ordered the demolition of the Church of the Holy Sepulcher in Jerusalem, the most revered church in the Christian world, as well as a number of other churches and at least one convent.[59]

True to his mercurial, supposedly mad nature, after 1012 he allowed unwilling apostates to return to their Christian and Jewish faiths and rescinded most of his anti-Christian, anti-Jewish edicts, but by then great damage had been done to his dhimmi subjects. Al-Hakim was hard on Sunni Muslims, as well, and came to a mysterious and apparently violent end in 1021. His successors were less relentlessly repressive than he, but the Christians remaining in the Holy Land, who might still have been as much as 40 to 50 percent of the population, were traumatized. Word reached the West fairly quickly of their sufferings and vulnerability, of the destruction of the Church of the Holy Sepulcher, and of the difficulties encountered by pilgrims to the Holy Land.[60] That news would color and inform Western attitudes toward Jerusalem and Muslims throughout the eleventh century and into the era of what we call the crusades.

The mid-eleventh century saw serious disruptions to the Muslim world of the Near East. In 1055, the Seljuk Turks, nomads from the steppes of Central Asia who were part of a larger group of Turkish peoples known as the Oghuz, effectively neutralized the weakened descendants of the Abbasid caliphate in Baghdad and began the process of replacing Muslim Arabs as overlords of the region.[61] Pagan at first, the Seljuks converted to the Sunni branch of Islam during this process of replacement. By the

57. Ibid., 297.

58. Vasiliev, *History*, 1:311.

59. F. E. Peters, *Jerusalem* (Princeton, NJ: Princeton University Press, 1985), 257–68, citing, inter al., William of Tyre, Ibn al-Qalanisi, and Yahya ibn Sa'id.

60. A good selection of primary sources on pilgrimage in the period before the crusades may be found in *Jerusalem Pilgrims before the Crusades*, trans. John Wilkinson (Warminster, UK: Aris & Phillips, 2002), as well as in various volumes of the *Palestine Pilgrims' Text Society*.

61. See Hugh Kennedy, *The Prophet and the Age of the Caliphates*, 2nd ed. (London: Pearson Longman, 2004), especially 156–73 and 343–45. The Turks belonged to a large constellation of Central Asian

latter part of the century, then, the Muslim Arab elite, which had forced itself on the diverse population of the Near East in the seventh century, found itself displaced by another foreign, and once again newly Muslim, elite. By 1065, the Seljuk Turks had captured part of Christian Armenia, devastated Byzantine Cilicia, and made inroads into Byzantine Anatolia. In 1067, they took Caesarea, in Cappadocian Anatolia.

In response, Emperor Romanus IV Diogenes assembled a large but patchwork army, drawing on pagan Pechinegs and other steppe peoples, Norman and Frankish mercenaries, and the various peoples of the empire, and carried off some reasonably successful counterattacks in 1068 and 1069. But in 1071, the world fell apart for the Byzantines when the Seljuk ruler Alp Arslan thrust into far eastern Anatolia, meeting an imperial army near the shores of Lake Van. On August 26, the Byzantine army was decisively defeated, and the emperor himself was taken prisoner.

The emperor was later ransomed for several cities—including the promise (never fulfilled) of Antioch and Edessa (which the Byzantines had recovered in 1031)—and an enormous sum of money. Romanus never recovered his throne, however, losing it in a palace coup that resulted in his blinding, exile, and death. Christian Byzantium was plunged into several decades of turmoil and instability. It lost its "breadbasket" and principal military recruiting grounds in Anatolia and, of course, those ancient Christian centers such as Antioch (which was taken again by the Turks in 1084) and Nicaea, both of which would not be recovered until the First Crusade. In the 1080s, Alp Arslan established his own Sultanate of Rum (Rome) with its eventual capital tauntingly near Constantinople, 125 miles away in the city of Nicaea.

In the chaos that followed Manzikert, Romanus' Norman mercenaries tried briefly to establish their own principality in Galatia, in central Anatolia. They failed, but the knowledge of this attempt probably made its way back to Norman territories in southern Italy, Sicily, and France. Here was territory that might be taken and perhaps even held.[62]

The Byzantines, in the person of the new emperor, Michael VII (r. 1071–1078), had begun sending off appeals to the West soon after Manzikert, primarily to the person they thought most likely to help, since—among other things—holders of his office had been involved in defensive actions against Muslim invaders in Italy for quite some time: the pope. Gregory VII (r. 1073–1085), current occupant of the See of Saint Peter, was favorably inclined[63] and immediately began to plan for an expedition to the eastern empire's aid.[64] Unfortunately for him and them, he was

---

nomadic peoples. Although the Arabs had contact with the Turks from the seventh century on, it was not until the eleventh that the latter began to supplant the former.

62. See Corliss Slack's treatment of the Norman crusader Bohemond of Taranto in her chapter in this book "The Quest for Gain: Were the First Crusaders Protocolonists?"

63. See *The Register of Pope Gregory VII 1073–1085: An English Translation*, trans. H. E. J. Cowdrey (Oxford: Oxford University Press, 2002), 20, no. 1.18, for Gregory's initial response to Michael.

64. Examples of documents supporting this planned expedition that occur in the *Register* include 1.46, 2.3, 2.31, and 2.37.

soon interrupted by a conflict with the German king and emperor elect, Henry IV, and embroiled in the Investiture Controversy (1075–1122). Documents mentioning any such rescue expedition thereupon ceased to be written by Pope Gregory's secretariat—he now had neither time nor resources to come to Constantinople's aid, as he was fighting, often literally, for his life.[65]

Meanwhile, the Seljuk Turks, avowed champions of Sunni Islam, continued their encroachments against Shi'a Muslims and Eastern Christians alike. They seized Jerusalem from the Fatimids in 1073[66] and took Damascus around 1076. The Fatimids seem to have retaken Jerusalem in 1076, only to lose it again to the Turks soon thereafter.[67]

The city still retained a substantial Christian population, even after the Turkish massacres of its inhabitants in the 1070s.[68] These residents of the Holy City were not just Eastern Christians of various loyalties but increasingly Latin Christians too. Charlemagne had taken an interest in the well-being of Eastern Christians in the eighth and ninth centuries,[69] and in the eleventh century not only pilgrims but also merchants such as Amalfitans from Italy were increasingly taking up residence in Jerusalem, despite the increased difficulties for, and pressure on, Christians in the area.[70]

Therefore, just because the area had fallen under Muslim rule did not mean that Christians had ceased to live there or had forgotten it or lost interest in its well-being and significance to their faith.[71] Recognizing the dangers, however, determined Western pilgrims increasingly began to band together and bear arms to ensure their safety and ability to reach and return from their destination. In 1064–1065, a large group of mainly German pilgrims made it to Jerusalem and back, though they were forced to fight for their lives and suffered losses.[72] Between 1087 and 1091 Count Robert of Flanders (later a leader of the First Crusade) led a major, and armed, pilgrimage to the Holy Land, stopped along the way to visit Emperor Alexius I Comnenus and swearing an oath to him to send five hundred Flemish knights, on his return, to help the Byzantines fight off the Muslims.

---

65. James M. Muldoon's chapter in this book, "Mad Men on Crusade: Religious Madness and the Origins of the First Crusade," also deals with Pope Gregory's planned expedition to the East.

66. Or 1071; the dates are a bit unclear. See Gil, *History of Palestine*, 409–11 and Adrian J. Boas, *Jerusalem in the Time of the Crusades* (London: Routledge, 2001), 8.

67. P. M. Holt, *The Age of the Crusades: The Near East from the Eleventh Century to 1517* (London: Longman, 1986), 14. The history of this period is not entirely clear, and experts differ on the exact chronology.

68. See the Introduction to this book, p. xxviii.

69. Gil, *History of Palestine*, 285–89, 437, 452–54.

70. Wilken, *Jerusalem*, 217–22, 271–76; Gil, *History of Palestine*, 478–82.

71. See Boas, *Jerusalem in the Time of the Crusades*, 9: "Several hundred years after the Islamic conquest, the Muslims may still not have been the majority and do not appear to have been entirely in control of the city. Christian and Jewish pilgrimages continued, in spite of the difficulties and dangers involved."

72. Brett Edward Whalen, ed., *Pilgrimage in the Middle Ages: A Reader* (Toronto: University of Toronto Press, 2011), 175-80.

In August 1098 the Fatimids recovered Jerusalem.[73] By this time the First Crusade was almost upon them. Bracing for the attack, the Fatimids expelled all Christians from the Holy City in 1099—probably (and reasonably) supposing that their sympathies would be more likely to lie with their fellow Christians than their Muslim overlords[74]—and waited for the arrival of the latest Christian attempt to recover their central city: the First Crusade.

Sicily and Italy

So much for peaceful coexistence between Islam and Eastern Christians such as the Byzantines—it is a myth. But the reader will recall the claim made in *U.S. News & World Report* and by others that the First Crusade represented the "first major clash" between *Western* Christians and Muslims. Let us turn now to two strategically important areas in the West, the islands of the central Mediterranean and Italy, and see if the historical evidence supports at least that claim.

In 700, Muslims attacked and occupied Pantelleria, an island midway between southwest Sicily and North Africa, and from about 704 on, Muslims repeatedly attacked and looted the far richer islands of Sicily and Sardinia.[75] The first Muslim raid on Corsica came in 713; this was followed by extensive and repeated raids in the region, especially by the 730s. The relics of Saint Augustine, which had been translated to Sardinia from North Africa in the late 600s to keep them out of Muslim hands, had to be rescued yet again and withdrawn to Pavia in northern Italy for safety.[76]

Berber revolts against harsh Arab rule in North Africa lessened the pressure on Byzantine Sicily for a time in the 740s and 750s by requiring the Muslims attacking Sicily to return to North Africa to deal with the revolts.[77] All the same, in 752–753 a Byzantine fleet had to fight off an apparent Muslim attempt to conquer Sicily entirely, though once again the Byzantines were aided by a timely Berber revolt.[78] Between 806 and 810, Charlemagne's navy tried to garrison Sardinia and Corsica against the Muslims but was unsuccessful.

In 827, at the behest of a rebellious Byzantine admiral, Muslim forces landed again in Sicily and began the final process of conquering it, taking until 902 to complete the

---

73. Peter Lock, *Crusading and the Crusader States* (London: Routledge, 2006), 15, 23, 412.

74. Thomas Madden, *The Concise History of the Crusades*, 3rd student ed. (Lanham, MD: Rowman & Littlefield, 2013), 31.

75. Alex Metcalfe, *The Muslims of Medieval Italy* (Edinburgh, UK: Edinburgh University Press, 2009), 6.

76. Ibid.

77. Ibid., 8.

78. Ibid.

conquest.[79] The long struggle for Sicily was a complicated matter, with various Christian and Muslim factions involved at times in a complex web of alliances that were forged with little or no thought to religious affiliation. However, there is no doubt that the initial assault of 827 was sparked by the juridical opinion of the eminent scholar of Islamic law, Asad ibn al-Furat, that this expedition was a holy jihad that would expand the borders of Islam. So convincing was his argument, he was made commander of the invasion force.[80] Sicily would only return to Christian hands in the late eleventh century when Norman French adventurers from southern Italy (which they had seized from Byzantine forces) captured the island in a series of campaigns that extended from 1061 to 1091—just a half decade before a significant number of Norman French from Italy and Normandy answered the call for the First Crusade.

The ninth century was disastrous for Italian Christians, as the fragile alliances of the often competitive Italian city-states fractured and their defenses against outside attack begin to crumble. During this time, trade relations and political concerns sometimes transcended religious or cultural ties, leading to the creation of occasional Muslim and Christian alliances against co-religionists. Indeed, in 837 Muslim armies made their first appearance on the Italian mainland at the request of the duke of Naples, who appealed for their help against a local enemy attacking his interests. The Neapolitans returned the favor by assisting Muslims in their attacks on Sicily, and the two maintained an alliance for much of the rest of the century, fending off efforts by popes and emperors to shatter it. Indeed, in 876–877 Naples allowed Muslim armies to use its ports for raids on other Sicilian and Italian cities and their markets for the disposal of booty collected during the raids.[81]

So there was no uniform Italian Christian front against these attacks by Muslim armies during the ninth century, and, consequently, the peninsula suffered greatly from the hardships of such conflict. Muslim forces, many of them acting essentially as pirates, racked up a string of victories during this time, occupying various towns along the Italian coast and using them as raiding bases. In 846 Rome itself, primal see of Christianity both by tradition and by decree of the First Council of Constantinople in 381, was attacked and the basilicas of Saint Peter and of Saint-Paul-outside-the-Walls were looted. Both were located on the right bank of the Tiber and, as the latter's name indicates, consequently outside the main walls of Rome, which had wisely been rebuilt by Pope Gregory IV (r. 827–844).

In response to the smash-and-grab tactics of their attackers, Leo IV (r. 847–855) had the walls further rebuilt and extended to encompass the area around Saint Peter's Basilica—walls that created the so-called Leonine City—and Pope John VIII (r. 872–882) would later fortify the Basilica of Saint Paul. In 849, another large Muslim

79. Hilmar Krueger, "The Italian Cities and the Arabs before 1095," in *History of the Crusades*, ed. Kenneth Setton, 2nd ed., 6 vols. (Madison: University of Wisconsin Press, 1969–1989), 1:4345, http://digital.library.wisc.edu/1711.dl/History.CrusOne (accessed July 9, 2014).

80. Metcalfe, Muslims of Medieval Italy, 9–12.

81. Karsh, Islamic Imperialism, 66–67.

The walls of the Leonine City. Completed in 852, these forty-foot-high walls, which encircled the entire Vatican Hill, extended three kilometers (1.86 miles). Photo: Courtesy of Alfred J. Andrea. All rights reserved.

fleet set out for Rome with, apparently, similar intentions. An allied Christian fleet met it and held it off until a storm wiped it out. A confused struggle, back and forth, for control of Christian southern Italy, with competing interests sometimes leading to Christian-Muslim alliances, then continued for the rest of the century.

Farther south, between Sicily and North Africa, the little island of Malta, where Saint Paul had been shipwrecked, had fallen by 870 (or perhaps earlier, as some scholars argue). It would not come under Christian rule again until it was reconquered by Norman troops in 1091, just before the First Crusade (though an uncertain but probably large proportion of its population remained Christian).

Weary of the raids, but growing in economic and military strength, several south Italian cities allied with Byzantine and papal troops in 915 and finally drove the Muslims out of their settlements on the Italian mainland. From this time on, the Italian cities began to exert ever-growing pressure on the Muslims of North Africa in an attempt to neutralize their ability to operate in Italy. Nonetheless, in 934 and 935, the Italian coast from Genoa to Pisa was subjected to a wave of Muslim attacks; the Genoese were massacred, their churches sacked, and their women and children enslaved.[82] In 965, Muslims inflicted a severe defeat on a Byzantine fleet near Messina.[83] Pisa was raided repeatedly, in 1004, 1011, and 1012, though it retaliated with a raid of its own against Muslim-occupied Reggio (at the southern tip of the Italian Peninsula) in 1004. In 1015, Spanish Muslims seized Sardinia and carried out more raids along the northwest Italian coast, but the Italian states were by now not entirely

---

82. Krueger, "Italian Cities," 51.

83. Ibid.

helpless; under the leadership of Pope Benedict VIII, the Pisans drove the Muslims off Sardinia and occupied it themselves.[84]

But Italy continued to be a battleground. Salerno, in southern Italy, came under siege in 1016–1017, a siege that was only raised when, not insignificantly, a band of armed Norman pilgrims returning from the Holy Land happened by and helped them out.[85] Bari and Taranto, also in the south, were targets; Bari had been saved in 1002 only by combined Byzantine-Venetian action.

Through the eleventh century, the Italian city-states, especially Pisa and Genoa, became steadily more powerful, more capable of defending themselves, and increasingly more able to take the fight to the enemy. In 1034 the Pisans, possibly with assistance from the Genoese and Provençals, mounted a raid on Bona in North Africa, perhaps the first instance of a Christian counterattack striking the south coast of the western Mediterranean. In 1062 or 1063, the Pisans also raided Palermo, on Sicily, and carried off an enormous quantity of loot.[86]

The greatest of these Italian counter-strikes came in 1087, with an allied raid on Mahdia in what is now Tunisia, a longstanding center of Fatimid power and a principal source of the torment that had been visited on the Frankish and Italian coasts.[87] Under the leadership of Pope Victor III and with the backing of Countess Matilda of Tuscany,[88] Pisa, Genoa, Rome, and Amalfi sent a large expeditionary force that had virtually taken the whole city by the time its ruler sued for terms, paying the Italians an enormous indemnity, freeing prisoners, and granting trade rights. Together the Pisans and Genoese also assisted in operations against Valencia (1092) and Tortosa (1093) in Spain.[89] After the Mahdia expedition, Muslim pressure on the Italian cities abated sharply. The historian Hilmar Krueger has noted:

> In the Pisan annals of Bernardo Maragone the next reference [after the Mahdia campaign] is to the call of Pope Urban II and to the Pisan participation in the First Crusade. It is not surprising. The Italian cities had fought and defeated the Arabs in the western Mediterranean, often upon the request of the Roman popes and under the leadership of papal legates. They had carried the battle to the Arab bases in Africa, Spain, and the Mediterranean lands, and in the last great campaign of 1087 they had won commercial rights and privileges. For them participation in the First Crusade was natural.[90]

---

84. H. E. J. Cowdrey, "The Mahdia Campaign of 1087," *English Historical Review* 92 (1977): 13.

85. Krueger, "Italian Cities," 51.

86. Cowdrey, "Mahdia Campaign," 13–14.

87. Ibid., 1–29.

88. Ibid., 16. Victor III (1086–1087) was pope between Gregory VII and Urban II; he and Matilda (a supporter of Gregory VII) were significant supporters of the militant, reformed papacy.

89. Krueger, "Italian Cities," 52.

90. Ibid., 53. See also Cowdrey, "Mahdia Campaign," 1–29.

From the point of view of the Italians, who had been engaged in resisting Islamic aggression for centuries, the transition to crusading against Muslims in the Holy Land in the late eleventh century—which was initially framed in large part as a defense of Eastern Christians, who had similar problems with Islamic foes—was seamless. Regardless of what developments in doctrine, church administration, or spirituality might or might not have facilitated the First Crusade, it is hard to see, at the very least, how the Italians could or would have viewed it as a particularly novel activity. They had been engaged for much too long in far too many protracted clashes with Islamic forces to conceive of them collectively as anything but part of a broader conflict. This long history of Italo-Muslim conflicts, however, is all too often unknown to or ignored by writers and videographers who begin the story of the crusades in 1095.

Spain and France

Christians in Italy and the nearby islands would therefore have found risible the argument that there were no "major clashes" between Western Christians and Islam before the First Crusade. But what about farther west, in Spain and France? Perhaps this area was what *U.S. News & World Report* and others referred to. Let us again examine the evidence.

If Italians apparently had little problem transitioning from the idea of conflict against Muslim enemies in Europe to conflict with Muslim enemies in the Holy Land, it is likely that Spanish Christians would have had even less of a problem. Like the Italians, Spaniards did not have to travel all the way to the eastern Mediterranean to find such a conflict. They had been engaged in an intermittent, but ongoing, struggle between Christians and Muslims at home for centuries before the calling of the First Crusade. This conflict had begun in 711, when the Muslim general Tariq bin Ziyad, in response to intrigue by a rebellious Christian governor of a Visigothic-Spanish enclave in North Africa, led an army across the straits of Gibraltar and invaded then Christian Spain.

Tariq defeated the Visigothic king of Spain in 712 near Toledo and effectively destroyed Christian control of the peninsula in one crushing blow. Cordoba and Granada fell immediately, Valencia, two years later. A small and tenacious group of Spanish Christians retreated into the mountainous area of far northwestern Spain. Thinking—correctly in the short term, though incorrectly in the long—that these Christian warriors represented no immediate threat, the Muslim armies bypassed them and headed northeast. "What are thirty barbarians perched on a rock? They must inevitably die," the Muslim chronicler Ibn Hayyan wrote contemptuously.[91] (Yet, according to one version of the story, the battered Christians had lured a Muslim army into a narrow valley and then defeated it by hurling down great boulders.)[92]

---

91. Joseph O'Callaghan, *A History of Medieval Spain* (Ithaca, NY: Cornell University Press, 1975), 99.
92. One version of the story may be found in *The Chronicle of Alfonso III*, in *Conquerors and Chronicles of Early Medieval Spain*, trans. Kenneth Baxter Wolf, 2nd ed. (Liverpool, UK: Liverpool University Press, 1999), 165–69.

Whatever the reason for their not completing the conquest of Spain, by 720 Muslim armies were crossing the Pyrenees into Narbonne, in present-day southern France, and raiding deeper and deeper into the Frankish kingdom. The process was not entirely without setbacks. In 731, Munnuza, the Berber commander of the passes through the Pyrenees, "conspired with Duke Eudo of Aquitaine to overthrow the Arabs because of the way they were treating his people"[93]—an incident that suggests that even the Berbers, North African tribesmen, were not yet entirely pacified or resigned to Islam.

The next year,[94] Charles Martel, mayor (chief minister) of the Frankish kingdom, met a major Muslim incursion somewhere between Tours and Poitiers and defeated it. Although at the time it probably did not seem to be a major turning point, in fact Muslim armies never again penetrated so deeply into Frankish territory; the high point of their campaigns receded steadily thereafter. By 769, the Franks had driven the Muslims out of their kingdom, and in 795, Charlemagne crossed the Pyrenees and set up a buffer region in the northern part of present-day Catalonia, reaching as far south as the Ebro River.[95] Thereafter the Franks offered intermittent assistance to the rump of unconquered Spanish Christians as they fought to cling to the remnants of their peninsula. They eventually began to push the Muslims south in what came to be known later as *Reconquista*, or "reconquest," of Christian Spain from its Muslim conquerors, a process that was not complete until Ferdinand and Isabella recovered Granada in 1492. The story, briefly told, of early Muslim-Christian conflict in the Iberian Peninsula down to the mid-eleventh century is as follows.[96]

Prior to the eleventh century, Christian power was confined to northern Spain. Asturias, a small kingdom that had emerged around 750, expanded to include the entire northwestern corner of Iberia. In the late eighth and early ninth centuries, Asturias had to endure three Muslim invasions, but it held on. Meanwhile, as already noted, the king of the Franks, Charlemagne, carved out by the year 810 a Spanish March (literally, a Spanish frontier or border zone) in the northeast. In the later ninth

---

93. Brett and Fentress, *Berbers*, 88. As the authors point out, this little known fact puts the relative success of the Frankish Christians at Tours the next year in an interesting light; the Muslims were having problems controlling their own rear areas.

94. Scholars have argued over whether the correct date for Tours is 732, 733, or 734. The best evidence suggests that the traditional date of 732 is correct.

95. Krueger, "Italian Cities," 41.

96. The sources for this story are Benjamin W. Wheeler, "The Reconquest of Spain before 1095," in *History of the Crusades*, ed. Kenneth Setton, 2nd ed., 6 vols. (Madison: University of Wisconsin Press, 1969–1989), 1:31–39, http://digital.library.wisc.edu/1711.dl/History.CrusOne (accessed July 9, 2014); Nikolas Jaspert, "Reconquista," in *The Crusades: An Encyclopedia*, ed. Alan V. Murray, 4 vols. (Santa Barbara, CA: ABC-Clio, 2006), 4:1013–19; Bernard F. Reilly, *The Medieval Spains* (Cambridge: Cambridge University Press, 1988); Joseph F. O'Callaghan, *Reconquest and Crusade in Medieval Spain* (Philadelphia: University of Pennsylvania Press, 2002); and O'Callaghan, *A History of Medieval Spain*.

century, Asturias captured and repopulated a region that today encompasses northern Portugal and the northern areas of present-day León-Castile, all of which in time became centers of new Christian kingdoms.

Against this background and during the same century, chroniclers in the kingdom of Asturias began to articulate the concept of *Reconquista,* a reconquest of Christian lands that had been unjustly seized by non-Christians, thereby inaugurating an ideology that became, for centuries thereafter, a central motif in Spanish-Christian literature and eventually a driving force in the Spanish psyche.[97] The ideal of reconquest was not immediately consonant with political-military reality, however, as the Christians were in no position to effect it.

After about the year 950, the Umayyad Caliphate of Córdoba was able to extend its temporary influence over the small Christian states to the north, turning them into dependencies. For example, in 956 Abd al-Rahman III (r. 912–961), the greatest Muslim ruler of the land known as Al-Andalus (Muslim Spain) and first proclaimed caliph of the Spanish Umayyads, helped place Sancho I on the throne of the Christian kingdom of León, although Sancho soon fell out with his Moorish patron. In 997 Muslim raiders destroyed the Christian shrine of Santiago in far northwestern Galicia to punish King Vermudo II of León for breaking his word. This was a particularly bitter blow for the Christians of Spain inasmuch as the shrine held (and continues to hold) what are believed to be the bones of the apostle Saint James (Santiago) the Greater, a relative of Jesus, making it one of the most revered sites of pilgrimage in the Christian West.

Later, toward the mid-twelfth century,[98] the apostle metamorphosed into Santiago Matamoros (Saint James the Moor-Killer), who was believed to miraculously appear at critical moments in battle, seated on a white horse and brandishing a weapon and a banner, to lead Christian forces to victory over their Moorish enemies.

The attack on the shrine of Saint James was a high-water point for the caliphate, which soon thereafter began to dissolve due to internal disorder. In 1031 the caliphate collapsed and Al-Andalus was divided into more than twenty *taifa* (factional) petty states. In the midst of this breakdown of central authority, Al-Andalus experienced a foreshadowing of the crusades when in 1064 an army of Christian Spaniards and French captured and plundered the stronghold of Barbastro, with perhaps the moral and spiritual support of Pope Alexander II.[99] The *Reconquista* had begun in earnest.

---

97. O'Callaghan, *Reconquest,* 4. As he also points out, "Reconquest was not a static concept brought to perfection in the ninth century, but rather one that evolved and was shaped by the influences of successive generations." Ibid., 3–4.

98. Or in the thirteenth century; the evidence is ambiguous.

99. Jonathan Riley-Smith, *Crusades,* 3rd ed., 30, notes that although it used to be thought that Alexander II gave an indulgence to the Christian soldiers going to besiege Barbastro, thereby prefiguring the crusade indulgence granted by Urban II in 1095, it has been argued that this indulgence was for pilgrims, not warriors.

Just as Muslim-Christian conflicts were becoming ever more frequent and heated in Iberia during the ninth century, the region of what is today southern France also became a battleground late in that same century and remained so for close to a hundred years. Balked for the time being on the land front, in about 888 Muslim forces began to establish nests along the coast of Provence, especially in La Garde-Freinet. These bases proved a major thorn in the side to the Christians and a dangerous staging point for Muslim raids and campaigns for most of the next century. Once having taken La Garde-Freinet, the Muslims promptly used it to exert control over the Alpine passes between France and Italy.[100] The Byzantine navy, in concert with local Christian forces in Provence, launched an attack to try to neutralize La Garde-Freinet in 931 but failed. A few years later, around 935, Muslims from La Garde-Freinet penetrated as far inland as present-day Aix-en-Provence and sacked it. Once again the Christians attempted to neutralize the source of the problem, attacking La Garde-Freinet in 942; once again they failed to dislodge its Muslim conquerors.

In 972, the Muslims of La Garde-Freinet pulled off a great coup against their Christian neighbors, but in so doing, they over-reached and provoked a growing power into fatal retaliation: they kidnapped and held for ransom Abbot Maiolus, leader of the most respected Western monastery, Cluny.[101] The count of Provence, exasperated beyond endurance, joined with Italian forces from Turin to clean out both the Alpine passes and—finally—the base at La Garde-Freinet itself, ending that particular threat.[102]

Back in Spain, the weak *taifa* kingdoms suffered a number of defeats at the hands of resurgent Christian kingdoms. Following the loss of their key city of Toledo in 1085, the Muslims of Al-Andalus called on the Almoravids from North Africa. These tough, fanatical Sunni Muslim Berbers from the Sahara soon took over the *taifa* kingdoms, holding up the Christian advance for a time but also making life more difficult for the significant Christian and Jewish populations of their domains. By 1090, they were even driving Christians north again, though not without setbacks; the semi-legendary Christian hero El Cid took Valencia in 1092, and it remained in Christian hands until 1102, when the Almoravids recaptured it. This was followed up with the Almoravid capture of Zaragoza in 1110. Around 1100, the lines stabilized for a time. Alfonso VI of Leon and Castile retook Valencia briefly but was unable to hold it, and by 1109 the Almoravids had it again. This, however, takes us beyond the First Crusade of 1095–1099.

So to answer the question of whether there were "major clashes" between Muslims and Christians in Spain and France before the First Crusade: yes, there certainly were "major clashes" there too, from 711 to the beginning of the First Crusade and beyond.

---

100. Kruger, "Italian Cities," 51.

101. An abbey at which Odo of Châtillon-sur-Marne would serve as prior (second in charge) before moving on to Rome, where he became Pope Urban II.

102. Kruger, "Italian Cities," 51.

The First Crusade

The Byzantines, who, as we have seen, had been calling for assistance for a couple of decades, finally induced the papacy to take action in the 1090s. At the Council of Piacenza in early 1095, Pope Urban II allowed a delegation from the Byzantine emperor Alexius I Comnenus to address the assembled churchmen and plead for military aid. Carrying this message across northern Italy and southern France, and consulting with prominent nobles and churchmen along the way, Urban ended up in Clermont in central France in late 1095. There, on November 27, he made his famous speech calling for aid to Eastern Christians and the Holy Land. He was answered by cries of "God wills it!" and a popular response of a magnitude that neither he nor anyone else anticipated. The First Crusade had begun, and with it a new stage in the ongoing conflict between Islam and the Christian West.

Conclusion

Within a scant 120 years from initial Muslim attacks, Islamic forces had taken control of lands from the Hindu Kush Mountains (located in present-day Pakistan and Afghanistan) to the Atlantic Coast, ripping away control of some two-thirds or more of the Christian world. In the following centuries, they launched continual attacks on Christian territory, forcing the "House of Islam" ever farther into Christian lands.

In 1095, after centuries of attacks, and a few tentative responses of their own, Western Europeans were finally ready to mount a major counteroffensive: a *counter offensive*, not an initiation of hostilities and certainly very far from the "first major clash" between Islam and Christianity. It was merely the latest phase in the long-running conflict between the two faiths that had begun with the Muslim conquest of Christian Syria in 633. There had been nearly continual conflict between the two from then on, with the Christians giving ground with disastrous swiftness and only later mounting counterattacks to recover their lost territories as it became possible.

The crusades were not the beginning of these counterattacks—the earliest genuinely successful ones were undertaken by the Byzantines in the ninth century in an effort to recover historic Christian lands, though there were significant successful efforts in the lands of the Franks, Italians, and Spaniards, as well. The ideas that the crusades represented the "first major clash" between Islam and Christianity, as *U.S. News & World Report* put it, that Islam established itself only through "enthusiasm and persuasion," as Voltaire put it, or that the crusades were merely the result of an "imperial-papal power play" that ended "five centuries of peaceful coexistence," as John Esposito put it, are simply and entirely wrong, as a careful examination of the historical evidence makes clear. The crusades were merely another aspect of the conflict that had existed between Islam and Christianity (and Islam and Judaism) since Islam's inception. As the First Crusade began, a new chapter was indeed being written . . . but in a book that was already very old.

2. MAD MEN ON CRUSADE: RELIGIOUS MADNESS AND THE ORIGINS OF THE FIRST CRUSADE

James M. Muldoon

Every age has its peculiar folly; some scheme, project, or phantasy into which it plunges, spurred on either by the love of gain, the necessity of excitement, or the mere force of imitation. Failing in these, it has some madness, to which it is goaded by political or religious causes, or both combined. Every one of these causes influenced the Crusades, and conspired to render them the most extraordinary instance upon record of the extent to which popular enthusiasm can be carried. History in her solemn page informs us, that the Crusaders were but ignorant and savage men, that their motives were those of bigotry unmitigated, and that their pathway was one of blood and tears.[1]

With these dramatic words, the mid-nineteenth-century journalist Charles Mackay summed up the medieval crusades in his often-reprinted *Extraordinary Popular Delusions and the Madness of Crowds*, one of the most famous and widely quoted discussions of mass irrational behavior ever published.[2] For Mackay, mass movements were

---

1. The first edition was in three volumes, had several chapters that were not reprinted, and arranged the chapters in a slightly different order than later editions. See Charles Mackay, *Memoirs of Extraordinary Popular Delusions,* 3 vols. (London: Richard Bentley, 1841); see also Charles Mackay, *Memoirs of Extraordinary Popular Delusions and the Madness of Crowds,* 2nd ed., 2 vols. (London: National Illustrated Library, 1852); reprint ed., 1 vol. (Boston: L.C. Page, 1932), 354. The second edition is available online at http://www.econlib.org/library/Mackay/macEx.html (accessed March 10, 2014).

2. The most famous chapters of the book deal with the Mississippi and South Sea bubbles that are often discussed in general histories, especially textbooks, when dealing with the economic and financial problems that faced early modern governments, particularly England and France. The chapter dealing with the Dutch Tulip Mania of the seventeenth century is less often discussed, although it has been mentioned in economic texts. See, for example, Herbert Heaton, *Economic History of Europe* (New York: Harper & Brothers, 1936), 280–81. The revised edition of this text, (New York: Harper & Row, 1948, 1965), 282, still mentions the tulips but in a shorter space than the earlier edition. See also Niall Ferguson, *The Ascent of Money* (New York: Penguin, 2008), 136–57. For criticism of Mackay on economic topics, see Peter M. Garber, *Famous First Bubbles: The Fundamentals of Early Manias* (Cambridge, MA: MIT Press, 2000), 29–30, 127–31 and Anne Goldgar, *Tulipmania: Money, Honor, and Knowledge in the Dutch Golden Age* (Chicago: University of Chicago Press, 2007), 135, 314.

a common phenomenon in the past because "nations . . . like individuals, . . . have their whims and their peculiarities; their seasons of excitement and recklessness" when "the population acts in frenzied multitudes. . . ."[3] He also suggested that in the nineteenth century Europeans had overcome the tendency toward such irrational behavior so that Europeans were now rational and sensible, unlike their medieval and early modern ancestors.[4] The book has remained in print almost continuously since 1841, when the first edition appeared.[5]

Many popular writers on the crusades since Mackay have shared his opinion of the crusaders as frenzied madmen even if they have not cited him directly, and the same is true of some authors of Western civilization textbooks, who likewise present the crusades as the product of mass delusions.[6] As the editors of this book indicate in the Introduction and as Thomas Madden, a leading historian of the crusades, pointed out some years ago, in spite of the great amount of scholarly research on the crusades in the past fifty years or so, popular writers still see the crusades as "a series of brutal wars of intolerance in which the cynical, voracious, superstitious, and gullible waged insensible war against a peaceful, sophisticated Muslim world, crushing the opulent Byzantine Empire in the bargain."[7] Moreover, as Daniel Franke shows in detail in his

---

3. Mackay, *Madness*, xix.

4. The experience of the twentieth century with irrational mass movements would suggest otherwise. Norman Cohn, *The Pursuit of the Millennium*, rev. ed. (Oxford: Oxford University Press, 1970), 285–86.

5. At the moment, amazon.com lists several editions in print, usually with introductions by well-known figures in the financial world. The edition used here has an introduction by Bernard M. Baruch.

6. See, for example, George Burton Adams, *Civilization during the Middle Ages* (New York, 1906), 263–67. More recently, the crusades were described by Edward McNall Burns as the consequence of "the impassioned preaching of Peter the Hermit, who went among the peasants rousing them to a frenzied enthusiasm for the holy cause." See his *Western Civilizations: Their History and Their Culture*, 4th ed. (New York: W. W. Norton, 1954), 315. A more recent edition of the text was even more emphatic: the crusaders "were whipped up by preachers into a religious frenzy that approached mass hysteria." Robert E. Lerner, Standish Meacham, and Edward McNall Burns, *Western Civilizations: Their History and Their Culture*, 11th ed. (New York: Norton, 1988), 344. The scholarly literature about the crusades has tended to ignore Mackay's chapter on the crusades. There is, however, a brief but insightful discussion of it in Elizabeth Siberry, *The New Crusaders: Images of the Crusades in the Nineteenth and Early Twentieth Centuries* (Aldershot, UK: Ashgate, 2000), 29–30.

7. Thomas F. Madden, "Crusaders and Historians," *First Things* (June/July, 2005): 26–31 at 26. Madden was referring to the very influential work of Steven Runciman, whose *History of the Crusades*, 3 vols. (Cambridge: Cambridge University Press, 1951–1954) is one of the most widely read modern histories of the crusades. While Runciman and those influenced by his work may not have read Mackay, they reflect his views. The long life of this line of criticism of the crusades, in spite of more nuanced scholarly views, is quite similar and indeed even related to the long-standing belief in the Middle Ages as the Dark Ages. Two recent enthusiastic rejections of this position are Rodney Stark, *The Victory of Reason: How Christianity Led to Freedom, Capitalism, and Western Success* (New York: Random House, 2005) and Thomas E. Woods, Jr., *How the Catholic Church Built*

chapter of this book, a number of popularizers have mistakenly drawn a straight line between the anti-Judaic madness of the crusaders and the anti-Semitic madness of the Nazis. According to Harvard Law School professor Alan Dershowitz, the "Crusades, after all, were the prelude to the Holocaust."[8]

Given Mackay's opinion that every era is characterized by a "particular folly," it is not surprising that his book contains a lengthy chapter on the medieval crusades, in his view a movement rooted in religious fanaticism and a prime example of the way in which irrational mass movements lead to disaster on a large scale. This was, by the way, a view shared by medieval Latin clerics regarding certain movements not initiated or blessed by the Church, as David Sheffler points out in his chapter on the Children's Crusade and a fact that would have surprised Mackay.[9] From his perspective, the crusades were characteristic of the entire Medieval Era that engulfed European society until modernity arrived to rescue Europe from this benighted condition as Europe finally cast "off the slough of superstition in which the Roman clergy had so long enveloped it" and so "became prepared to receive the seeds of the approaching Reformation."[10] In his reading of history, the crusades were not just one element in the fabric of medieval European society; they were *the* characteristic feature of the entire medieval world.

Just how accurately did Mackay judge the crusades? Were the crusaders as deluded as he claimed or did he misunderstand them because of his basic premise that societies possess some inherent form of madness? Is it possible to argue *contra* Mackay that, despite the irrefutable presence of individuals and groups gripped by apocalyptic fantasies during at least some of these expeditions, crusaders on the whole were not mad or rendered irrational by religious frenzy, superstition, and delusion and that the ultimate failure of the movement was not rooted in an apocalyptic craze—what Mackay characterized as "this European madness"—that supposedly initiated and drove the

---

Western Civilization (Washington, D.C.: Regnery, 2005). For a recent more positive view of the crusades, see Rodney Stark, *God's Battalions: A Case for the Crusades* (New York: HarperCollins, 2009). Several words of caution are in order. Woods is not a crusade historian or even a medievalist. A historian of the United States, who has written on the Catholic Church in the Progressive Era, Woods should be counted among the cohort of conservatives who have overstated the case of the European Middle Ages and the medieval Church in reaction to assaults by Protestant apologists of the Reformation and Humanists of every era. Stark, a sociologist whose historical books are derivative, must be counted as both an apologist for Western Christianity and among the Traditionalists, according to the four-part division of crusade historians that the editors outline in the Introduction. He deals only with the factors leading up to the First Crusade and crusading in the Middle East and Egypt in the period, 1096–1291.

8. Alan Dershowitz, "My crusade against crusading," http://www.jewishworldreview.com/0899/crusades1.asp (accessed March 11, 2014).

9. Mackay's 150-page chapter, "The Crusades," is at http://www.econlib.org/library/Mackay/macEx9.html#Ch.9 (accessed March 10, 2014).

10. Mackay, *Madness*, 460.

entire movement?[11] For the most part, today's crusade historians do not employ terms such as "insanity" and "madness" to characterize the crusades as a whole, although the term "frenzy" is often used to describe the behavior of some groups of crusaders, especially during the First Crusade. But are they wrong to be so moderate in their use of language and so apparently balanced in their conclusions, and are Mackay's more colorful language and judgment basically correct?

Mackay's book provides little evidence to support his views and few dates to demonstrate the time span involved. He does cite the words of a number of chroniclers, Guibert of Nogent, Fulcher of Chartres, William of Tyre, and Anna Comnena, among others, but without indicating the texts used or page numbers or displaying any understanding whatsoever of the contexts of their works, the authors' perspectives, or the genres in which they were writing. In other words, he provides no firm evidence from which readers can judge the accuracy of his statements and judgments. He also mentions several modern historians who dealt with the crusades but, again, without any indication of which of their texts he used. For example, he refers to Edward Gibbon (1737–1794) and Friedrich Wilken (1777–1840) in passing but without specific citations.

This oversight is all the more frustrating because some of his information about the First Crusade seems to have come from Gibbon's chapter 58, "Origin and Numbers of the First Crusade."[12] Clearly, even more of the information that he dispenses originated in Wilken's multi-volume *Geschichte der Kreuzzüge* (History of the Crusades).[13] Mackay's vague references to Wilken's work are especially interesting because Wilken was "the first scholar to combine Western and Eastern materials in a critical source-based account [of the crusades] up to the early fourteenth century."[14] Mackay, however, does not appear to have actually read Wilken's work but apparently knew of it by way of an article in the *Foreign Quarterly Review* (1830) that reviewed Wilken's first four volumes and two works by the French author Joseph François Michaud.[15]

---

11. See the discussion of the Popularist School of crusade historians in the Introduction. Several crusade historians have essentially agreed with Mackay's view of an apocalyptic fantasy as the driving element behind the crusades: Paul Alphandéry, *La Chrétiente et l'idée de croisde*, 2 vols., ed. A. Dupront (Paris: A. Michel, 1954–1959) and Jay Rubenstein, *Armies of Heaven: The First Crusade and the Quest for Apocalypse* (New York: Basic Books, 2011). It is still a minority view. The overall role of apocalyptic fervor and other elements of religious enthusiasm as a major force in medieval Latin society has been the subject of a great deal of scholarly effort in recent years. In addition to Norman Cohn's fundamental study, *Pursuit of the Millennium*, see a recent challenge to Cohn's views: Gary Dickson, *Religious Enthusiasm in the Medieval West* (Aldershot, UK: Variorum, 2000).

12. Edward Gibbon, *The History of the Decline and Fall of the Roman Empire*, 4 vols. (New York: Harper and Brothers, 1836), 4:106–41.

13. Friedrich Wilken, *Geschichte der Kreuzzüge*, 7 vols. (1803–1832). Christopher Tyerman, *The Debate on the Crusades* (Manchester: Manchester University Press, 2011), 127–37, passim, places Wilken's work into a historiographical context.

14. Jonathan Riley-Smith, *The Crusades: A Short History* (New Haven, CT: Yale University Press, 2005), 299.

15. *Foreign Quarterly Review* (1830), Art. X, 623–54.

Mackay also refers to the work of Charles Mills, a self-taught English historian who wrote on the crusades.[16] Clearly, the title of Mackay's work echoes lines from Gibbon and Mills and from the review article in the *Foreign Quarterly Review*. Gibbon refers to "the popular madness of the times."[17] Likewise, Mills characterized the crusades as "the extremist idea of madness," which "retarded the march of civilisation."[18] On its part, the review article in the *Foreign Quarterly Review* opens with the statement "The most extraordinary phenomena beyond question which the history of the world presents are the Crusades to the Holy Land."[19] In essence, Mackay presented a derivative and, worse, ill-constructed scholarly veneer—an academic Potemkin village that was all façade and no substance—to "support" his extravagant claims.

In dealing with the crusades, in one of the longest chapters in his work, Mackay created not one but several myths that were embraced in popular narratives of the crusades for many years to follow. The first myth in Mackay's telling concerns the origin of the crusades. For Mackay the crusades emerged "at the close of the tenth and commencement of the eleventh century" when Europeans began to believe that the end of the world was near and that all "Christendom was in commotion. A panic terror seized upon the weak, the credulous, and the guilty, who in those days formed more than nineteen-twentieths of the population."[20] According to Mackay, this apprehension of the Apocalypse and the expected return of Christ to Earth led many Christians to march to Jerusalem to meet their Lord. Once there the pilgrims discovered that the city was now in the hands of the fierce Turks who harassed Christian pilgrims.

The amount of putative terror surrounding the year 1000 has been a matter of scholarly debate, with the most recent scholarship demonstrating that there was no widespread terror.[21] Yet, one still reads popular accounts of the crusades that maintain that the First Crusade was launched against a background in which "the air was thick with future marvels. Europe had been swept by millenarianism. It was being said that

---

16. Charles Mills, *The History of the Crusades for the Recovery and Possession of the Holy Land*, 2 vols. (London: 1820).

17. Gibbon, *Decline*, 3:107.

18. Quoted in Tyerman, *Debate*, 118–19.

19. *Foreign Quarterly Review*, 623.

20. Mackay, *Madness*, 357–58. Compare chapter 5 ("Modern Prophecies") of the second edition, which begins with the supposed apocalyptic terrors that gripped Europe at the coming of the year 1000. Mackay almost never gives a precise date, preferring to use vague general terms.

21. See Henri Focillon, *The Year 1000*, trans. Fred. D. Wieck (New York: Harper & Row, 1971). The approach of the year 2000 generated a good deal of scholarly interest in medieval theories of the Apocalypse and the Millennium. Much of this work rejected the notion that such thought had any effect on the crusades. See Richard Landes, Andrew Gow, and David C. Van Meter, eds., *The Apocalyptic Year 1000: Religious Expectation and Social Change, 950–1050* (Oxford: Oxford University Press, 2003); Frederick S. Paxton, "History, Historians, and the Peace of God" in *The Peace of God: Social Violence and Religious Response in France around the Year 1000*, ed. Thomas Head and Richard Landes (Ithaca, NY: Cornell University Press, 1992), 21–40, at 37–38.

a huge body of Christian pilgrims assembling in Jerusalem could hasten the return of the Messiah."[22] We shall return to the issue of the myth of the terrors of the year 1000 toward the end of this chapter.

Mackay further claimed that this combination of supposed apocalyptic terror and Turkish occupation of Jerusalem was the ultimate cause, or necessary precondition, for the mass movement that was much later termed "the crusades."[23] The proximate, or immediate, cause was when Peter the Hermit, "a monk of Amiens . . . [who] had served as a soldier," returned from a pilgrimage to Jerusalem to inform the pope of the persecution of Christians in the East. According to Mackay, Peter was "enthusiastic, chivalrous, bigoted, and, if not insane, not far removed from insanity," but he was exactly suited to the age, "the very prototype of the time."[24]

Seeing what he judged to be the horrible condition of Christians in the East and of the Holy City in Turkish hands, Peter approached the Greek patriarch of Jerusalem and suggested that he write a letter to the pope "and to the most influential monarchs of Christendom, detailing the sorrows of the faithful, and urging them to take up arms in their defence." Returning to Europe, Peter approached Pope Urban II and presented him with the patriarch's letter. Moved by Peter "whose zeal was so unbounded," the pope "sent him abroad to preach the holy war to all nations and potentates of Christendom."[25]

According to Mackay, "The Hermit preached, and countless thousands answered to his call," causing large groups of unarmed people to speed eastward to a land the location of which they did not know, people without "discipline, principle, or true courage" who "rushed through the nations like a pestilence, spreading terror and death wherever they went."[26] The assorted groups of this first wave of crusaders were composed of "three hundred thousand men, women, and children . . . the vilest rascality of Europe."[27]

---

22. Terry Jones and Alan Ereira, *Crusades* (New York: FactsOnFile, 1995), 28. See the editors' Introduction for an analysis of Jones' portrayal of the crusades and crusaders.

23. See the editors' Introduction for a discussion of the origin of this term and the continuing debate among historians as to what constituted a crusade. For the purposes of this discussion, campaigns against Muslim societies will be labeled crusades unless otherwise indicated.

24. Mackay, *Madness*, 358.

25. Ibid., 361.

26. Ibid., 361–70.

27. Ibid., 370. He provides no evidence for this figure but appears to have borrowed it from Albert of Aachen, not realizing that medieval chroniclers tended to grossly exaggerate the numbers of people in any situation. John France, *Victory in the East: A Military History of the First Crusade* (Cambridge: Cambridge University Press, 1994), 127–42, provides the best estimate of crusade numbers to date. He estimates that about 80,000 crusaders—fighters and non-combatants combined—ever reached Anatolia (present-day Asian Turkey). At no time did the combined armies of the second wave (the Crusade of the Nobles) number more than 50,000–60,000, whereas the main force of the so-called Peasants' or People's Crusade was about 20,000. If about 80,000 in both waves of the First

The eventual result of this first stage of the First Crusade, a movement often mistermed the Peasants' Crusade of 1096, was a disaster leading to the death of most of these crusaders. To Mackay, the career of Peter the Hermit thus demonstrated not only the madness of the crusades but also the corruption of the medieval Church that kept humanity in the kind of ignorance and superstition that provided fertile ground for mass delusions, such as the crusades that drove people totally unprepared and untrained for combat to undertake such a foolhardy expedition.

Mackay's tale of Peter the Hermit and his role in initiating the crusades is largely mythical. In the first place, evidence for a mass delusional great fear of the imminent end of the world in and around 1000 just does not exist. There is also no definite evidence that Peter the Hermit ever met the pope, and indeed the pope did not need any encouragement from a wandering preacher to call upon Latin Christians to support their Eastern brethren. It is also more than just a vast exaggeration to state in regard to Peter the Hermit that "the train that was to explode so fearfully was now laid" because he possessed "the hand to apply the torch." Moreover, there is no evidence whatsoever that he preached throughout Europe encouraging "countless thousands" to heed his words.[28] It was Urban's call to assist the Christians of the East that inspired preachers of the crusade, not Peter the Hermit's experiences and actions, although Peter did preach the crusade following Urban's call for an expedition to Jerusalem and did manage to raise a sizeable army—but not hundreds of thousands.

Mackay's picture of a deluded, possibly insane pilgrim inspiring Pope Urban II to call the Latin Christian world to arms in defense of the oppressed Christians of the East can be found in two twelfth-century sources for the First Crusade. William of Tyre (c. 1130–1186), one of the most important crusade chroniclers, writing in the late twelfth century discussed the role of Peter but more calmly than Mackay. Basing his account upon that of the early twelfth-century crusade chronicler Albert of Aix (also known as Aachen), who wrote his account of the First Crusade sometime after 1121, or more than a quarter century after the event, William describes Peter as "a certain priest named Peter, from the kingdom of the Franks" who had gone on pilgrimage to Jerusalem, where he learned of the "existing perils, but also the persecutions" that the Christians living there had long endured.

Subsequently Peter conferred with the patriarch of Jerusalem, who informed the pilgrim of "all the evils which the people of God had suffered while dwelling in Jerusalem." Peter convinced the patriarch to write a letter to the "lord Pope and the Roman church and to

---

Crusade actually crossed the Bosporus from Constantinople, then the total mass of initial crusaders must have exceeded 100,000, considering the numbers who died, returned home, or permanently detoured before ever reaching Asia. Added to this 100,000 were the unknown numbers who arrived as reinforcements at ports in Anatolia and Syria-Palestine. Peter Lock, *The Routledge Companion to the Crusades* (London: Routledge, 2006), 139, estimates about 100,000 persons initially set off on crusade.

28. Mackay, *Madness*, 358–61.

the kings and princes of the West" that will "inform them of the greatness of your sufferings and to urge them to hasten to your relief." Peter then took the letter, returned to Italy, "proceeded to Rome, and found the lord Pope Urban in the vicinity," where he presented the pope with the patriarch's letter."[29] Mackay retold this basic story, but in keeping with his theme of the insanity of the crusades, he retold it in vivid, gory colors, transforming the story of a pious pilgrim scandalized by the fate of his fellow Christians under Muslim rule into the tale of a madman who applied a torch to the tinder provided by the supposed apocalyptic currents present within the Latin Church.

Pope Urban II preaching the First Crusade from an engraving in the 1841 edition of *Extraordinary Popular Delusions and the Madness of Crowds*. The person in black, who has the facial expression and body language of an unbalanced person and stands directly behind the pope, is undoubtedly Peter the Hermit. Note the stern-faced churchmen who stand high above the masses. The few faces from the crowd that we can see display rapt attention. The two knights in the foreground are anachronistically dressed in thirteenth-century armor, but that aside, note how they and the two lords with their backs to us are also set far apart from the "mad" crowd. Photo source: Wikimedia.

Both versions, that of Albert and William and that of Mackay, emphasize that the pope did not know of the cruelties being perpetrated in the East until Peter told him about the situation. But this was surely not the case. Pope Gregory VII (r. 1073–1083), who had made holy war a tool of the papal reform movement of the eleventh century, had announced in 1074, in response to Byzantine pleas for aid against the Seljuk Turks, that he planned to lead in person a vast relief expedition to the East that would push forward all the way to Jerusalem.

Subsequent momentous events in Europe, namely the Investiture Controversy, prevented Gregory from acting on this plan, but he set in place as papal policy four of the primary elements of what later became the First Crusade: relief of embattled

---

29. William of Tyre, *History of Deeds Done beyond the Sea*, trans. E. A. Babcock and A. C. Krey (New York: Columbia University Press, 1943, 1976) as excerpted in Edward Peters, ed., *The First Crusade*, 2nd ed. (Philadelphia: University of Pennsylvania Press, 1998), 108–9.

Eastern Christians through a military campaign, reconciliation of Eastern Christians with the Church of Rome, papal leadership over all Christendom, and the liberation of Jerusalem.[30] The papal court, which has a long institutional memory, never forgot this program, and twenty-one years later Pope Urban II, who had been one of Gregory's most trusted cardinals and confidants, put Gregory's plan into action, as Urban's twelfth-century biographer made clear.[31]

Consequently, modern scholars reject or greatly diminish the role of Peter the Hermit in the First Crusade that Mackay and others who followed him have promulgated. A leading specialist in the history of crusading warfare, John France, for example, put it this way: "For much of the nineteenth century it was thought that the crusade was generated by the frustrations of a pilgrim, Peter the Hermit," who "promised the Patriarch of Jerusalem that he would return to his own land and recruit a great army to liberate" the oppressed Christians of the East. His preaching in turn aroused great enthusiasm and generated the First Crusade.[32] As France sees it, Peter was a successful preacher, one of many who preached holy war in the East, not a madman, and the range of his preaching was quite limited. Another modern scholar observed that the story of Peter the Hermit's meeting with the pope "was believed by one or two of Peter's contemporaries and probably assiduously propagated by himself," encouraging the opinion "that the crusade was his brainchild."[33]

Furthermore, those who followed Peter the Hermit and other leaders of the so-called Peasants' Crusade on the trek east in 1096 were not a frenzied mob. As John France has pointed out, "It is a mistake to see these elements of the crusading movement as being different from those that followed them."[34] They formed a body well

---

30. One of several letters that Pope Gregory sent out on this issue is available in *The Correspondence of Pope Gregory VII: Selected Letters from the Registrum*, trans. Ephraim Emerton (New York: W. W. Norton, 1960), 56–58. See also H. E. J. Cowdrey, *Pope Gregory VII, 1073–1085* (Oxford: Oxford University Press, 1999).

31. I. S. Robinson, *The Papacy, 1073–1198* (Cambridge: Cambridge University Press, 1990), 325.

32. John France, *The Crusades and the Expansion of Catholic Christendom, 1000–1714* (London: Routledge, 2005), 23. Mackay's book certainly was one of the books that popularized this nineteenth-century view of Peter the Hermit's importance in the crusades. France returned to the issue of Peter's putative role in *Victory in the East*, 88, n. 28, arguing that the roots of the First Crusade lay in preexisting papal policy and Urban's own thinking. E. O. Blake and Colin Morris have examined the issue of Peter's supposed role in "A Hermit Goes to War: Peter and the Origins of the First Crusade," in *Monks, Hermits and the Ascetic Tradition*, ed. W. J. Shiels (Oxford: Oxford University Press, 1985), 79–107. They conclude that we cannot reject out of hand the notion that Peter influenced Pope Urban, but they go no further than that. See also Christopher Tyerman, *God's War: A New History of the Crusades* (Cambridge, MA: Belknap Press, 2006), 78–81, where he argues that Peter's role in initiating the crusade cannot be totally dismissed. For the origins of the story of Peter the Hermit, see Tyerman, *Debate*, 15–18.

33. Riley-Smith, *Crusades History*, 26. See also France, *Victory*, 88.

34. France, *Crusades and Catholic Christendom*, 65.

enough organized "to manage a long march and they fought well enough against the Turks."[35] In addition, "Peter the Hermit was well-received by the Byzantines" certainly not the response they would have given to a crazed mob led by a lunatic.[36] Yet, despite the fact that this was "not just a crusade of lesser people which collapsed through lack of skill in arms and military leadership,"[37] the myth remains, and is often retold in popular accounts of the crusade, that the "horde that Peter led into Anatolia . . . was not really an army."[38]

A miniature painting from the *Abreviamen de las Estorias*. This fourteenth-century depiction of Peter the Hermit leading a crusade contingent shows a body of followers consisting of a large number of men-at-arms, a mounted knight, and three women (one of whom is largely obscured). Photo source: Wikimedia.

Having demonstrated to his own satisfaction that the initial stage of the crusades "was the worst paroxysm of the madness of Europe," Mackay then generated another myth. He pointed to the feudal nobility of Europe, "her chivalry," who at this moment stepped upon the scene, "employing their cool heads, mature plans, and invincible courage . . . to lead and direct the grand movement of Europe upon Asia."[39] In other words, there was some rationality within the crusading community, but it was associated with secular, not clerical, leaders, and it certainly did not include "the masses." Although influenced by religious enthusiasm, these hardheaded noble warriors, according to Mackay, brought some sense of realism to the crusading movement, thus saving it from the worst excesses of enthusiasm. They were not "crazy like Peter the Hermit" because "their valour being tempered by caution, their religious

---

35. Ibid., 65–66.

36. Ibid., 65.

37. France, *Victory*, 88.

38. Jones and Ereira, *Crusades*, 37–38. The widely read world history textbook by Jerry H. Bentley and Herbert F. Ziegler, *Traditions and Encounters: A Global Perspective on the Past* (Boston: McGraw Hill, 2003), 541, characterizes the force raised by Peter the Hermit as "a ragtag army of poor knights and enthusiastic peasants . . . [who] set out for Palestine without proper training, discipline, weapons, supplies, or plans." This charge was laid against Peter the Hermit's army by the daughter of Emperor Alexius I in her *Alexiad*, a work composed to magnify the deeds of her father in which she displayed antipathy toward the crusaders. Peters, *First Crusade*, 151. See John France, "Anna Comnena, the *Alexiad*, and the First Crusade," *Reading Medieval Studies* 10 (1984): 20–38.

39. Mackay, *Madness*, 377.

zeal by worldly views, and their ferocity by the spirit of chivalry,"[40] they reshaped the crusading movement. In other words, these chivalrous, level-headed nobles were very much like the British gentlemen who were laying the base for a global empire in 1841.

In stressing the religious fanaticism of Peter the Hermit and those like him, namely clerics and the deluded masses, and countering that spirit with a more rational, experienced, and worldly spirit associated with the feudal nobility, Mackay was able to glide over the role of the papacy in the crusades. In fact, however, despite being shunted off to the sidelines by Mackay, Urban II best reflected the role of rational planning in the initial stage of the First Crusade.

As already noted, given the policy established by Pope Gregory VII, Urban II needed no letters from Eastern clerics or firsthand reports by scandalized pilgrims to consider calling for a campaign against the Muslims in the Near East. Wars against the Muslims were not new. From about 1050, Christians in Spain, often supported by French warriors, fought against the Muslims who had overrun Spain in the early eighth century.[41] When Urban II addressed the issue of calling for a crusade, he was operating within an existing tradition and was not moved to sudden dramatic action by the apocalyptic visions of a madman as Mackay would have us believe.

While the text of Urban's speech at Clermont does not exist, five chroniclers and historians, some of them eyewitnesses to the event, composed versions of it written a number of years after the event that present the main themes as they were understood by listeners and by the writers themselves.[42] Only one of the versions, possibly written later than the other four and probably by someone who did not hear Urban's speech at Clermont, mentions the apocalyptic theme that Mackay saw as central to the crusade. Abbot Guibert of Nogent's version of Urban's speech, composed by a churchman with a theological agenda, includes a brief reference to "the approaching time of the Antichrist" and the prophesies associated with the biblical Book of Daniel as motivations for going on this expedition to the East, but this was only a small part of the speech and, as noted, does not appear in any other version of the speech.[43]

What the various versions of Urban's speech do uniformly emphasize is the belief that the Turks were inflicting terrible evils upon the Christians of the East and that the Latin Christian world ought to go to their assistance. The address is not to unarmed

---

40. Ibid.

41. Joseph F. O'Callaghan, *Reconquest and Crusade in Medieval Spain* (Philadelphia: University of Pennsylvania Press, 2003). Chapter 1 of this book, "The First Crusade: Unprovoked Offense or Overdue Defense?" by Paul Crawford outlines in detail pre-crusade conflicts between Muslim and Christian forces.

42. For a brief introduction to the problem of reconstructing Urban's words, a problem universally recognized by crusade historians, see H. E. J. Cowdrey, "Pope Urban's Preaching of the First Crusade," *History* 55 (1970): 177–88. Corliss Slack investigates what we can infer about Urban's message in her chapter of this book, "The Quest for Gain: Were the First Crusaders Proto-Colonists?"

43. Peters, *First Crusade*, 35; Andrew Holt and James Muldoon, eds., *Competing Voices from the Crusades* (Oxford: Greenwood World Publishing, 2008), 20–21.

and untrained masses but to those who by birth and training bear arms, those best prepared to assist the Eastern Christians.

This appeal to the warriors of Christian Europe is best expressed in the version of Urban's speech provided by Robert of Rheims, a clerical chronicler who may well have heard the pope give it. According to Robert, the pope appealed to the nobles of France as a "race chosen and beloved by God" to act as their ancestors had acted in support of the Church. Having described the Turkish atrocities in the East, the pope charged his listeners to "let the deeds of your ancestors move you and incite your minds to manly achievements" and to follow in the footsteps of Charlemagne and the other French monarchs who "have extended in these lands the territory of the holy church." They should turn the weapons that they are accustomed to employ "to murder one another" to a better use, to "wrest that land from the wicked race, and subject it to yourselves." Urban told those who would go on this great campaign that they will not only gain earthly rewards, such as land, but also "remission of your sins" and "the imperishable glory of the kingdom of heaven."[44]

Urban made it clear that he was calling for experienced warriors to answer his call when he declared that "the old or feeble, or those unfit for bearing arms, not undertake this journey, nor ought women to set out at all, without husbands or brothers or legal guardians. For such are more of a hindrance than an aid, more of a burden than an advantage." In addition, priests are not to go "without the consent of their bishop."[45] This theme is repeated in later papal calls for crusaders as well. In his letter to the monks of Vallombrosa, written in October 1096, the pope was unambiguous in stating that he was "stimulating the minds of knights to go on this expedition, since they might be able to restrain the savagery of the Saracens by their arms and restore the Christians [of the East] to their former freedom." He had heard that some monks of this congregation wanted to accompany those knights to Jerusalem. While the sacrifice of this dangerous journey was proper, monks were "the wrong kind of persons" to undertake it. Therefore, no cleric or monk was to rush off on crusade without proper permission from a superior.[46] Clearly, Pope Urban thought that while some clerics were needed as chaplains (after all, he had appointed Bishop Adhemar of Puy as his personal representative to and the spiritual leader of the expedition to Jerusalem),[47] this expedition was best served by practical-minded and skilled fighting men, and the vast majority of clerics and monks would best serve Christendom by remaining at home and tending to their spiritual duties. Likewise, he counseled a number of Spanish nobles and their vassals that they best served the Christian cause by staying in Spain and fighting Islam there. Their work in recovering Spain from the Muslims would earn them the same spiritual merit as that

---

44. Peters, *First Crusade*, 26–29; Holt and Muldoon, *Voices*, 14–16.

45. Peters, *First Crusade*, 29.

46. Ibid., 44–45.

47. "Letter to the Faithful in Flanders of December 1095." Peters, *First Crusade*, 42.

of those who went east to aid the Asian Church.[48] What all of this reflects is the cool-headed planning of a pragmatic pope.

Subsequently, Pope Innocent III (r. 1198–1216) restated Urban's principles in a papal decree involving those who took a vow to go on crusade but proved unable to do so by reason of age, health, or family responsibilities. Such individuals could fulfill their vows by paying the expenses of warriors who wished to go but lacked the necessary funds.[49]

The warriors and others who heard Urban's speech at Clermont in November 1095 responded, "It is the will of God! It is the will of God!"[50] Yet the hard-minded and eminently practical warriors who were roused to action at Clermont did not march immediately eastward in a burst of religious frenzy. Neither did the many more who subsequently learned of this expedition from the sermons of preachers, who spread the word from Eastern and Central Europe to Greenland, and decided to march east. They responded enthusiastically to the pope's call, not in an insane fashion but in a rational one. Warriors know that logistics trumps grand strategy and tactics, and the most vulnerable warrior is one who races off without adequate preparation.

Research on crusading charters by Jonathan Riley-Smith and Marcus Bull, among others, has demonstrated how rather than blindly rushing off to the East in a religious frenzy, individual crusaders of means carefully considered the costs and logistics of crusading as they made preparations for the management of their affairs in their absence.[51] The greater lords who wished to go had to arrange financing for themselves and their followers, often borrowing the funds from local moneylenders or mortgaging their estates to obtain the necessary funds.[52] Furthermore, leaders had to be designated, travel routes determined, and large amounts of equipment and animals

---

48. Ibid., 45–46, letter sent between January 1096 and July 1099.

49. *Decretales*, 3.34.8., *Quod super*. This brief decretal generated a lengthy commentary on the legitimacy of the crusades by Pope Innocent IV (1243–1254) in which he argued that peaceful relations between Christian and non-Christian societies were quite possible. See James Muldoon, *Popes, Lawyers, and Infidels: The Church and the Non-Christian World 1250–1550* (Philadelphia: University of Pennsylvania Press, 1979), 6–16. A translation of part of the commentary is in *The Expansion of Europe: The First Phase*, ed. James Muldoon (Philadelphia: University of Pennsylvania Press, 1977), 191–92.

50. Robert of Rheims in Peters, *First Crusade*, 28.

51. Jonathan Riley-Smith, *The First Crusade and the Idea of Crusading* (Philadelphia: University of Pennsylvania Press, 1986, 2009), 43–47; Marcus Bull, *Knightly Piety and the Lay Response to the First Crusade: The Limousin and Gascony, c. 970–c. 1130* (Oxford: Clarendon Press, 1993).

52. On the financing of the First Crusade, see France, *Victory*, 84–87. For a detailed analysis of the recruitment of crusaders in the early thirteenth century, see James Powell, *Anatomy of a Crusade, 1213–1221* (Philadelphia: University of Pennsylvania Press, 1986), 67–87. For a detailed discussion of the costs of crusading, see Norman Housley, "Costing the Crusade: Budgeting for Crusading Activity in the Fourteenth Century," in *The Experience of Crusading.* Vol. 1: *Western Approaches*, ed. Marcus Bull and Norman Housley (Cambridge: Cambridge University Press, 2003), 45–59.

to transport men and materials acquired and organized.[53] The pope sought to arouse enthusiasm for the effort among those most capable of achieving military success in the East, not among suicidal fanatics. And he largely succeeded in doing so, although some fanatics did join the crusade, as the attacks on Jews in 1096 and various other atrocities bear witness.[54]

A weakness in Urban's strategy as set forward in his sermon at Clermont and a problem for the crusading movement in general was not that it articulated an apocalyptic vision of a great war against Islam but that it had several goals that were not always clearly articulated and that were, to some extent, in conflict with one another. As Jonathan Riley-Smith has noted, "It was not until after the [First] crusade was over that a coherent and internally consistent body of thought was to be distilled."[55]

In the first place, on the ecclesiastical level, how would the crusade fit with one of the chief goals of the eleventh-century reformed papacy—an assertion of papal jurisdiction over the Eastern Christian churches? Was Western support for the Byzantine Empire contingent upon a willingness to accept papal authority and the Latin rite?

On the secular level, there were two crucial issues that were never adequately addressed. Was the goal simply to restore Jerusalem and the rest of the Holy Land to Christian control or was the goal to strengthen the Byzantine Empire against the Muslim advance or was it to accomplish both goals? Related to this was the question of the relation of the crusaders to the Byzantine imperial forces. Were the crusaders going in support of the Byzantines and serving under imperial command and restoring to the Byzantines lands lost to the Muslims, or were they an independent force whose members could carve out principalities for themselves from the lands retaken from the Turks and colonize them with migrants from Europe?[56] Who, indeed, would rule the reconquered lands, especially Jerusalem: the Byzantine emperor or the crusaders who fought the Turkish occupiers? This ambiguity probably was responsible for the initial resistance of Godfrey of Bouillon and Raymond of Toulouse to join the other leaders of the various "armies of the nobles" that arrived in Constantinople in 1097 in swearing an oath of loyalty to Emperor Alexius I and guaranteeing that they would return captured imperial territories to him.[57]

Another fundamental issue that neither Urban nor anyone else appears to have raised in any serious way was the question of organization and leadership, in modern

---

53. France, *Victory*, deals with all of this in-depth in chapter 4, "Preparations and Prelude," 80–121.

54. See the editors' discussion of the charge of crusader genocide and barbarism in the Introduction.

55. Riley-Smith, *Idea of Crusading*, 30.

56. Corliss Slack deals with the issue of crusader colonization in a chapter of this book (note 42 above).

57. Jonathan Harris, *Byzantium and the Crusades* (London: Hambledon and London, 2003), 61–62.

terms, the question of command and control of the assembled crusaders. How would the various contingents be raised and coordinated? Who was in command of the crusading forces, and what control would he or they have over the troops? A closely related question was the question of financing these expeditions. Who would bear the costs of the campaigns, and how would the money be raised? Normally pilgrims bore their own expenses, and the Church treated persons going on this expedition as pilgrims, but pilgrim armies would be massively expensive—far more expensive than purely religious pilgrimages.

The apparent failure of Urban to spell out in detail the goals of the proposed crusade, specifically the territorial goals, and to deal with the relation of the crusaders to the Byzantines, along with the lack of unified leadership, and the lack of a plan for the financing of the crusades led to one of the most dramatic scenes in the entire history of the crusades: the response of the Byzantine emperor to the coming of the first crusaders. The ambiguity regarding crusader-Byzantine relations continued to poison relations between the empire and these warriors from the West throughout the twelfth century, resulting in a number of misunderstandings and conflicts. Ultimately the army of the Fourth Crusade would capture and pillage Constantinople in 1204 due to a combination of unforeseen circumstances that intensified in magnitude as incident piled upon incident until a point of no retreat was reached. Propelling this set of circumstances forward to its tragic conclusion was a mood of mutual distrust that had built up and intensified over more than a century.[58]

Tension between the Latins and the Byzantines theologically and militarily went back a long way. Although Emperor Alexius I and Pope Urban had enjoyed a friendly exchange of correspondence and embassies before 1095 and the pope's sermon at Clermont was his way of responding positively to the request for military assistance from the West that Alexius had made in March 1095 at the Council of Piacenza,[59] the Byzantines had long been at odds with the papacy for several reasons. There was political conflict stemming from Pope Leo III's crowning of Charlemagne as Roman emperor in 800.[60]

There was also the longstanding conflict over papal claims to headship of the Church, a difference highlighted in 1054 when papal legates publicly excommunicated the patriarch of Constantinople, and the patriarch responded by excommunicating the

---

58. See Harris, *Byzantium and the Crusades*, 53–162; Donald E. Queller and Thomas F. Madden, *The Fourth Crusade: The Conquest of Constantinople*, 2nd ed. (Philadelphia: University of Pennsylvania Press, 1997); Jonathan Phillips, *The Fourth Crusade and the Sack of Constantinople* (New York: Viking, 2004).

59. Tyerman, *God's War*, 61–62.

60. Werner Ohnsorge, "The Coronation and Byzantium," in *The Coronation of Charlemagne: What Did It Signify?*, ed. Richard E. Sullivan (Boston: D.C. Heath, 1959), 80–91; see also Roger Collins, *Charlemagne* (Toronto: University of Toronto Press, 1998), 148–53.

legates but not the pope.[61] By themselves, these issues did not dominate the question of whether or not to support the Byzantines. What did cause a deep division between the Latins and the Byzantines was the unexpected development during the First Crusade of Byzantine resentment of the crusaders as interlopers intent on seizing Byzantine territory for themselves, a threat equal to that posed by the advancing Turks.[62]

Ultimately the crusaders, after experiencing some initial success, failed to stop the Muslim advance, and in 1291 the last significant crusader outpost on the mainland of Syria-Palestine, the port city of Acre, fell to the Mamluks of Egypt and Syria. Mackay traced this failure of the crusades to the fact that "the popular mania had run its career" and "that fanaticism that originated, and the folly that conducted the Crusades faded."[63] The fanaticism that Peter the Hermit had putatively inspired was long gone.

In order to make that case, Mackay had to conflate several different aspects of the history of the eleventh, twelfth, and thirteenth centuries, making them causally related and presenting them as having affected every part of Christendom equally. His discussion of the supposed apocalyptic movement of around the year 1000 is a good example of this. His picture is of the entire European population overcome with terror at the thought of the end of the world. While it is true that apocalyptic themes do appear in some literature of the First Crusade, Guibert of Nogent's version of Urban II's speech at Clermont, for example,[64] it is not present everywhere nor is apocalypticism a major motif.[65] Modern scholarship has demonstrated that while there certainly were apocalyptic movements in this period, it was not a single, universal movement.[66] Furthermore, once the initial stage of the crusades ended there was little

---

61. The impact of the events in 1054 on relations between the Eastern and Western branches of the Christian Church has been downplayed in modern historical literature. See George Every, *The Byzantine Patriarchate, 451–1204*, 2nd rev. ed. (London: Society for Promoting Christian Knowledge, 1962), 153–59; George Every, *Misunderstandings between East and West* (Richmond, VA: John Knox Press, n.d.); Yves Congar, *After Nine Hundred Years: The Background of the Schism between the Eastern and Western Churches* (New York: Fordham University Press, 1959). Alfred J. Andrea, "The Myth of the Schism of 1054," in *Crusades: The Illustrated History*, ed. Thomas F. Madden (London: Duncan Baird, 2004), 30.

62. For an example of the Byzantine view of the crusaders, see Anna Comnena, *The Alexiad*, trans. E. R. A. Sewter (London: Penguin Books, 1969), 438–39. But this was probably an exaggerated view, given the partisan nature of her book, which glorified her father, Alexius I. The very title of Anna's book implies that he was a Homeric-like hero beset by enemies on all sides.

63. Mackay, *Madness*, 460.

64. Note 43 above and Robert Levine, trans., *The Deeds of God through the Franks: A Translation of Guibert de Nogent's "Gesta Dei per Francos"* (Woodbridge, UK: Boydell Press, 1997), 42.

65. For a contrary view, see note 11 above.

66. Cohn, *Pursuit*, 61–70. Excellent and more recent works on medieval apocalypticism, based on much deeper research, include Richard K. Emerson and Bernard McGinn, eds., *The Apocalypse in the Middle Ages* (Ithaca, NY: Cornell University Press, 1992); Bernard McGinn, *Apocalypticism in the Western Tradition* (Aldershot, UK: Variorum, 1994); Brett E. Whalen, *Dominion of God: Christendom and Apocalypse in the Middle Ages* (Cambridge, MA: Harvard University Press, 2009).

apocalyptic energy involved, although apocalyptic elements did reappear from time to time thereafter.[67] Mackay also seems quite unaware that there was a good deal of criticism of the crusades in Latin circles for several reasons, including the charge that the crusades interfered with the evangelization efforts of missionaries in the East.[68]

A war against Muslims was nothing new and did not require Urban II's meeting with a fanatical preacher to move him to act, as Paul Crawford demonstrates in his chapter in this book. Mackay overlooked the fact that for centuries there had been conflict between Christians and Muslims as the Arabs defeated Byzantine armies and moved across North Africa and into Spain up to the Pyrenees and then on to the kingdom of the Franks, where they encountered Charles Martel in 732. At sea Muslim ships dominated portions of the Mediterranean for long periods of time.[69] This advance did not go unchallenged. In the eleventh century, at the western edge of the Muslim advance, Spain, the "balance of power, so long weighted against the Christians, seemed to shift decisively in their favor after the fall of Toledo in 1085."[70] The Norman conquest of Sicily (1061–1091) was another example of Latin Christian success against the Muslims.

By placing the blame for the crusades on the benighted Latin Christians as if they began the crusades because of some religious mania, Mackay no doubt appealed to smug Protestant Victorians secure in their belief that they were so much superior to their ancestors who had succumbed to the superstition and irrationality that Victorians associated with medieval Catholicism. It was not, however, an accurate statement of the circumstances that led to the crusades.

Mackay's focus on the dramatic elements of the crusade, his emphasis on charismatic and legendary figures such as Peter the Hermit, and the picture he drew of masses of ignorant peasants wandering off to Jerusalem is at great odds with current scholarly discussion. More specifically, to MacKay's narrow focus on the participants of the misnamed Peasant's Crusade, contemporary chroniclers might have dismissed them as "mere rabble," because they failed, but these initial crusaders were, as John

---

67. For the use of apocalyptic crusade rhetoric by a pope on the eve of the Fifth Crusade, see Alfred J. Andrea, "Innocent III, the Fourth Crusade, and the Coming Apocalypse," in *The Medieval Crusade*, ed. Susan J. Ridyard (Rochester, NY: Boydell Press, 2004), 97–106.

68. Palmer A. Throop, *Criticism of the Crusade: A Study of Public Opinion and Crusade Propaganda* (Amsterdam: Swets and Zeitlinger, 1940). Elizabeth Siberry, *Criticism of Crusading: 1095–1274* (Oxford: Clarendon Press, 1985), questions and modifies but does not negate Throop's thesis.

69. Joseph F. O'Callaghan, *A History of Medieval Spain* (Ithaca, NY: Cornell University Press, 1975), 89–190. The significance of the Muslim advance for the long-term development of Europe has been the subject of intense scholarly debate since the publication of Henri Pirennes's *Mohammed and Charlemagne* (New York: Norton, 1939). There is a very useful introduction to the debate: Alfred F. Havighurst, ed., *The Pirenne Thesis: Analysis, Criticism, and Revision* (Boston: Heath, 1958).

70. O'Callaghan, *Medieval Spain*, 194. Another element of the Christian reaction to the Muslim advance was the Norman conquest of Sicily. See Paul Chevedden, "'A Crusade from the First': The Norman Conquest of Islamic Sicily, 1060–1091" *Al-Masāq* 22 (2010): 191–225.

France has argued, sufficiently well organized and not an inchoate mass that was incapable of fighting. Their disastrous defeat at the hands of the Turks was not due to any
lack of military vigor or ability but to a lack of strong leadership. In other words, their
"fatal weakness was command."[71] In practice, this initial wave of crusaders consisted
not of a unified body led by competent leaders but of a number of small groups with
a variety of leaders who did not work well together and had their own agendas.

The same lack of command and control that characterized the initial waves of
the so-called Peasants' Crusade (more properly, the Popular or People's Crusade) also
marked the crusade armies that Mackay's "chivalry" led, namely the second wave of
the First Crusade, or the Crusade of the Nobles. The conflicts among the various
nobles on the First Crusade reflected the complex political situation in Latin Europe:
kingdoms composed of multiple small units held together by bonds of personal loyalty at all levels, with local lords fiercely protective of their lands, rights, and authority. Anna Comnena tells of one Latin lord, who, daring to sit on Alexius' imperial
throne in the very presence of the emperor, declared, "I am a pure Frank and of noble
birth."[72] Friction and factionalism, which were part and parcel of the European political landscape, were built into the makeup of the First Crusade and almost all subsequent crusades. During the Third Crusade two kings, as well as lesser lords, would be
in conflict with one another.

At first glance, the crusades can appear as the blindly fanatical religious movement
that Mackay and others have described. There really was a Peter the Hermit, and there
were many other such preachers as well. Large numbers of people did initially rush
off to the East inspired by apocalyptic visions of the coming end. Furthermore, influenced by their religious positions, the leaders of the Latin and the Byzantine churches
insisted on stressing the theological and liturgical differences that separated them even
in the face of Turkish expansion and conquest. These examples, graphic as they are
and satisfying to modern readers who see the people of the Middle Ages as bigoted
fools blinded by religious beliefs, however, do not tell the full story. The various elements of the crusading era that Mackay conflated have to be carefully distinguished
and placed in context if we are to understand them correctly.

In the final analysis, Mackay's conclusions about the crusades rest on several false
assumptions and are to some extent contradictory. On the one hand he appears to
have assumed that any religious motivation is fundamentally a sign of madness and
that this is the fundamental characteristic of the entire crusading movement. While
there were in the course of the crusades vivid examples of religious mania, fanatical
frenzy, and horrible behavior, there is no evidence that the vast majority of crusaders
were mad or deluded. It is true that some fanatics were said to have followed "a goose
and goat" that were believed to embody the Holy Spirit, but that was not the case for

---

71. France, *Catholic Christendom*, 65–66.

72. Harris, *Byzantium and the Crusades*, 62.

the vast majority of crusaders, even though Mackay and others would have us believe that this was typical of those who flocked to the "Peasants' Crusade."[73]

On the other hand, even Mackay asserted that when the crusades acquired lay leadership the religious madness that had putatively prevailed to that point was replaced by more rational direction. And what about that supposed "religious madness?" In the long run, Mackay seems unable to distinguish between apocalyptic fantasies and religious enthusiasm. He also seems unable to see how any program or movement that had religious roots could be rational. Yet, contrary to what Mackay would have his readers believe, Urban II was motivated by a conception of papal power, jurisdiction, and spiritual responsibility that had been developing for some time.[74] Given that context, he and other ecclesiastics had developed a program for church reform, which included a holy war that was rationally planned and implemented. Likewise, the laity who went on crusade were motivated by a mixture of eminently rational religious and personal motives. Equally so, the Byzantines had religious motives that were consonant with contemporary standards of rational behavior. For that matter, so did the Muslims.

---

73. Mackay, *Madness*, 376. The clerical chronicler of the crusade Albert of Aachen contemptuously reported that some delusional individuals followed a goose and a she goat, which they believed contained within themselves the Holy Spirit, and he denounced the act as a detestable and hateful crime against the Lord. Peters, *First Crusade*, 111. Abbot Guibert of Nogent termed the tale "a vulgar fable" but also noted that the story had been circulated by reliable authors. *Deeds of God*, 156. Both texts are available online at http://themedievalworld.blogspot.com/2010/05/goose-who-led-crusade-well-sort-of.html (accessed March 13, 2014). Terry Jones' video program, *The Crusades*, which is analyzed in the editors' Introduction, makes much of this incident, and he pretends to try to interview a direct descendant of that goose of Cambrai of 1096, turning history into low comedy.

74. Although there is some exaggeration in the argument, a good brief introduction to the papal view of its role is Walter Ullmann, *Medieval Papalism* (London: Methuen, 1949). Ullmann's views have been strongly criticized, most forcefully by Francis Oakley, "Celestial Hierarchies Revisited: Walter Ullmann's Vision of Medieval Politics," *Past & Present* 60 (August 1973): 3–48. An excellent general survey of the medieval papacy is Brett Whalen, *The Medieval Papacy* (Basingstoke, UK: Palgrave Macmillan, 2014).

3. The Crusades and Medieval Anti-Judaism: Cause or Consequence?

Daniel P. Franke

> Those popes, kings, generals and other leaders who ordered Christian soldiers to put
> non-believers to the sword deserve a special place in hell and in infamy. The Crusades,
> after all, were the prelude to the Holocaust. Entire undefended communities [of] babies,
> pregnant mothers, and the aged were all slaughtered in the name of religious cleansing.
> —*Alan M. Dershowitz Attorney and activist*[1]

> Myth #5: No pope ever called a Crusade against Jews. During the First Crusade
> a large band of riffraff, not associated with the main army, descended on the
> towns of the Rhineland and decided to rob and kill Jews they found there.
> —*Thomas Madden, Professor of medieval history*[2]

> It would seem that the Crusades were not felt at the time as a major landmark
> in Jewish life. Only in retrospect, in light of the medieval expulsions, the pre-
> modern massacres in seventeenth-century Poland, and the Holocaust, the Crusades
> took on a life of their own as the beginning of the end of European Jewry.
> —*Daniel J. Lasker Professor of Jewish culture*[3]

In May 1096, an army of the First Crusade launched a series of attacks against Jewish
communities in the Rhineland, starting with the community of Speyer. The violence
was contained by Bishop John's ability to offer the Jews protection and to punish some
of the perpetrators. The persecutors, checked by the bishop's stern defense, moved on
to Worms, where they found townsfolk more ready to assist in the work of murdering
Jews and a bishop with less power (or willingness) to protect the Jews sheltering in his
palace. Several massacres followed. By May 25, the persecutors were at Mainz, one of
the chief cities of the empire and home to a large Jewish community.

---

1. "My crusade against 'crusading,'" 1999, August 2, 1999 http://www.jewishworldreview.
com/0899/crusades1.asp (accessed November 9, 2013). A less angry and more poignant column
on what the crusades meant to Jewish communities is found in Larry Domnitch, "Commemo-
rating the Crusader Attack upon Jerusalem," *Jewish Magazine* August 2003, http://jewishmag.
com/70mag/tishabav/tishabav.htm (accessed November 9, 2013).

2. Thomas F. Madden, "Crusade Myths," *Catholic Dossier* Jan/Feb 2002, http://www.ignatiusinsight.
com/features2005/tmadden_crusademyths_feb05.asp (accessed January 31, 2013).

3. "The Impact of the Crusades on the Jewish-Christian Debate," *Jewish History* 13 (1999): 33.

The crusaders systematically annihilated their victims, perpetrating massacres in the city, assaulting castles where local authorities had given Jews shelter, and finding and murdering Jews who had gone into hiding with their Christian neighbors. A significant number of Jews chose to kill themselves and their loved ones to escape the profanation of forced baptism or murder at the hands of the crusaders. This done, the army finally began to turn east to Hungary; other groups had broken off earlier and assaulted Jewish communities in Trier and Metz. Others proceeded down the Rhineland, murdering Jewish communities at Cologne, Xanten, and elsewhere. Subsequently, pogroms took place in Prague and Regensburg by these or allied groups.[4]

Who were these murdering groups, and did they initiate a new age in medieval Jewish history? The Jewish chronicles are very clear on who they were: those who had "placed an idolatrous sign on their clothing—the cross," intending to reach Jerusalem and "to drive out the Muslims who dwell in the land and to conquer the land." While passing through towns with Jewish communities, "they said to one another: 'Behold we journey a long way. . . . But here are the Jews dwelling among us, whose ancestors killed him and crucified him groundlessly. Let us take vengeance first upon them. Let us wipe them out as a nation; Israel's name will be remembered no more. Or else let them be like us. . . .'"[5] So, as the Hebrew chroniclers knew, the persecutors were those who responded to the papacy's call for a military pilgrimage to Jerusalem, what we now know as the First Crusade. Whether the crusaders initiated a "new age" of "persecutions as a concomitant of a Crusade" has been widely debated.[6]

This chapter triangulates a position suspended among the three quotations above: the crusades had everything to do with Latin Christian attitudes and actions toward medieval Jews and were a watershed in the history of European Jewry; the crusades had nothing to do with medieval Jews; and the crusades, whatever their immediate impact, were not a turning point in Jewish-Christian relations and were not seen as such until

---

4. The most concise description of these events is Chapter 6, "'In Witness to the Oneness': The First Crusade and the Jews of the Rhineland" in Leonard B. Glick, *Abraham's Heirs: Jews and Christians in Medieval Europe* (Syracuse, NY: Syracuse University Press, 1999), 91–110.

5. Robert Chazan, *European Jewry and the First Crusade* (Berkeley: University of California Press, 1987), 243–44. See also Schlomo Eidelberg, *The Jews and the Crusaders* (Madison: University of Wisconsin Press, 1977). Unfortunately, as of publication we are still waiting for an English edition of Eva Haverkamp's magisterial *Hebräische Berichte über die Judenverfolgungen während des Ersten Kreuzzugs* [Hebrew Accounts of the Jewish Persecutions during the First Crusade] (Hannover: Hahnsche Buchhandlung, 2005).

6. Eva Haverkamp, "Jews in Christian Europe: Ashkenaz in the Middle Ages," in *The Wiley-Blackwell History of Jews and Judaism*, ed. Alan T. Levenson (London: Blackwell, 2012), 169–206, at 175. This is the most recent overview of northern medieval Jewish history. See also Jeremy Cohen, *Sanctifying the Name of God: Jewish Martyrs and Jewish Memories of the First Crusade* (Philadelphia: University of Pennsylvania Press, 2004); Robert Chazan, *Reassessing Jewish Life in Medieval Europe* (Cambridge: Cambridge University Press, 2010); and "'Let Not a Residue or a Remnant Escape': Millenarian Enthusiasm in the First Crusade," *Speculum* 84 (2009): 289–313.

the modern period. There is some truth in each proposition, and to argue exclusively for one or the other, as many do, runs the risk of mythologizing the crusades. As should become clear as we study the issue, at times the crusades inspired and activated medieval Christians' latent anti-Judaism, but in general they had only an erratic influence on the development and prosecution of Christian-Jewish antagonism.[7]

It is always important to remember that the crusades did not themselves create medieval anti-Judaism but were the product of an anti-Jewish society that had been busy reviewing its relationship with Judaism well before Urban II's sermon at Clermont in 1095. Given the vast scope of the scholarship on these topics, it is impossible to explore every aspect in the compass of a brief chapter, but the sources cited in the footnotes are given with an eye toward providing the most concise, but at the same time thorough, guide to further reading.[8]

Ultimately, the topic boils down to two main myths. One, the "inherency myth," tends to be more popular in nature (as the quotation from Dershowitz suggests) and insists that the medieval crusades were inherently anti-Jewish, that the persecutions inflicted during the crusades were precursors of the Holocaust, and that the creation of the idea of the Jew as subversive "Other" was a product of the First Crusade. Consider the Reconciliation Walk, a four-year pilgrimage of Christians (1995–1999) that followed the route of the First Crusade "in apology for [our forefathers'] deeds and in demonstration of the true meaning of the Cross." Appropriately, the group visited the Jewish communities in the Rhineland and asked forgiveness for the slaughter of Jews there in 1096.[9] Although the organizers of the Reconciliation Walk project were careful in the way they phrased their summary of events that had taken place in 1096, Dershowitz mentions its reception in Jerusalem in 1999 by Israel's Chief Rabbi Yisrael Meir Lau, who was reported as saying, "This evil century which we are leaving started with those evil events of 900 years ago."

The chain of causation from 1096 to 1933 has become almost an article of faith for some.[10] Karen Armstrong's best seller *Holy War* expresses it most directly: "Despite the Church's disapproval, hatred of the Jews continued to be an essential element in crusading. . . . The Crusades made anti-Semitism an incurable Western disease, which persisted

7. For various reasons I have chosen to use the term "anti-Judaism" rather than "anti-Semitism" to describe medieval Christian prejudice against Jews; this follows a fairly standard practice among medieval scholars, for example, Cohen in *Sanctifying*.

8. See also the Suggested Readings at the end of this book.

9. "The Apology," The Crusades Anniversary Project, http://www.crusades-apology.org/Crusades%20Project/walk.htm (accessed April 2, 2015).

10. See David Nirenberg, "The Rhineland Massacres of Jews in the First Crusades: Memories Medieval and Modern," in *Medieval Concepts of the Past: Ritual, Memory, Historiography*, ed. Gerd Althoff, Johannes Fried, and Patrick J. Geary (Washington, D.C.: German Historical Institute), especially 299–309. This is one of the most important articles on how historians have written about 1096.

long after the Middle Ages. . . ."[11] Likewise, James Carroll's 2002 best seller *Constantine's Sword: The Church and the Jews: A History* claims that the Trier pogrom functioned as "Europe's rehearsal for the extermination of Jews who would not conform."[12]

In a more muted fashion, many scholars have accepted, or at least not questioned, these connections. In summarizing the reasons behind the vicious pogroms that surrounded Richard I's coronation in 1189, John Gillingham says simply, "The spirit of crusade was in the air."[13] R. I. Moore's classic study, *The Formation of a Persecuting Society*, is the most eloquent expression of this viewpoint: "From the beginning, then, the crusades undoubtedly stimulated hostility to the Jews and provided the most appalling occasions of its expression."[14] In Helen J. Nicholson's excellent 2004 volume *Palgrave Advances in the Crusades* both the great French medievalist Jean Flori and James Muldoon, a leading canon law scholar, unequivocally state that crusade was intimately bound up with the growth of religious oppression and persecution in the twelfth and thirteenth centuries. "The crusade," writes Muldoon, "became a fundamental instrument of what R. I. Moore termed a 'persecuting society.'" Flori argues that the eschatological motivations of many crusaders in 1095 cannot be dismissed as many scholars would like and that such feelings, expressed in popular movements to kill, convert, or otherwise isolate the non-Christian "Other," characterized "almost all major expeditions to the Holy Land."[15] Finally, a popular undergraduate sourcebook on the crusades claims that "every major medieval crusade would be accompanied by pogroms against the Jews of Europe."[16]

At the opposite end of the spectrum is a smaller body of work reacting against the "inherent" school of thought. Typically, it focuses on a close examination of the ideology of the First Crusade and the large crusading armies that had little recorded role in the persecutions. Often the "completely separate" model is more implicit than explicit and is most readily seen in studies that omit mention of the part attacks on Jews played in the crusades.[17] On a popular level, Thomas F. Madden's many short

---

11. Karen Armstrong, *Holy War: The Crusades and Their Impact on Today's World*, 2nd ed. (New York: Anchor Books), 74.

12. James Carroll, *Constantine's Sword: The Church and the Jews: A History* (New York: Houghton Mifflin, 2002), 247–48.

13. John Gillingham, *Richard I* (New Haven, CT: Yale University Press, 2002), 108.

14. R. I. Moore, *The Formation of a Persecuting Society*, 2nd ed. (Malden, MA: Blackwell Publishing, 2007), 30.

15. James Muldoon, "Crusading and Canon Law," and Jean Flori, "Ideology and Motivations in the First Crusade," in *Palgrave Advances in the Crusades*, ed. Helen J. Nicholson (New York: Palgrave Macmillan, 2004), 37–57 and 15–36.

16. S. J. Allen and Emilie Amt, *The Crusades: A Reader* (Peterborough, Ontario: Broadview Press, 2003), 47.

17. Notable examples include Thomas F. Madden's edited volume, *The Crusades: The Essential Readings* (Oxford: Blackwell, 2002) and I. G. Robinson's *The Papacy 1073–1198: Continuity and Innovation* (Cambridge: Cambridge University Press, 1990).

pieces since 9/11 appear in publications whose audience is predisposed to listen and where the need for conciseness inevitably simplifies an extremely complex, violent phenomenon.[18]

In a similar vein, an important article from 2002 "Were the Crusades Anti-Semitic?" makes a number of excellent points, such as noting how "most Christian sources for our information on the First Crusade are silent about the pogroms. If anti-Jewish activity was inherent to or championed by the crusading movement, it would stand to reason that these writers would include it in their histories." However, the author moves to shakier ground when asking, "And yet, if this sort of anti-Semitic outlook was inherent to the movement, as some argue, why did the pogroms occur only in the Rhineland?"[19] In reality, the persecutions were more widespread than that, a point of fact that many crusade historians are not anxious to explore.[20]

Given this complex background, perhaps the best way to clarify the relationship of crusading to anti-Judaism is to first examine the so-called Peasants' Crusade—its origins, actions, and reception by medieval Christians and most importantly its connection to the "main" crusade armies. We should question also whether 1095 and 1096 represent a break with the past or instead demonstrate continuity. Second, what were the actual consequences of 1096 on anti-Judaism and Jewish communities in the twelfth century and beyond?

The "Peasants' Crusade" and Jewish-Christian Relations before 1096

Why did the persecutors of 1096 do what they did, and what was their connection to the main crusade armies? For many years, most crusade historians (with the exception of Jonathan Riley-Smith)[21] effectively side stepped the issue by doggedly insisting

---

18. Among Madden's other well-written responses to "common misconceptions" are the following: "Crusade Propaganda: The Abuse of Christianity's Holy Wars," *The National Review*, November 2, 2001, http://www.nationalreview.com/article/220747/crusade-propaganda-thomas-f-madden (accessed March 16, 2013); "Crusade Myths," *Catholic Dossier*, January/February 2002, http://www.ignatiusinsight.com/features2005/tmadden_crusademyths_feb05.asp (accessed January 31, 2013); "The Real History of the Crusades," *Crisis Magazine*, March 19, 2011, http://www.crisis-magazine.com/2011/the-real-history-of-the-crusades (accessed March 16, 2013); and "The Church and the Jews in the Middle Ages," *Crisis Magazine*, March 5, 2011, http://www.crisismagazine.com/2011/the-church-and-the-jews-in-the-middle-ages (accessed March 16, 2013).

19. Vince Ryan, "Were the Crusades Anti-Semitic?" *Catholic Dossier*, January/February 2002, http://www.ignatiusinsight.com/features2006/vryan_jewscrusades_nov06.asp (accessed March 21, 2014).

20. The most important analysis of crusade historians' handling of 1096 is Benjamin Z. Kedar, "Crusade Historians and the Massacres of 1096," *Jewish History* 12 (1998): 11–31.

21. Jonathan Riley-Smith, *The First Crusade and the Idea of Crusading* (London: Continuum, 1986), 50–52.

that the persecutors were undisciplined riffraff who were motivated solely by greed; any valid theological motivation, such as apocalyptic expectations that *required* the death or conversion of Jews, was largely discounted or minimized.[22] Without a legitimate ideological motive, then, the "Peasants' Crusade" must have had purely material goals, and such extreme rhetoric and actions must have been confined to a minority. At any rate, the "peasants" had little to do with the main armies who form the center of the First Crusade narrative. According to one eminent crusade historian, "The rhetoric [of the persecuting "peasants"] . . . was religious, but the motive may have been financial."[23]

In the past fifteen years, however, a newer generation of scholars has questioned these conclusions, emphasizing the apocalyptic (and by extension anti-Judaic) motives of the First Crusade by connecting the "peasant" armies to the main crusading forces.[24] The spotlight has fallen particularly on the ringleader of the crusaders at Worms and Mainz, Emicho of Flonheim, whom Rabbi Eleazar described in his chronicle as being the "chief persecutor" who informed his followers that upon reaching Constantinople he would receive a royal diadem and "overcome his enemies."[25]

If this was indeed Emicho's motivation, and if it reflected a widespread cultural understanding of the eleventh century, then our questions change considerably. Where did the Jews figure in this legend, and how would such an understanding have melded with Urban II's call for crusade? Matthew Gabriele's important study of Emicho not only renders the apocalyptic aspects of the movement concrete but also places them more at the center of the First Crusade enterprise than previously imagined. Emicho now emerges as the leader of a potent army that was attempting, in its persecution of the Jews, to bring about their conversion to Christianity as the first act

---

22. Ibid. See also Steven Runciman, *A History of the Crusades, Volume 1 The First Crusade and the Foundation of the Kingdom of Jerusalem* (Cambridge: Cambridge University Press, 1951; reprinted London: The Folio Society, 1994), 111–17, for a broadly similar assessment. See also Bernard McGinn, "Apocalypticism and Church Reform: 1100–1500," in *The Continuum History of Apocalypticism* (New York: Continuum, 2003), 273–98; McGinn's collection of medieval apocalyptic sources, *Visions of the End: Apocalyptic Traditions in the Middle Ages* (New York: Columbia University Press, 1979); and the very influential "*Iter sancti Sepulchri*: The Piety of the First Crusaders," in *The Walter Prescott Webb Memorial Lectures: Essays on Medieval Civilization*, ed. Bede Karl Lackner and Kenneth Roy Philip (Austin: University of Texas Press, 1978).

23. Christopher Tyerman, *God's War: A New History of the Crusades* (Cambridge: The Belknap Press of Harvard University Press, 2006), 103. For similar assessments, see Hans Eberhard Meyer, *The Crusades*, 2nd ed, (Oxford: Oxford University Press, 1992), 41 and Jean Richard, *The Crusades, c. 1071–c. 1291* (Cambridge: Cambridge University Press, 1999), 39.

24. Jay Rubenstein, *Armies of Heaven: The First Crusade and the Quest for the Apocalypse* (New York: Basic Books, 2011), 47–53, clearly places the perpetrators of the First Crusade's pogroms into this context.

25. For Rabbi Eleazar's account of Emicho, see Chazan, *European Jewry*, 250–51.

of End Times. This process would conclude with the army capturing Jerusalem and Emicho emerging as the "Last Emperor," a legendary hero to come.[26]

Thus Christian anti-Judaism, popular apocalyptic legends, and the papacy's Jerusalem project were fused into a single deadly force. "The actions of the Rhenish crusaders," argues Gabriele, "were very much a part of the First Crusade—not some unfortunate byproduct."[27] This conclusion is reinforced by Conor Kostick's study of the younger warriors, the *iuvenes*, of the First Crusade, several of whom had served under Emicho in the Rhineland before joining the main crusade armies and gaining fame as great warriors.[28]

If the 1096 persecutions drew their inspiration from ideas about End Times and the Jews' place in that narrative, we can wonder why the persecutions were localized to the Rhineland. In fact, they were not, although how extensive and serious they were outside the Rhineland continues to be debated. Norman Golb has argued that persecutions and pogroms were much more widespread in France than is commonly assumed. While his reading of Hebrew manuscripts has been questioned over the years, his analysis of fragmentary Christian and Jewish sources presents a compelling argument that Jews in France suffered widespread pogroms during the First Crusade and allows us to understand Rabbi Eleazar's description of the persecutors as French *and* German and to understand Godfrey of Bouillon's famous threat to murder the Jews in his lands before leaving for Jerusalem.[29]

Indeed, the Jewish communities within Godfrey's duchy of Lower Lorraine felt sufficiently threatened that they secured from Emperor Henry IV a charter of protection, which in turn caused the duke to declare that he had never really meant the

---

26. For the Last Emperor legend, its prevalence, and its impact on the First Crusade, see Matthew Gabriele, *An Empire of Memory: The Legend of Charlemagne, the Franks, and Jerusalem before the First Crusade* (Oxford: Oxford University Press, 2011), chapter 4, "The Franks' Imagined Empire," and chapter 5, "The Franks Return to the Holy Land."

27. Matthew Gabriele, "Against the Enemies of Christ: The Role of Count Emicho in the Anti-Jewish Violence of the First Crusade," in *Christian Attitudes Toward the Jews in the Middle Ages: A Casebook*, ed. Michael Frassetto (New York: Routledge, 2007), 66. One issue not addressed in this interpretation is the crusaders' tendency to turn first to murder, rather than conversion; see David Malkiel, "Destruction or Conversion: Intention and Reaction, Crusaders and Jews, in 1096," *Jewish History* 15 (2001): 257–80.

28. Conor Kostick, "*Iuvenes* and the First Crusade (1096–1099): Knights in Search of Glory?" *The Journal of Military History* 73 (2009): 369–92; see also his *The Social Structure of the First Crusade* (Leiden: Brill, 2008).

29. Norman Golb, *The Jews in Medieval Normandy: A Social and Intellectual History* (Cambridge: Cambridge University Press, 1998), 115–36. Reaction to Golb's work has been extremely mixed. Paul Hyams' important "The Jews of Medieval England, 1066–1290," in *England and Germany in the High Middle Ages*, ed. Alfred Haverkamp and Hanna Vollrath (Oxford: Oxford University Press, 1996), treats Golb's conclusions cautiously. For other reactions, see Sophia Menache's generally positive review in *Speculum* 75 (2000): 468–70 and William Chester Jordan's negative review in *The Jewish Quarterly Review*, n.s. 89 (1999): 437–38.

Jews any harm. Whatever had been his initial intention (and it seems likely that it had been a ploy to extort money from these Jewish communities), as Godfrey marched through the Rhineland sometime after the massacres there, the Jews of Mainz and Cologne gave him hefty bribes to leave them in peace.[30] They, like their coreligionists of Lower Lorraine, thought they had good reason to fear Duke Godfrey.

Revisionist scholarship of the past fifteen years has presented us with compelling evidence that, although Urban II's preaching made no known mention of Jews, thousands of crusaders considered it natural and a matter of course to include the murder or persecution of Jews in their crusading. Since spontaneous persecution of Jews occurred in most subsequent crusades, we have to ask: Why was there this almost reflexive inclusion of Jews in crusading? To answer this question, we need to examine Christian-Jewish relations before 1096.

Most scholars who study the Jewish experience in the long term conclude that the crusades were a symptom, rather than a cause, of the changes that swept Western Europe in the eleventh century. "Historians," writes Leonard Glick, "often point to 1096 . . . as a pivotal year, after which Jews in Christian Europe began a slide downward from which they would never recover. The fact is, though, that the entire eleventh century was pivotal. . . ."[31] Similarly, Robert Chazan notes, "The animosities which exploded so viciously in 1096 did not spring up overnight. There are signs of antipathy throughout the previous century."[32] Chazan points to the destruction of the Holy Sepulcher in 1009 by the Fatimid caliph as a key event in this antipathy, as it was widely believed in the West that Jews had instigated this destruction.

It could be argued that the resultant persecutions set a complicated chain of causation in motion—the association of Jews with the Muslim enemy, followed by the first major persecution of Jews in Western Christendom; a lingering sense of fear and injury that resurfaced in many First Crusade chronicles; and the gradual refocusing of Christian spiritual energy on the salvation narrative and the physical places associated with it. To these could be added a growing fear of Judaism as a proselytizing religion, illustrated by the notorious case of a Christian convert to Judaism in the reign of German king Henry II.[33] These trends were strengthened by the Spanish campaigns of the mid-eleventh century.

---

30. Chazan, *European Jewry*, 53.

31. Glick, *Abraham's Heirs*, 77.

32. Robert Chazan, "1007–1012: Initial Crisis for Northern European Jewry," *Proceedings of the American Academy for Jewish Research* 38/39 (1970–1971): 101–17, at 101.

33. See Alpert of Metz's account in *Warfare and Politics in Medieval Germany, ca. 1000: On the Variety of Our Times by Alpert of Metz*, trans. David S. Bachrach (Toronto, Canada: Pontifical Institute of Medieval Studies, 2012). For an analysis of the reported Jewish-Christian disputation, see Anna Sapir Abulafia, "An Eleventh-Century Exchange of Letters between a Christian and a Jew," *Journal of Medieval History* 7 (1981): 153–74, reprinted in *Christians and Jews in Dispute: Disputational Literature and the Rise of Anti-Judaism in the West (c. 1000–1150)* (Aldershot, UK: Ashgate, 1998).

A late-thirteenth-century French manuscript painting depicting the crucifixion of Jesus, Urban II's preaching of the First Crusade, a pious Christian king (Godfrey of Bouillon? Baldwin I?) praying at the Holy Sepulcher in Jerusalem, and five persons in Jerusalem worshipping a pagan idol who holds a shield. Note that each of the two soldiers at the crucifixion and two of the pagan idol-worshippers is depicted wearing a peaked *Judenhut* (Jewish hat), a hat that Christian Europeans associated with male Jews. Photo Source: Walters Art Museum, Baltimore, MD. W137.1 *Histoire d'Outre Mer*, William of Tyre, French, ca. 1295–1300, parchment with ink, paint, and gold. H: 13 3/8 3 W:9 5/8.

Anti-Jewish persecutions marked the mobilization and progress of French armies to the Spanish frontier, eliciting a strongly worded response from Pope Alexander II "that [Jews] should not be destroyed by those who went out against the Saracens in Spain. Inspired by stupid ignorance or perhaps out of blind cupidity, they wanted to kill them in their rage, though divine piety might have predestined them to salvation."[34] Even Carroll, in *Constantine's Sword*, subscribes to this view when he writes, "No one knew it, but Europe was ready for something like the Crusades."[35]

The fact is Jews had figured for centuries in Christian writing and in liturgy in ways that preserved Christian resentment for their supposed role in the Crucifixion.

---

34. Amnon Linder, ed. *The Jews in the Legal Sources of the Early Middle Ages* (Detroit: Wayne State University Press, 1997), 452–53.

35. Carroll, *Constantine's Sword*, 239.

For example, the *Vindicta Salvatoris* (the Savior's Vengeance), the Christian celebration of the destruction of Jerusalem by the Romans, had long had a place in the Mass eleven weeks after Pentecost, paralleling the Jewish day of mourning for that event; in the eleventh century, we find a French Easter sermon elaborating on this destruction.[36]

La Chanson d'Antioche (The Song of Antioch), part of a larger French song cycle originating in the decades after the First Crusade, opens the tale of the First Crusade with the Crucifixion, during which Demus, the righteous thief, says that Christ should be avenged on the Jews. In reply to this, he is assured that "a new race will come from over the sea to avenge the death of their Father . . . the Franks will liberate the whole land." This is then followed by a description of the Romans' campaign against Jerusalem, strongly suggesting that, for some Christians, 1099—and perhaps 1096?—was a reenactment of that earlier conflict and that in the popular mind crusade and anti-Judaism were connected in a very fundamental way.[37]

In addition to liturgy and theology, we should also not underestimate the impact of the eleventh-century reform movement on Western Christian views of Judaism. As David Hay states, "The ideology of Church reform, which at this time was producing more and more aggressive justifications of pious violence, appears to have functioned in a manner similar to that of the ideology of religious pollution/purification."[38] This was the thrust of Gregory VII's letter to Alfonso VI of Castile in 1081, urging him not to employ Jews in any trusted positions at his court: "For to place Christians under Jews or to subject them to their jurisdiction—what is this but to oppress the Church of God, to exalt the synagogue of Satan, and in aiming to please the enemies of Christ to throw contempt upon Christ himself?"[39]

The Church was also becoming more interested in Jewish beliefs and critiques of Christianity, as reflected in Gilbert Crispin's polite *Disputatio Iudei et Christiani* (Debate between a Jew and a Christian), composed in the decade before 1095, and in Anselm's famous defense of the Christian faith, *Cur Deus homo* (Why God Became Man), whose "adversaries" were almost certainly meant to be Jews and which was most likely written while the First Crusade was underway. This growing sensitivity to Jewish criticisms of the doctrine of the Incarnation, among other points of faith,

---

36. See Israel Jacob Yuval, *Two Nations in Your Womb: Perceptions of Jews and Christians in Late Antiquity and the Middle Ages* (Berkeley: University of California Press, 2006), 38–49.

37. See Susan B. Edgington and Carol Sweetenham, trans., *The Chanson d'Antioche* (Farnham, UK: Ashgate, 2011), 106–7, stanzas 12–14. See also Jonathan Riley-Smith, *The First Crusaders 1095–1131* (Cambridge: Cambridge University Press, 1997), 41–42.

38. David Hay, "Gender Bias and Religious Intolerance in Accounts of the 'Massacres' of the First Crusade," in *Tolerance and Intolerance: Social Conflict in the Age of the Crusades*, ed. Michael Gervers and James M. Powell (Syracuse, NY: Syracuse University Press, 2001), 7.

39. Ephraim Emerton, trans., *The Correspondence of Gregory VII* (New York: W. W. Norton, 1969), 177–78.

is perhaps best reflected in twelfth-century crusade historian Guibert of Nogent's vicious attack on the count of Soissons, who was suspected of being a "Judaizer."[40]

There was thus an enormous amount of material, both before and (in Guibert's case) immediately after 1095, for Christian society to associate the Jews with the crusade, some of it originating from the papacy. Yet despite the growing militancy of Christianity, most of that militancy had nothing to do with Jews, and most Christian crusade chroniclers did not think the Rhineland persecutions worth mentioning.[41] In fact, the eleventh century was generally a time of Jewish growth, such as when the bishop of Speyer, "wish[ing] to make a city out of the village," chartered a Jewish settlement in the town.[42] And the Church did not waver in its support of Jewish communities that came under threat during this time, as Pope Alexander's decree, mentioned above, indicates.

After 1096: Policy and Subsequent Persecutions, 1099–1421

Just as the story of the First Crusade is a complex one, so too is the relationship of subsequent crusades to later outbursts of persecution. After the capture of Jerusalem in 1099, many, if not most, subsequent crusades witnessed some kind of anti-Jewish persecution, whether by random crusaders or by organized groups. Some were spectacularly vicious, such as the pogroms of the Second Crusade and the massacres in England in 1189–1190. Others were noted by only a few observers and, thereby, appear to have been limited in scope, such as the lament of Rabbi Eleazar of Worms over a pogrom by Henry VI's crusaders in 1196.[43] Yet while crusading might have provided an opportunity for violent anti-Judaism to manifest itself, it did not much influence anti-Judaism's development. Rather, anti-Judaism followed a course that sometimes converged with crusading but more often operated according to its own dynamic.

---

40. See Margery Chibnall's useful overview in *The World of Orderic Vitalis: Norman Monks and Norman Knights* (Woodbridge, UK: Boydell, 1996, reprint of Oxford, 1984), 152–61. See also *The Works of Gilbert Crispin, Abbot of Westminster*, ed. G. R. Evans and Anna Sapir Abulafia (London: British Academy, 1986).

41. Fulcher of Chartres, Baldric of Dol, the *Gesta Francorum*, Ralph of Caen's *Gesta Tancredi*, and Robert the Monk do not mention them at all. In fact, as Rudolf Hiestand notes, they are absent from *any* French or Italian chronicle. Rudolf Hiestand, "Juden und Christen in der Kreuzzugspropaganda und bei den Kreuzzugspredigern" [Jews and Christians in Crusade Propaganda and Crusade Preaching], in *Juden und Christen zur Zeit der Kreuzzüge* [Jews and Christians at the Time of the Crusades], ed. Alfred Haverkamp (Sigmaringen, Germany: Jan Thorbecke, 1999), 160.

42. Robert Chazan, ed., *Church, State, and the Jew in the Middle Ages* (West Orange, NJ: Behrman House, 1979), 57–63, Bishop Rudiger's 1084 charter, and Emperor Henry IV's 1090 confirmation.

43. The best survey of these episodes is still Gerd Mentgen, "Kreuzzugsmentalität bei antijüdischen Aktionen nach 1190" [Crusade Mentality in Anti-Jewish Actions after 1190] in *Juden und Christen* (note 41 above), 287–326.

What kind of legacy did the persecutions of 1096 leave to subsequent generations? In terms of population, they had little effect on the development of Jewish settlements throughout Catholic Europe—on the contrary, the period from 1100 to 1250 saw the number of settlements and networks in Germany alone grow many times over. The Rhineland communities were rebuilt, and more were established (or at least formally chartered), mostly along the Rhine and Main rivers, but after 1200 reaching as far north as the Baltic Sea and as far east as the Oder River. What ultimately decimated the Jews of Germany was not the crusades but the persecutions that came with the Black Death in 1348 and immediately following.[44]

Medieval chroniclers were divided on how to interpret the persecutions of 1096. To many the crusade demonstrated once and for all the superiority of Christianity over all rivals, not least Jews and Judaism. This was mirrored in the female sculptural personifications of *Ecclesia* (Church) and *Synagoga* (Synagogue) that graced many churches, with the latter growing more broken and disheveled as time went on.[45] Some scholars have argued that Christian writers emphasized Christian superiority out of fear and insecurity, which is a difficult

Replicas of early-thirteenth-century allegorical statues of *Ecclesia* (the Church) and *Synagoga* (the Synagogue), Strasbourg cathedral, France. In her left hand, the blindfolded *Synagoga* holds a representation of the Torah, the Jewish Law of the Old Covenant. *Ecclesia* holds a chalice, representing the Blood of Christ of the New Covenant. The original statues were placed in prominent niches on the cathedral's façade. Photo source: Wikimedia.

---

44. The figures and geography of medieval Jewish demographics in Germany can be found in Michael Toch's article "The Formation of a Diaspora: The Settlement of Jews in the Medieval German Reich," originally published in *Aschkenas* 7 (1997): 55–78, reprinted in *Peasants and Jews in Medieval Germany: Studies in Cultural, Social, and Economic History* (Aldershot, UK: Ashgate/Variorum, 2003). Toch's analysis is not without its critics; for a less statistical, more readable analysis, see Alexander Patschovsky, "The Relationship between the Jews of Germany and the King (11th–14th centuries). A European Comparison," in *England and Germany in the High Middle Ages* (London: Oxford University Press, 1996), 235–65.

45. Glick, *Abraham's Heirs*, 52–54. See also Monika Winiarczyk's post, "The Fallen Woman: Shifting Perceptions of Synagoga," http://monikawiniarczyk.wordpress.com/2012/10/28/the-fallen-woman-shifting-perceptions-of-synagoga/, October 28, 2012 (accessed March 19, 2014).

assertion to sustain in the face of the triumphant atmosphere after 1099.[46] The very success of the crusade worked to disassociate Jews from the earthly Jerusalem, now clearly in Christian possession, and the prestige of the papacy kept crusaders focused on fighting the Eastern enemy and not in interfering with the divinely protected unbelievers in their midst.[47]

More than thirty Christian references to the persecutions of 1096 survive, some in chronicles very far from the Rhineland, and many show contrasting shades of approval or disapproval.[48] The most prominent Christian chronicler to accord space to the Rhineland pogroms was the German cleric Albert of Aachen, whose *History of Jerusalem* collected accounts and documents from a wide variety of participants. Albert displayed "remarkable sympathy" toward the persecuted, and his direct criticism of his fellow Christians was "unique."[49] He interpreted the defeat of Emicho's army in Hungary as proof that the persecutors had suffered divine judgment on account of "excessive impurities and fornicating unions" and for punishing "the exiled Jews (who are admittedly hostile to Christ) with great massacre, rather from greed for their money than for divine justice, since God is a just judge and commands no one to come to the yoke of the Catholic faith against his will or under compulsion."[50]

Most other Christian chroniclers were more equivocal in their assessments, most prominently Frutolf of Michelsberg (near Bamberg), whose account of the persecutions is unabashedly anti-Jewish. To Frutolf, the crusaders were good, honest common folk of the kingdoms of the West who were peacefully marching to the Holy Land when they took it upon themselves, in their zeal, to destroy the "truly innermost enemies of the church." None of the army commanders received criticism for his behavior in the massacres, and even Godfrey of Bouillon, whose conduct toward the Jews in his dominions was mentioned above, is commended for his actions. Perhaps, however, bowing to a general atmosphere of disapproval, Frutolf ends his account diffidently: "Whether it pleased [God] has to be left up to Him."[51] Frutolf's influential chronicle appears to have been used by authors of the *Chronicle of Würzburg*, the *Annals of St. Albans*, and the *Annals of Harsefeld*, among others.

However, for his entry on 1096 the St. Albans chronicler used a different account of the massacres that recorded a bitterly angry verdict on the crusaders' conduct: it was "murder" on a mass scale, and divine justice was visited on the city of Mainz

---

46. Kenneth Stow, "Conversion, Apostasy, and Apprehensiveness: Emicho of Flonheim and the Fear of the Jews in the Twelfth Century," *Speculum* 76 (2001): 911–33, at 912 and 926–27.

47. Liebeschütz, "The Crusading Movement," 270.

48. See Eva Haverkamp, "What Did the Christians Know? Latin Reports on the Persecution of Jews in 1096," *Crusades* 7 (2008): 59–86.

49. Albert of Aachen, *Historia Ierosolimitana*, ed. and trans., Susan B. Edgington (Oxford: Clarendon Press, 2007), xxxv.

50. Albert of Aachen, I:29.

51. Haverkamp, "What Did the Christians Know?" 71–73.

soon after, when a fire destroyed the greater part of the city. Rather than use Frutolf's inflammatory account, the Harsefeld author, for reasons known only to him, chose to omit any mention of the persecutions in 1096, focusing instead on Peter the Hermit's preaching, and recording for 1097 that "King" Henry of Germany had allowed baptized Jews to return to their faith, namely those Jews who had been forcibly baptized in 1096.[52]

The persecutions may have resulted in a permanent "elimination of trust" between Christians and Jews, but it is hard to detect in Christian chronicles much sense that something decisive had occurred in Christian-Jewish relations.[53] Subsequent theological controversies between Christians and Jews infrequently mentioned crusading, reinforcing the impression that "ultimately the issues which divide[d] Judaism and Christianity transcend[ed] history."[54]

Chroniclers aside, church policy toward the Jews also remained stable in the first century of crusading. In fact, the papacy reiterated the doctrine of toleration for Jews and took steps to prevent, or at least discourage, persecutions during subsequent crusades. After 1096, the most pressing issue was deciding what to do with the Jews forced to convert to Christianity. As noted above, in 1097 Emperor Henry IV allowed them to return to their faith, a decision also supported by his enemy Urban II, although to some observers this seemed to officially sanction apostasy. Continued concern with persecutions and forced conversions led Pope Calixtus II to issue the bull *Sicut Judeis* (And Thus to the Jews) sometime around 1120. This reaffirmed the standard papal policy toward the Jews and was reissued by no fewer than twenty-three popes into the fifteenth century. "We . . . offer them the shield of our protection," reads the earliest version. "We decree that no Christian shall use violence to force them into baptism while they are unwilling and refuse. . . . Moreover . . . no Christian shall presume to wound their persons, or kill them, or rob them of their money. . . . Furthermore, while they celebrate their festivals, no one shall disturb them in any way. . . ."[55] By the 1170s, the Jews of Rome regarded *Sicut Judeis* as the cornerstone of their prosperity. "They have heard of the Franks' massacres of Jews to the north," wrote Benjamin of Tudela during his Mediterranean tour,

---

52. Ibid., 74–76.

53. Stow, "Emicho of Flonheim," 929.

54. See Lasker, "Impact of the Crusades," 33. However, see Chazan, "Crusading in Christian-Jewish Polemics," in *The Medieval Crusade*, ed. Susan J. Ridyard (Woodbridge, UK: Boydell, 2004), 33–51 and Chazan, *Jewish Identity in Medieval Western Christendom* (Cambridge: Cambridge University Press, 2004). See also Elchanan Reiner, "A Jewish Response to the Crusades: The Dispute over the Sacred Places in the Holy Land," in *Juden und Christen* (note 42 above), 209–31.

55. The standard analysis in English remains that of Solomon Grazel, "The Papal Bull *Sicut Judeis*," in *Studies and Essays in Honor of Abraham A. Neuman*, ed. Meir Ben-Horin, et. al. (Leiden, Netherlands, 1962), 243–80, reprinted in *Essential Papers on Judaism and Christianity in Conflict: From Late Antiquity to the Reformation*, ed. Jeremy Cohen (New York: New York University Press, 1991), 231–59.

but that was long ago and far away, and in a sense the atrocities against Jews in the Rhineland redounded to the benefit of the Jews in Rome, because . . . the pope issued [*Sicut Judeis*]. He issued it twenty years after the massacres, to be sure; we thank God that subsequent popes have honored it.[56]

On the other hand, the Church's tolerance of Judaism had limits. *Sicut Judeis* left a loophole for persecution by only protecting "those [Jews] who do not presume to plot against the Christian faith." At the Third Lateran Council in 1179, Alexander III, who had reissued *Sicut Judeis* a short time previously, made clear Jews' social and legal inferiority to Christians.[57] Further, the papacy's ability to actually protect Jews was limited. Celestine III (r. 1191–1198), for example, could do little to protect the Jews of France from Philip II's depredations.[58] His successor Innocent III (r. 1198–1216) was much less friendly than his predecessors toward Jews, and his church reforms strengthened the link between crusading and common Christian devotion.[59]

The Fourth Lateran Council of 1215, the culmination of Pope Innocent's III's attempts at reforming Latin Christendom, established as law several important regulations in regard to the Jews, although some of these conciliar canons were already traditional practices. It forbade reversion to Judaism after voluntary conversion to Christianity and mandated coercion to keep former Jews in the Church; it made a matter of Christian policy the physical demarcation of Jews and Muslims through the wearing of distinctive garments; it banned Jews from public offices; and it identified Jews exclusively with "the cruel oppression" of usury.[60]

On their part, secular rulers saw their taxing of Jewish usury as a ready source of crusade funding, thus keeping Jews before the crusading public's eye while possibly diluting the motive to persecute.[61] Despite Innocent's antipathy toward Jews and Judaism, this pope's crusades to the East, the fourth (1202–1204) and

---

56. Benjamin of Tudela, *The World of Benjamin of Tudela: A Medieval Mediterranean Travelogue*, ed. and trans. Sandra Benjamin (London: Associated University Presses, 1995), 87.

57. Canon 26 of the council, http://www.intratext.com/ixt/eng0064/_P2.HTM (accessed March 19, 2014). For an abbreviated version of *Sicut Judeis*, http://people.umass.edu/~juda102/outlines/sicutJudaeis.html (accessed March 19, 2014).

58. See Marie Therese Champagne, "Celestine III and the Jews," in *Pope Celestine III (1191–1198)*, ed. John Doran and Damian J. Smith (Farnham, UK: Ashgate, 2008), 271–85.

59. See Christoph T. Maier, "Mass, the Eucharist and the Cross: Innocent III and the Relocation of the Crusade" in *Pope Innocent III and His World*, ed. John C. Moore (Aldershot, UK: Ashgate, 1999), 351–60.

60. See canons 67–70 of the Fourth Lateran Council, http://www.fordham.edu/halsall/basis/lateran4.asp (accessed August 10, 2013). For a concise account, see Robert Chazan, "Innocent III and the Jews," in *Pope Innocent III and His World*, ed. John C. Moore, 187–204.

61. Regarding usury and crusade, see Jessalynn Bird, "Reform or Crusade? Anti-Usury and Crusade Preaching during the Pontificate of Innocent III," in *Pope Innocent III and His World*, 165–85, and Rebecca Rist, "The Power of the Purse; Usury, Jews, and Crusaders, 1198–1245," in *Aspects of Power and Authority in the Middle Ages*, ed. Brenda Bolton and Christine Meek (Turnhout, Belgium: Brepols, 2007), 197–213.

the fifth (1217–1221), saw no major outbreaks of anti-Jewish persecution, and a study of thirteenth-century papal crusading documents shows that for the most part crusading and Jewish affairs occupied separate spheres of thought.[62] Churchmen tasked with preaching and recruiting the crusade occasionally declared that those who hesitated to take the cross were worse than Jews, but in general Jews did not figure in crusade preaching.[63] The Albigensian Crusade (1209–1229) into southern France, however, saw widespread casual persecutions and massacres of Jewish communities in Languedoc, including Simon de Montfort's looting of the synagogue in Toulouse, the massacre of the community at Béziers, and a stipulation in the final treaty of 1229 that the count of Toulouse could not employ Jews in his government, a prohibition that was consonant with Canon 69 of the Fourth Lateran Council.[64]

"National" narratives of crusade and anti-Jewish agitation are similarly complex. In 1189, Richard I of England's coronation took place in the midst of his preparations for the Third Crusade, and when a delegation of London's Jewish community arrived at the palace to offer the customary gifts to the new king, a series of riots broke out, culminating in massacres throughout England, especially in Norfolk and Yorkshire. In his brief account of the events, Gillingham summarizes the persecutors' motivations as "the crusading spirit" and a desire to seize Jewish wealth that "could help many a poor but pious man on his way" to Jerusalem. Older scholarship tended to "discuss [the persecutions], if they do, within important but circumscribed discussions of anti-Semitism or debt."[65]

Recent studies, however, have argued that Christian chroniclers, such as William of Newburgh, saw the massacres as a central event of their times, and "the English expression of [the] pogroms . . . first in 1096 and 1146 . . . [then of] the murder of thirty Jews at Blois in northern France in 1171 and [then of the] attempted violence

---

62. For papal documents of the thirteenth century, see Solomon Grazel, *The Church and the Jews in the XIIIth Century* (Philadelphia: The Dropsie College, 1933). For a summary of major papal decrees on Jews, see Solomon Grayzel, "Bulls, Papal," in the *Encyclopaedia Judaica* (the Gale Group, 2008), http://www.jewishvirtuallibrary.org/jsource/judaica/ejud_0002_0004_0_03728.html (accessed March 19, 2014).

63. See the sermons and letters in the so-called *Ansbert Chronicle* in *The Crusade of Frederick Barbarossa*, ed. and trans. Graham Loud (Farnham, UK: Ashgate, 2010). For the thirteenth century, see Jacques de Vitry, Sermo I, p. 97; Gilbert of Tournai, Sermo I and Sermo III, in *Crusade Propaganda and Ideology: Model Sermons for the Preaching of the Cross*, ed. and trans. Christoph T. Maier (Cambridge: Cambridge University Press, 2000), 179, 183, and 205.

64. See Mark Gregory Pegg, *A Most Holy War: The Albigensian Crusade and the Battle for Christendom* (Oxford: Oxford University Press, 2008), 151; for the synagogue in Toulouse, 76–78, 189–190 for the massacre at Béziers and 180 for the Treaty of Meaux-Paris in 1229.

65. Gillingham, *Richard I*, 108; Sethina Watson, "Introduction" in the extremely valuable *Christians and Jews in Angevin England*, ed. Sarah Rees Jones and Sethina Watson (Woodbridge, UK: Boydell, 2013), 4.

at Mainz in 1188."[66] Certainly the massacres, particularly the suicides and murders of the York community in 1190, shocked contemporaries and revealed not simply a "crusading" zeal but a deep and vicious anti-Judaism that had been building for some time. Outside London, Richard proved largely powerless to stop the murders (or perhaps he did not care to), and it is hard to escape the conclusion that the Third Crusade acted as a direct catalyst to anti-Jewish persecution.[67]

Of course, the monetary concerns of the persecutors should not be discounted, as England's relations with its Jewish community tended to orbit around encouraging Jewish financial activities, such as the lending of money, and seizing the profits when the crown needed them.[68] This pattern recurred until 1290, when Edward I expelled the Jewish community, which departed English shores in a storm of persecution and murder. Edward was an enthusiastic crusader, and his persecution of the Jews was ideologically, not financially, motivated.[69] In the case of England, it is hard to escape the conclusion that crusading was, in fact, a major contributor to anti-Judaism.[70]

---

66. Watson, *Christians and Jews*, 5 and 2.

67. By contrast with the Third Crusade, consider the effective royal orders in England during the Second Crusade in Ephraim of Bonn's chronicle, in Eidelberg *Jews and the Crusaders*, 131. The Fordham Internet Sourcebook contains two extracts on the Third Crusade persecutions: Roger of Hoveden, http://www.fordham.edu/halsall/source/hoveden1189b.asp (accessed March 19, 2014), and Ephraim of Bonn, http://www.fordham.edu/halsall/source/ephr-bonn1.asp (accessed March 19, 2014). For an efficient overview of the Jewish experience in England, with relevant citations, see *The Jews of Medieval Britain: Historical, Literary, and Archaeological Perspectives*, ed. Patricia Skinner (Woodbridge, UK: Boydell & Brewer, 2003).

68. Paul R. Hyams, "The Jews in Medieval England, 1066–1290," in *England and Germany in High Middle Ages*, 173–92, which, though old, remains an excellent overview. See also the *Dialogue of the Exchequer* (ca. 1179), II:10 and 25, http://avalon.law.yale.edu/medieval/excheq.asp (accessed January 26, 2014). Also W. L. Warren, *Henry II* (Berkeley: University of California Press, 1973), 546–47, 382–83. Consider also the anti-Jewish clauses of *Magna Carta*, all of which were directed toward Jewish financial interests, discussed in J. C. Holt, *Magna Carta*, 2nd ed. (Cambridge: Cambridge University Press, 1992), 211–14, 335–36, 452–55.

69. The latest account of the expulsion of England's Jews is Robin R. Mundill, *The King's Jews: Money, Massacre, and Exodus in Medieval England* (London: Bloomsbury Academic, 2010). It received a mixed review from the leading scholar Robert Stacey, http://www.history.ac.uk/reviews/review/1077 (accessed August 15, 2014). See also Hyams, "The Jews in Medieval England," 191 and Michael Prestwich, *Edward I* (New Haven, CT: Yale University Press, 1997; original London, 1988), 343–46. See Kate McGrath, "English Jews as Outlaws or Outcasts: The Ritual Murder of Little St. Hugh of Lincoln in Matthew Paris's *Chronica Majora*," in *British Outlaws of Literature and History*, ed. Alexander L. Kaufman (Jefferson, NC: McFarland, 2011), 11–27. For a quick overview of Edward I's Jewish policy, see Colin Richmond's 1999 review of *England's Jewish Solution: Experiment and Expulsion, 1262–1290* by Robin R. Mundill, http://www.history.ac.uk/reviews/review/70 (accessed March 19, 2014).

70. In addition to all of the more recent and focused works cited above, see Christopher Tyerman, *England and the Crusades, 1095–1588* (Chicago: University of Chicago Press, 1988), who deals with the Jews and English crusading, passim.

On the other hand, it is harder to establish the same relationship in France—French persecutions coincided less with crusade activity, though persecutions occurred in Normandy during the Second Crusade, and Louis VII was persuaded to cancel any Jewish debts his crusaders might have incurred. In 1171, a spectacular persecution occurred at Blois but was not connected with crusading. Philip II (r. 1180–1223) persecuted Jews throughout his reign, occasionally out of a lingering "crusading zeal," but while scattered violence occurred in France during his preparations for the Third Crusade, he had already expelled Jews from royal lands. After a period of relative quiet, anti-Jewish policies became a hallmark of Louis IX (r. 1226–1270), who believed that government reform required, among other things, isolating and persecuting French Jews prior to launching his crusades.[71] The 1251 "Shepherds' Crusade," a popular, apocalyptic movement, made a special target of Jewish communities, basically continuing these policies.[72] Even Louis IX, however, spent relatively little time on the Jews, being consumed with larger issues of war and government.

Medieval Germany's treatment of its Jewish communities presents similar inconsistencies in Christian victimization of Jews.[73] Throughout the twelfth century, persecution in Germany was sporadic and became general only once, during preparations for the Second Crusade, when renewed persecutions took place in the Rhineland and in the Main River Valley in the spring and autumn of 1146 and in February 1147. It would have been much worse but for Abbot Bernard of Clairvaux's strenuous efforts to halt the preaching of the monk Rudolf, whose "carelessly sown" anti-Jewish ideas were a dangerous perversion of Church teaching.[74]

---

71. For the pogrom at Blois, see Robert Chazan, *God, Humanity, and History: The Hebrew First Crusade Narratives* (Berkeley: University of California Press, 2000), 1–17. The classic English-language study of medieval French Jews is William Chester Jordan, *The French Monarchy and the Jews: From Philip Augustus to the last Capetians* (Philadelphia: University of Pennsylvania Press, 1989), which argues that the persecutions in Philip II's reign stemmed partly from the gradual acceptance of anti-Jewish libels by the population at large, including the king.

72. The most recent annotated collection of sources is in *The Seventh Crusade, 1244–1254: Sources and Documents*, trans. Peter Jackson (Farnham, UK: Ashgate, 2009), 180–93. See also William Chester Jordan, *Louis IX and the Challenge of the Crusade: A Study in Rulership* (Princeton, NJ: Princeton University Press, 1979).

73. Still the best overview of Jews in medieval Germany is Alexander Patschovsky's "The Relationship between the Jews of Germany and the King," cited in note 44. Although dated, Patschovsky's discussion of the German emperors' growing authority over "his" Jews and the concept of *servi camerae* (chamber serfs) retains considerable value.

74. The passage is in Otto of Freising, *The Deeds of Frederick Barbarossa*, trans. Christopher Mierow (New York: W. W. Norton, 1966, reprint of the 1953 edition by Columbia University Press), 74, book I, chapter 38, p. 37. See also Shlomo Eidelberg's translation of R. Ephraim of Bonn's *Sefer Zekhirah*, in *The Jews and the Crusaders: The Hebrew Chronicles of the First and Second Crusades* (Madison: University of Wisconsin Press, 1977). For the *Würzburg Annals*, with their ritual murder accusation, see the *Annales Herbipolenses* (in Latin), MGH SS XVI, 3.

In 1189, similar persecutions threatened to develop in the Rhineland. However, not only were these disturbances broken up by imperial officials, but in the Emperor Frederick I's decrees we see the only explicit secular rejection of the idea that a persecutor could also be a legitimate crusader. Those who persecuted Jews were to be stripped of their crusader status and any privileges pertaining thereto. It was the strongest German decree in favor of the Jews; it would not be sustained by Frederick's son Henry VI (r. 1190–1197).[75] On the other hand, Henry's son Frederick II (r. 1220–1250) took a fairly detached view of Judaism during his reign, mostly regarding Jews as his personal resource for funds.[76] Not surprisingly, much anti-Jewish violence in Germany had no direct association with crusading: more typical is the *Erfurt Annals*' record of major riots in Frankfurt in 1241, occasioned by a young Jewish man wishing to convert to Christianity but forbidden to do so by friends and family. The resulting violence saw nearly two hundred Jews slaughtered and, with the support of the bishop, twenty-four baptized.[77]

Conclusion

At the end of the day, who has the better of the argument: Dershowitz or Madden? Did "the ideology of crusading and anti-Judaism [go] hand in hand?" Was anti-Jewish persecution a "concomitant of crusade?"[78] Were the crusades even the "prelude to the Holocaust?" The answer must remain a rather unsatisfying "It depends," because we can find examples of positive and negative answers for each question. After the Third Crusade, it is difficult to demonstrate a direct causal link from crusading to most anti-Jewish violence. Before the Third Crusade, it is a somewhat different story. To claim more or less is to verge toward myth-making.

Whether Salo W. Baron was right to claim, "In many ways 1096 marked a turning point in Jewish history"[79] is still debated. Certainly the mere occurrence of the massacres exerted its own influence on the way medieval Christians and Jews thought

---

75. Robert Chazan, "Frederick I, the Third Crusade, and the Jews," *Viator* 8 (1977): 83–93, particularly 89–91.

76. See John P. Dolan, "A Note on Emperor Frederick II and Jewish Tolerance," in *Jewish Social Studies*, 22 (1960): 165–74 and David Abulafia, "Ethnic Variety and Its Implications: Frederick II's Relations with Jews and Muslims," in *Intellectual Life at the Court of Frederick II Hohenstaufen*, ed. William Tronzo (Washington, D.C.: National Gallery of Art, 1994), 213–24.

77. *Annales Erphordenses,* MGH SS XVI, 34.

78. Cohen, *Sanctifying the Name of God*, 3; Haverkamp, "Jews in Christian Europe," 175.

79. Baron, *A Social and Religious History of the Jews*, 2nd ed. (Philadelphia, 1957), 4:89, quoted in Daniel J. Lasker, "The Impact of the Crusades on the Jewish-Christian Debate," *Jewish History* 13 (1999): 23. See also David N. Myers' thoughtful analysis of the Jewish historiography of the 1096 persecutions in the nineteenth and twentieth centuries, in "'*Mehabevin et ha-tsarot*': Crusade Memories and Modern Jewish Martyrologies," *Jewish History* 13 (1999): 49–64, especially 52–56, http://www.sscnet.ucla.edu/history/myers/cvfin3_files/Mehabevin%20et%20ha-tsarot.pdf (accessed August 19, 2014).

about persecution, and it taught them to associate crusading with anti-Judaism. It is also quite possible that 1096 bequeathed to Christian Europe the ritual murder libel, which first appeared in the 1140s in England and Germany and is often linked to some Jews' slaughter of their own children in Mainz in 1096 (rather than let them fall into the hands of the Christian mob).[80] The "Peasants' Crusade" also had stronger connections to the "real" crusaders of the second wave, known popularly as the Crusade of the Nobles, than many historians like to admit.

These connections derived from anti-Judaic rituals such as the "Savior's Vengeance," a heightened sense of the importance of the Holy Sepulcher and the Christian salvific narrative, changing perceptions of the Mass, a sense of destiny connected to the Frankish *gens* (folk), and a need, somewhat obscure in its origins, on the part of Christian theologians to address Jewish criticisms of Christianity in powerful and influential tracts. Moreover, several key figures of the 1096 pogroms later appear as honored and valuable crusaders in the Levant. Even optimistic historians would have to admit that while Jews may have benefitted from the Twelfth-Century Renaissance, more and more often access to justice in the face of robbery, murder, and casual oppression proved, with increasing frequency, "entirely beyond their [the Jews'] reach."[81]

But despite these points, when we examine the evidence closely it becomes difficult to identify 1096 as a decisive event in Christian and Jewish history. Jewish-Christian disputes followed well-trodden paths after the First Crusade, and they only infrequently mentioned crusading as a point of contention. Jewish populations and prosperity increased throughout the twelfth century despite periodic persecutions, many of which had no connection to crusading. Jewish theologians responded to the challenge of a militant reformed Christianity by crafting a robust model of Jewish heroic piety. "Crusading," whether one believes it a new phenomenon in 1095 or an evolving concept, stood recognizably apart from anti-Judaism intellectually, politically, and religiously, although the continued association of crusading with anti-Judaic persecutions suggests it appealed to medieval logic. But since anti-Judaism long preceded the First Crusade, it is not too much to say that insofar as the crusades were anti-Judaic, they were so because the society that produced them was anti-Judaic, had been for centuries, and had begun to reassess its Jewish minority well before 1096.

Perhaps that is why, rightly or wrongly, so many crusade histories spend little time discussing the Jewish experience. The goal and purpose of the crusade was *not* to murder or convert Jews; it was, as has been shown elsewhere in this volume, to promote the primacy of the Roman papacy, to bring aid to the Christian communities in the eastern Mediterranean, and to regain control of the Christian holy places in the Levant. At the end of the day, crusading was produced by the Reform Papacy's "persecuting society," not the other way around. As Henry Leibeschütz wrote in 1959,

---

80. See Yuval, *Two Nations*, chapter 4 "Intersecting Stories: From Martyrdom to Ritual Murder Accusations," 135–204.

81. Glick, *Abraham's Heirs*, 129.

"This combination of enthusiasm and primitive instincts was rather a presupposition of the Crusades than their consequences."[82] The crusading concept as expounded by the Church and practiced by many rulers took no account of anti-Judaism in its execution.

At the very least, there really is no convincing way to link the crusades to Nazi Germany, despite the occasional description of 1096 as the "first Holocaust."[83] That this idea persists is due in large part to controversial popular works such as Daniel Goldhagen's *Hitler's Willing Executioners* or otherwise excellent sourcebooks that, in the interests of brevity, advance unsubstantiated and unsustainable claims that after a thousand years "without significant physical contact," the crusades turned "toleration [of Jews] . . . to mass violence."[84] Then, just as unsustainably, one has to believe that an unbroken tradition of murderous persecution of Jews in Western Europe extended for more than eight hundred years from 1096 to the Holocaust under the Nazis. That is quite a stretch, especially given the fact that the theological, philosophical, ideological, and cultural priorities of medieval Christianity do not line up very well with Nazi ideology, as Steven T. Katz has argued at great length.[85]

Ultimately, what one believes on the issue depends partly on whether one gives any agency to the persecutors in determining the meaning of "crusade" or if, instead, one accepts papal pronouncements as the last word on the subject. After all, papal crusade policy was both evolving and experimental, and popular piety could and often did diverge quite widely from papal governance. Were it possible to triangulate the truth of the matter, we would probably see the magnet drift toward Lasker's statement, rather than toward Dershowitz's or Madden's, as quoted at the start of this chapter. The First Crusade was the product of an anti-Judaic society that by 1096 had already begun to reassess the Jewish communities in their midst, and the crusades, with their intense focus on the physical sites of the Christian salvation narrative, especially the

---

82. H. Liebeschütz, "The Crusading Movement in Its Bearing on the Christian Attitude towards Jewry," *Journal of Jewish Studies* 10 (1959), 97–111, reprinted in *Essential Papers on Judaism and Christianity in Conflict*, ed. Jeremy Cohen (New York: New York University Press, 1991), 271.

83. Jonathan Riley-Smith, *A History of the Crusades*, 2nd ed. (New Haven, CT: Yale University Press, 2005), 23–25. See also his perceptive comments in *The Crusades: A History*, 3rd ed. (London: Bloomsbury, 2014), 43–45, where he argues that "holy war has a tendency to turn inwards" (45) and forced baptism was perceived a means of "creating a uniformly Christian society" (ibid.).

84. Steven Hochstadt, ed., *Sources of the Holocaust* (New York: Palgrave Macmillan, 2004), 8.

85. Steven T. Katz, *The Holocaust in Historical Context*, vol. 1: *The Holocaust and Mass Death Before the Modern Age* (Oxford: Oxford University Press, 1994). Katz's two chapters on crusade and medieval anti-Judaism are exhaustively footnoted and constitute a resource in themselves. However, see the 2012 research by Nico Voigtländer and Hans-Joachim Voth, "The Medieval Origins of 20th Century Anti-Semitism in Germany," which suggests a correlation between sites of medieval and modern persecutions, http://blog.oup.com/2012/07/medieval-pogrom-origin-20th-century-anti-semitism-germany/ (accessed August 14, 2014).

Crucifixion, for which the Jews were blamed, simply gave these evolving beliefs and emotions an outlet, although their purpose had nothing to do with Jews or Judaism.

Attempts by church and state authorities to balance the social subordination of Jews as enemies of God, while at the same time forbidding murder and persecution (since Jews were the living proof of Christianity) met with repeated failure, as the persecutions of the Second and Third Crusades demonstrate. Yet, somewhat surprisingly, the development of medieval anti-Judaism and crusading followed separate and very distinct paths, and neither influenced the other very much. Even R. I. Moore, despite the earlier statements quoted above, writes of Jewish victimization, "But they [the crusades] did not cause it, and may too easily serve as a portmanteau explanation of events whose real causes and connections with each other are obscure."[86]

As Robert Chazan has written, "Simplistic imageries have enormous appeal. They make the work readily understandable; they usually involve the establishment of clearly demarcated good and evil; they eliminate much of the difficulty associated with complex judgments."[87] But history is not simple. The weight of evidence suggests that *correlation* not causality was the dominant relationship between crusading and medieval anti-Judaism, although the influence of 1096 on subsequent persecutions was real and cannot be discounted. Given the continued ability of the medieval crusades to inflame passions and to shape identity in (post)modern times, understanding this relationship retains considerable importance, and will continue to do so.

---

86. Moore, *Persecuting Society*, 30.
87. Chazan, *Reassessing Jewish Life in Medieval Europe*, 14.

4. The Quest for Gain: Were the First Crusaders Proto-Colonists?

Corliss Slack

> The leaders [of the First Crusade] set out with the idea of forming a new kingdom *at* Jerusalem. The crusade was migration as well as war.[1]

Harold Lamb, a writer of popular high-adventure nonfiction and novels and a consultant for Cecil B. DeMille's wildly ahistorical film *The Crusades* (1935), initially penned these words in the early 1930s, but by then it was a commonplace notion that the military leaders of the First Crusade and the thousands of professional warriors who formed their retinues went east in search of land and wealth, many of them, so the story went, being the landless younger sons of Europe's feudal leadership. In essence, it was a migration of would-be colonizers, not unlike the waves of European and American colonists who, in search of better lives and riches in the nineteenth and twentieth centuries, flocked to distant lands that were held in servitude by a mother country. Was that the case? One argument in favor of such an interpretation is the fact that four crusader states emerged during and in the immediate wake of the First Crusade—the County of Edessa, the Principality of Antioch, the Kingdom of Jerusalem, and the County of Tripoli—and remnants of them persisted down to 1291.[2]

It is easy to discover this idea still percolating today. A perfect mix of contemporary principles and concerns, including a contempt for colonialism in all of its forms, can be found in the four-part *Crusades* (1995) miniseries, which has been extensively critiqued in the Introduction and which several other authors of chapters in this book have taken to task. As noted by many, *Crusades* is staged as part Monty Python routine and part almost-serious historical overview, and that latter aspect can seduce the unwary viewer into incorrectly assuming that the story line and judgments contained therein are mainstream and represent up-to-date scholarship.

To give credibility to that misperception, the director has interjected brief comments by a number of "talking heads," several of whom (but certainly not all) have

---

1. Harold Lamb, *The Crusades: Iron Men and Saints* (New York: New Home Library, 1942), 327.

2. The list of solid historical studies of these states is long. One of the best, which, however, only takes their story down to 1192 and the end of the Third Crusade, thereby overlooking a full century of continued existence, is Malcolm Barber, *The Crusader States* (New Haven, CT: Yale University Press, 2012). A brief overview of the states that traces their fortunes from 1098 to 1291 in fewer than one hundred pages is P. M. Holt, *The Crusader States and Their Neighbours* (London: Pearson Education Limited, 2004).

standing as eminent crusade historians.[3] Two historians in that category are Jonathan Riley-Smith and Christopher Tyerman, who emphasize in the seconds allotted to them the religious motivation that drove participants of the First Crusade. Yet, somehow their voices are almost muted by a contrary message that resounds throughout the film: the crusaders were barbaric fanatics led by greedy, self-serving lords "on the make." Therefore, the establishment of crusader states in the Levant was a goal even before the crusade armies of 1096 left Europe. Judicious editing and constant repetition of a single theme, no matter how ill conceived, can drown out the voices of those whose insights are based on so much more than contempt for crusaders and crusading.

Although its characterizations of many individuals and incidents, its assumptions and conclusions, and many of its made for comic effect scenes raise the ire of professional crusade historians, the *Crusades* series seems almost sober and scholarly when compared with other video products available to the serious viewer who wishes to learn about the crusades. A case in point is Ridley Scott's *Kingdom of Heaven* (2005), which also caused a ruckus among informed commentators, who variously bemoaned its fictional story line, adorned with the names of actual people, and its anachronistic and hostile portrayal of religious belief in twelfth-century Europe.[4]

On another level of criticism, crusade enthusiasts who are not trained historians happily debate the historicity of the film's depiction of medieval interiors, battle scenes, armaments, and costumes, and, depending on their proclivities, ridicule the central romance and deplore or celebrate the portrayal of Sultan Saladin as, essentially, "the good guy."[5] The official hero of the movie is a fictional character with

---

3. Karen Armstrong is one such non-historian.

4. The History Channel produced a documentary, directed by Steven Jack, on the inaccuracies of the film as episode 21 of *Hollywood vs. History*, forty-three minutes, May 5, 2005. In it, historians defend the idea that the crusaders were largely driven by piety and a desire for salvation rather than colonialism or greed. The episode was packaged with the two-disk special edition of the DVD for *Kingdom of Heaven* (directed by Ridley Scott, 144 minutes, Twentieth Century Fox Film Corporation, 2005). Charlotte Edwardes, "Ridley Scott's New Crusades Film 'panders to Osama bin Laden,'" *The Telegraph*, January 18, 2004, quotes scathing criticism by crusade historians Jonathan Riley-Smith and Jonathan Philips, and the journalist Amin Maalouf of the film's inaccuracies and gross misrepresentations, http://www.telegraph.co.uk/news/worldnews/northamerica/usa/1452000/Ridley-Scotts-new-Crusades-film-panders-to-Osama-bin-Laden.html (accessed April 17, 2014). For a movie critic's view of the film, see William B. Parrill, *Ridley Scott. A Critical Filmography* (Jefferson, NC: McFarland & Co., 2011).

5. For example, on August 2, 2006, H. J. Spivak wrote an amazon.com review that included the observation "Oh, and the heraldry was (I'm pretty sure) right for a change. King Richard's standard on his chest was the one he adopted during the crusades, the 2 Lions Rampant and Countered, not the Lion Rampant and Roaring that always gets used but was only used by him when at home." http://smile.amazon.com/Kingdom-Heaven-2-Disc-Widescreen-Edition/product-reviews/B000AARKOO/ref=cm_cr_pr_btm_link_next_2?ie=UTF8&pageNumber=2&showViewpoints=0&sortBy=byRankDescending (accessed April 23, 2014).

a historical name, Balian, a humble French blacksmith who is the bastard son of a crusader and the heir to the property his father won in the Kingdom of Jerusalem.[6] A sympathetic murderer of a repellant priest at home in France, the fictional Balian, whose faith is lost, seeks redemption in the Holy Land. He improves the land he inherits to benefit his serfs, but in the end, he goes home to Europe, leaving Saladin in charge of a region that the film depicts as Muslim. Scott does so without dealing with the Christian claims to the region that undergirded the morality of the crusades for medieval Europeans, whose claims to the "Holy Land" were based on the Christian past as they understood it, part of a complex medieval worldview, essentially a theological interpretation of history, that is not reflected in the film.

The movie's story line confirms the lessons of Terry Jones's BBC miniseries in two essential ways: the religious claims of the Europeans are overshadowed by their brutality, and there is no reasonable explanation for a crusade into the Holy Land other than greedy colonialism. In short, crusaders and colonists of the Latin Kingdom alike are brutal hypocrites. To add a bit of romantic counterpoise to the film, the sensible (and sensitive) hero takes the woman he loves (a former queen of Jerusalem) home to their land of origin, leaving the "Kingdom of Heaven," formerly an ill-gotten colony, to its rightful Muslim occupants, who had fairly and chivalrously reclaimed their land.

The audiences of both films can feel virtuous, broad-minded, and well informed, thinking that they have learned a bit, and in the Hollywood film, have seen a stirring visualization of the fall of Jerusalem in 1187 to Saladin and his Egyptian-Syrian army. They can also feel superior, since the crusaders in general seem akin to stereotypical Western colonialists of the modern era, who exploited and brutalized hapless natives (although the fictional Balian, who runs counter to the stereotype, somewhat miraculously finds water for his parched farmland and its endangered native farmers). Crusaders from Europe and those Westerners who were born in the crusader states were nothing more than the first wave of a hateful era of European history—colonists driven by greed, a totally erroneous sense of cultural superiority, and racism—an era that many do not see as over and that some think is now dominated by the intertwined political and economic agendas of the United States.

Having examined several examples of popular uses of crusade history, centered in one way or another around the issue of colonial greed, it is time to ask how academic historians of the medieval crusades, many of whom who have devoted a lifetime of study to the issue, view the role of greed and colonialism in the expeditions. What use do they make of the sources left by the participants? How do their judgments differ from popular views?

---

6. The historic Balian II of Ibelin was a high-born, powerful lord of the Kingdom of Jerusalem who spent his entire life in the kingdom (ca. 1143–1193?). He was married to former Queen Maria Comnena, the widow of King Amalric of Jerusalem, which made him stepfather to Queen Isabella I, her daughter. The only thing that Ridley Scott got right was that Balian led the defenses of Jerusalem against Saladin in 1187.

The Evolving Views of Historians on the Motivations of the First Crusaders

The views of historians change over time. New sources are discovered, but also—as a new generation of historians, armed with new experiences, looks at the sources—new questions are asked. One constant remains in looking at medieval civilization: medieval Europeans (as well as many other contemporaneous peoples, such as Byzantines and Muslims), whether they were aristocrats or commoners, clergy or laity, simply did not define and differentiate politics and religion as we do. In his overview of the crusades, Hans Eberhard Mayer begins with a survey of the Mediterranean region that emphasizes Europe's "fierce internecine struggles" even as it "gathered its strength for a vigorous counter-attack on the Muslims." Thus, the problem was uniting Europeans for the task of pushing Islam back.[7] The Roman Church, although beset with its own difficulties, offered the leadership that was lacking among European secular rulers.

According to Mayer, the two political and religious centers of Christendom, Rome and Constantinople, had become estranged over matters of doctrine, liturgy, and primacy in 1054.[8] Nevertheless, in Mayer's view, Pope Gregory VII (r. 1073–1085) believed that an overarching identity as Christians mandated a response by the Roman Church to the attack by the Seljuk Turks on the Christian Byzantine Empire. To this end, Gregory proposed launching an armed expedition to the East led by the pope himself. A few years later, in an attempt at effecting a reconciliation between Byzantium and the Normans, who were consolidating their hold on the former Byzantine lands of southern Italy, he worked to arrange a marriage alliance between a Byzantine princess and the Norman leader Robert Guiscard. Due to circumstances, neither plan bore fruit.[9] It remained for Gregory's successor once removed, Pope Urban II (r. 1088–1099), to bring to fruition two decades later the expedition to rescue Eastern Christians and liberate Jerusalem.

For Mayer, these papal initiatives were motivated by a mixture of the spiritual and the political. Spiritual concerns, as far as both Pope Gregory and Urban were concerned, included the unity of Christendom and the role of the papacy in the world.

---

7. Hans Eberhard Mayer, *The Crusades*, 2nd ed., trans. John Gillingham (Oxford: Oxford University Press, 1988), 1–2. Mayer originally composed the book in 1965 and then published it in a second edition in 1988. Gillingham's English translation of the 1965 edition only appeared in 1972. The page references to Mayer in this note and in notes below are valid for both editions.

8. Ibid., 2–3. Contrary to this view, many historians have argued that 1054 was not the epochal moment of irrevocable schism. See Henry Chadwick, *East and West. The Making of a Rift in the Church: From Apostolic Times until the Council of Florence* (New York: Oxford University Press, 2003), 206–18. James Muldoon provides further bibliography in his discussion of the thorny issue of 1054 and the schism in his chapter "Mad Men on Crusade: Religious Madness and the Origins of the First Crusade," note 61.

9. Mayer, *Crusades*, 3. See this book's opening chapter by Paul Crawford, "The First Crusade: Unprovoked Offense or Overdue Defense?" for a survey of the events that led up to the First Crusade.

Pope Urban's main political concern in 1095 was how to combine and redirect the European powers in the face of ongoing controversies over the choice and election of bishops with the German emperor Henry IV (r. 1056–1105), the excommunication of King Philip I of France (r. 1060–1108) over his marital status, and the "extremely anticlerical" policies of King William II Rufus of England (r. 1087–1100).

How could the pope convince these rulers to accept his leadership in planning an attempt to rescue Constantinople from the Turks' aggression? How open would the Byzantines be to papal allies who answered the call for help? Regime change had brought in a new Byzantine emperor, Alexius I Comnenus (r. 1081–1118), who, as he took the throne, was fighting the Normans of southern Italy at Epirus (present-day Albania and northwestern Greece), which was imperial territory. Alexius was not likely to look with favor on the papal proposal of an alliance with his Norman enemies, who clearly were the aggressors. The motives of those Normans who joined the First Crusade, especially Bohemond of Taranto, who had been second in command of the Norman invasion of the Balkans as recently as 1085, would always be suspect to the Byzantines.[10]

Writing in the first half of the twelfth century and well after the First Crusade, Anna Comnena, daughter of Emperor Alexius I, noted that this Norman adventurer turned crusader, Bohemond of Taranto, who seized the Byzantine city of Antioch for himself in 1098 and established there the state known as the Principality of Antioch (1198–1268), had gone on the crusade "to win power for himself—or rather, if possible to seize the Roman [Byzantine] Empire itself."[11]

Indeed, Western European motives for crusading in general were subject to Greek suspicion. Alexius would insist in 1097 that every leader of the First Crusade take an oath to return all captured territory to him. Oaths were eventually taken, some under duress and, correspondingly, much of Anatolia (present-day Asian Turkey), including the ancient and important Christian city of Nicaea, which had recently been conquered by the Turks, was restored to Byzantine rule due to the combined efforts of the crusaders and Emperor Alexius's forces. Yet crusade leaders also later embraced rationales that allowed them to justify establishing themselves as rulers at Edessa, Antioch, Jerusalem, and Tripoli, as well as replacing Byzantine clerics with Latin churchmen in the pilgrimage churches of Jerusalem and neighboring lands. But was all of this *colonialism*—either a colonialism that followed a preexpedition plan or an onsite, ad hoc colonialism that sprang up in a helter-skelter, unplanned fashion?

Crusade historians have debated for some time the question of whether these conquests can be labeled early examples of European colonialism. Four decades ago, the eminent Israeli scholar, Joshua Prawer, who, more than any other historian was

---

10. Mayer, *Crusades*, 2–3. The Norman attack on Byzantine territory in the Balkans (1081–1085) had enjoyed the support of Pope Gregory VII.

11. Anna Comnena, *The Alexiad of Anna Comnena*, trans. E. R. A. Sewter (Harmondsworth, UK: Penguin, 1969), 329.

Church of Saint Anne, Jerusalem. In addition to taking over a number of Eastern Christian churches and installing Latin clerics in them, crusaders and settlers in *Outremer* built new churches and religious establishments. One of the few remaining Latin-settlement structures is the Church of Saint Anne in Jerusalem, believed to be site of the birthplace of the Virgin Mary, daughter of Saints Anne and Joachim. Constructed probably between 1131 and 1138, the church joined French Romanesque elements to a domed, Byzantine-style basilica. The result was a distinctive crusader-settlement style that married Eastern and Western architectural elements and was more fully realized in the later reconstruction of the Church of the Holy Sepulcher. Saint Anne's was one of few Latin churches in Jerusalem not destroyed by Saladin following his conquest of the city in 1187. In 1192 he converted it into a madrasa (a religious school). In 1856 the Ottoman sultan bestowed the church on the French government in recognition of France's participation in the Crimean War. Today it is administered by the Roman Catholic Order of White Fathers. Photo source: Courtesy of Alfred J. Andrea. All rights reserved.

responsible for establishing the field of crusader states studies, concluded that "the crusades are the opening chapter of European expansion and foreshadow all later colonial movements."[12] Prawer was not alone in that judgment. As noted in the Introduction, a number of nineteenth-century apologists for European colonialism had seen the crusades as the first heroic act in Europe's "civilizing" colonial mission. Prawer was ideologically far removed from Michaud, Chateaubriand, and others of that ilk and was no apologist for colonialism, but this notion of crusader colonialism had been around for quite a long while before Prawer began to study what he saw as a "colonial society."

Recently, many, probably most, crusade historians have rejected the term when referring to the crusader states because of the baggage now associated with such modern instances of colonialism as establishment of the British Raj in India, the "Scramble for Africa," the carrying of the "White Man's Burden" into the Philippines, and the post–World War I division of the Middle East. Today no serious historian, whether a specialist in the crusades or not, would be so misguided as to equate the kings of Jerusalem, the princes of Antioch, or the counts of Tripoli and of Edessa with Cecil Rhodes or King Leopold II of Belgium, but even when the most hideous abuses

12. Joshua Prawer, *The Crusaders' Kingdom: European Colonialism in the Middle Ages* (New York: Praeger, 1972), 469.

Church of the Holy Sepulcher. When the crusaders captured Jerusalem in 1099, they found the ancient Church of the Holy Sepulcher, which encompassed the presumed sites of Jesus' crucifixion and burial, in a sad state. Following the church's destruction by Caliph al-Hakim of Egypt in 1009, the edifice had been partially reconstructed under Byzantine imperial patronage, but much remained to be done. The bulk of reconstruction, in a style that combined Byzantine and French Romanesque forms (see the Church of Saint Anne), took place between 1140 and 1149. The official dedication of the church was held on July 15, 1149, the fiftieth anniversary of the crusaders' capture of the city. Upon Saladin's capture of Jerusalem in 1187, he refused to destroy the church, citing the example of Caliph Umar, who had chosen to preserve the original Church of the Holy Sepulcher as a Christian site of worship when he captured the city in the seventh century. Saladin did, however, close the church to everyone except those who could pay the hefty fee of ten golden byzants. The fee was lifted in 1192 by reason of the treaty between Saladin and King Richard I. Photo source: Wikimedia.

of modern colonialism have been taken out of the equation, crusade historians now either refuse to affix that term on the crusader states or feel obligated to defend its use.

Thomas F. Madden is among those who see its application as totally inappropriate. In one of his several essays on crusade myths, Madden assails "Myth 4: The Crusades were just medieval colonialism dressed up in religious finery" by stating:

> It is important to remember that in the Middle Ages the West was not a powerful, dominant culture venturing into a primitive or backward region. It was the Muslim East that was powerful, wealthy, and opulent. Europe was the third world. The Crusader States, founded in the wake of the First Crusade, were not new plantations of Catholics in a Muslim world akin to the British colonization of America. Catholic presence in

Crusader graffiti on the exterior of the Church of the Holy Sepulcher in Jerusalem. The numerous crosses and names in a wide diversity of scripts and languages that pilgrims carved on the columns flanking the main door of the Church of the Holy Sepulcher that Latin settlers rebuilt in the twelfth century are testimony to the strong attraction of this site to Christians of every variety. Photo source: Courtesy of Alfred J. Andrea. All rights reserved.

the Crusader States was always tiny, easily less than ten percent of the population. These were the rulers and magistrates, as well as Italian merchants and members of the military orders. The overwhelming majority of the population in the Crusader States was Muslim. They were not colonies, therefore, in the sense of plantations or even factories, as in the case of India. They were outposts. The ultimate purpose of the Crusader States was to defend the Holy Places in Palestine, especially Jerusalem, and to provide a safe environment for Christian pilgrims to visit those places. There was no mother country with which the Crusader States had an economic relationship, nor did Europeans economically benefit from them. Quite the contrary, the expense of Crusades to maintain the Latin East was a serious drain on European resources. As an outpost, the Crusader States kept a military focus.[13]

In his recent work on crusader castles, the Israeli historian Ronnie Ellenblum has suggested that the question of colonialism, whether the historian defines it as benign or predatory, is not useful in studying the crusades. The framework of comparisons the word brings up, and the emotional impact of its implications, simply do not apply to the medieval period. Expectations that arise from a colonial model can shape historical conclusions in a way that falsifies the evidence. He concludes that the crusades do have a place in the history of Israel as well as of Europe and the broader Middle

13. Thomas F. Madden, *Crusade Myths*, http://www.ignatiusinsight.com/features2005/print2005/tmadden_crusades_print.html (accessed April 22, 2014).

East, that they were a complex phenomenon, and that they deserve to be studied on their own terms without recourse to anachronistic terms and without reference, no matter how unintentional, to latter-day movements and ideals.[14]

Despite such rejection of the term, some historians persist in using the term and seeing the crusader states as the first major instance of European overseas expansionism and its European settlers as colonists (although the colonies established in Iceland and Greenland were earlier, and a handful of Icelanders and Greenlanders even went on crusade).[15] As Alfred J. Andrea has pointed out in his lectures, the crusader states were dependent on a constant influx of settlers and crusaders from the West and the lifeline to Europe provided by its port cities and the Italian mercantile quarters in those cities. What is more, those quarters were, indeed, factories (trading stations), very much like the factories of the African and Asian portions of the later Portuguese overseas empire. Indeed, it is far from certain that the states, on balance, were an overall drain on the resources of Europe, but even if they were, this is not a reason for denying that they were cultural and economic colonies.[16]

Additionally, Paul Chevedden has posited the thesis that on both sides, Muslim and Christian, conquest was seen as the basis for the establishment of justice, or more properly the freedom to create a just society based on religious principles, and that the theme of justice is as much of a European crusade distinctive as is the papal indulgence.[17] If this was the case, then conquest of the Holy Land in order to establish a just society sounds mightily like colonialism—not colonialism motivated by nationalism, or a desire to "civilize," or a thirst for economic or imperial gain, but still colonialism motivated by an overriding religious mission. And even if one rejects Cheveddon's thesis, was not "the liberation of Jerusalem" a religious-colonial mission?

In 1995, Jonathan Phillips took up the question briefly, quoting the twelfth-century chronicler Abbot Guibert of Nogent to the effect that the crusaders who set up a kingdom at Jerusalem were "Holy Christendom's new colonists." Summarizing the findings

---

14. Ronnie Ellenblum, *Crusader Castles and Modern Histories* (Cambridge: Cambridge University Press, 2007), 43–61.

15. J. R. S. Phillips, *The Medieval Expansion of Europe*, 2nd ed. (Oxford, UK: Clarendon Press, 1998), 40–51, characterizes them as early European colonies.

16. Andrea has not yet composed a complete essay on this, but he has noted in print that "in some respects, [the crusader states] were Europe's first major overseas colonies," although he does point out that they were independent states answerable to no mother country. Alfred J. Andrea and James H. Overfield, *The Human Record: Sources of Global History*, 8th ed., 2 vols. (Boston: Cengage, 2015), 1:275. See also his *Encyclopedia of the Crusades*, 86–89 and 285–89.

17. Paul Chevedden, "The View of the Crusades from Rome and Damascus: The Geo-Strategic and Historical Perspectives of Pope Urban II and ʿAli ibn Tahir al-Sulami," *Oriens* 39 (2011): 257–329. See especially pp. 267, 292, 303, and 304 on the relative strength of Islam against Europe. For a shared perception that ancient Rome was the model for control of the Mediterranean, see pp. 297–98, notes 110, 111. Each side, Western Europe and Islam, saw the Roman Empire as an important precursor to its own rule.

of historians who worked with a narrow definition of colonialism as a system that politically directed or economically exploited territory for the benefit of a homeland, he concluded that "the Latin settlements in the Levant before 1291" could not be called colonies in either sense. Instead, he suggested a new concept of "religious colonization," by which the conquerors took Armenian and Byzantine territory to protect it more effectively from Muslim incursion, maintaining close ties with coreligionists in Europe because of their shared faith and their need for financial and military support.[18]

For Mayer and Phillips, who had articulated their interpretations thirty years apart from one another, the main outlines of the story were the same: the contest for the control of Mediterranean trade between Islamic and Christian powers; the divisions within Christendom that separated Rome and Constantinople; and the leadership of the papacy in organizing a response to Muslim attacks on Byzantine territory in 1095. But there was a significant difference. Between the original publication of Mayer's book in 1965 and the appearance of *The Oxford Illustrated History of the Crusades* in 1995, to which Phillips contributed his article, scholars, including Phillips, had worked to identify and describe the motivations of crusaders with greater precision and nuance, and since 1995, analysis of the crusades continued apace.

Today the considered judgment of most historians who study the chronicles, letters, songs, charters, and art works of every sort from the crusade period is that the Christian spirituality and religious fervor of the Middle Ages, rather than elements evident in European colonialism of the nineteenth and twentieth centuries, was the dominant factor in a complex mix of motives for crusading. Yet, as Jonathan Phillips recently wrote, "Religion was not the sole driving force for the crusaders . . . other ideas, such as the lure of land and money, a sense of honor and family tradition, a desire for adventure, and the obligation of service, all sat alongside—and sometimes smothered—religion."[19]

Both eras, the Age of the Crusades and the Age of Modern Colonialism, had their share of shocking events, outrages, and atrocities. The contexts for those events, however, were different. Greed, always a human motivation, certainly played a role in both eras. However, greed is not the whole story, particularly not in the context of the First Crusade (although a better argument for greed as a prime factor can be made regarding some later crusades, especially the Baltic Crusades).[20] In this case, "greedy

---

18. Jonathan Phillips, "The Latin East, 1098–1291," in *The Oxford Illustrated History of the Crusades,* ed. Jonathan Riley-Smith (Oxford: Oxford University Press, 1995), 112–13.

19. Jonathan Phillips, *Holy Warriors. A Modern History of the Crusades* (New York: Random House, 2009), xix.

20. Ane L. Bysted, et al., *Jerusalem in the North: Denmark and the Baltic Crusades, 1100–1522* (Turnhout, Belgium: Brepols, 2004); Eric Christiansen, *The Northern Crusades: The Baltic and Catholic Frontier, 1100–1525,* 2nd ed. (London: Penguin, 1997); Alan V. Murray, ed., *Crusade and Conversion on the Baltic Frontier, 1150–1500* (Aldershot, UK: Ashgate, 2001); William L. Urban, "Baltic Crusades," in *The Crusades: An Encyclopedia,* ed. Alan V. Murray, 4 vols. (Santa Barbara, CA: ABC-Clio, 2006), 2:145–51.

colonialism" invokes a range of ideas, institutions, and events that are rooted in the nineteenth century rather than the origins of the crusading movement in the late eleventh century.

Christopher Tyerman's massive new history of the crusades, which he offers as a corrective and update to Steven Runciman's equally monumental history of the crusades places religion squarely at the center of the crusading movement from start to finish.[21] Reflecting the general consensus of today's crusade historians, his Preface begins:

> Violence, approved by society and supported by religion, has proved a commonplace of civilized communities. . . . The crusades were wars justified by faith against real or imagined enemies defined by religious and political elites as perceived threats to the Christian faithful. The religious beliefs crucial to such warfare placed enormous significance on imagined awesome but reassuring supernatural forces of overwhelming power and proximity that were nevertheless expressed in hard concrete physical acts: prayer, penance, giving alms, attending church, pilgrimage, violence.[22]

Further reflecting the scholarship of the past half century, Tyerman notes that the outstanding innovation of the impoverished West was the Church. Ecclesiastical reform in the eleventh century produced a papacy that was "deliberately and innovatorily international in outlook and personnel . . . [with a belief that] the Church of Rome was synonymous with the universal church; [and] that the pope held temporal as well as spiritual jurisdiction on earth as the heir to St. Peter."[23]

The program of this reformed papacy led to a contest of wills with the German emperor, which culminated in an attack on Rome in 1084. Gregory VII, the pope with whom Hans Eberhard Mayer began his crusade story, fled from the emperor to the Normans for protection. Another "pope," Clement III (reigned as antipope, 1080–1100), seen as illegitimate by much of Latin Christendom, was installed and supported by the German Empire. On the opposite side of the contest, the pope elected by the reforming, anti-imperial party, Urban II (r. 1088–1099), preached the First Crusade in 1095, through which he "sought to use the mobilization of the expedition as a cover to reclaim the pope's position in Italy and demonstrate his practical leadership of Christendom."[24] For Tyerman and most of today's crusade historians, the call to liberate Jerusalem was deeply connected to the call to liberate the Church from secular control. The papacy's universalist claim to temporal and spiritual juris-

21. Christopher Tyerman, *God's War: A New History of the Crusades* (Cambridge, MA: Harvard University Press, 2006), xv. Steven Runciman, *A History of the Crusades*, 3 vols. (Cambridge: Cambridge University Press, 1951–1954).

22. Tyerman, *God's War*, xiii.

23. Ibid., 6.

24. Ibid., 7; for a more extensive study of the context surrounding the First Crusade, see Marcus Bull, "Origins," in *The Oxford Illustrated History of the Crusades*, 13–33.

diction allowed for the creation of crusading polities in lands conquered in the eastern Mediterranean. Not incidentally, the success of the call allowed Urban to reestablish the seat of papal power in Rome.[25]

Early Primary Sources and the Motivations of the Crusaders

A recent collection of crusade primary sources in translation contains four clerical accounts of Urban's call to the First Crusade, all of which offer a number of themes and ideas that are important indicators of what laity and clergy alike would have heard from the Church about crusade motivation.[26] Not included with them is the brief account in the *Gesta Francorum et aliorum Hierosolymytanorum* (The Deeds of the Franks and the Other Jerusalem Pilgrims), which was probably composed by a lay warrior who clearly had not been at Clermont, an inference that follows from the fact that this Italo-Norman follower of Bohemond of Taranto never mentions the council but refers only to the sermons that Pope Urban delivered "beyond the mountains," namely north of the Alps.[27] Unlike this nameless layperson, three of the clerical writers are credited with having been eyewitnesses at the Council of Clermont (Abbot Guibert of Nogent was the exception), where the sermon was delivered.

Despite their presence there, we must keep in mind that they crafted their accounts years after the sermon was given. In no case is any account of the sermon anything like a straightforward transcription. Strange as it may seem, that is the very value of these versions of what Urban reputedly said. They reflect not only the memories of the clerical chroniclers regarding the aims of the papacy as they were articulated that day in 1095, but the concerns and perspectives of these same clerical writers and their lay audiences long after the crusade had culminated in the capture of Jerusalem in 1099. In other words, the outcome of the First Crusade influenced the way in which people remembered the initial call to undertake this armed pilgrimage to Jerusalem.

---

25. Tyerman, *God's War*, 8.

26. These accounts of the sermon, written well after it was given (the earliest clerical account, that of Fulcher of Chartres, was composed no earlier than late 1100), are taken from translations in S. J. Allen and Emily Amt, eds., *The Crusades: A Reader* (Peterborough, Canada: Broadview Press, 2003), 39–47, and are available in other anthologies of translated crusade sources, such as Edward Peters, ed., *The First Crusade*, 2nd ed. (Philadelphia: University of Pennsylvania Press, 1998), 26–37, 52–53.

27. The *Gesta's* account is in Peters, *First Crusade*, 25–26. The *Gesta*, probably produced before 1104, is judged by scholars to be the oldest surviving account of the crusade and was composed in a style that suggests a lay author—in a linear "seemingly artless style which yet shows signs of careful construction" and fits more into the category of a vernacular epic than the clerical accounts, according to Christopher Tyerman's overview of the relationship among these texts in *The Debate on the Crusades, 1099–2011* (Manchester, UK: Manchester University Press/Palgrave Macmillan, 2011), 8. See also, Andrew Holt and James Muldoon, eds., *Fighting Words: Competing Voices from the Crusades* (Westport, CT: Greenwood World Publishing, 2008), 6.

This is not the place for an extensive analysis of the sermon accounts, their authors, and the relationship among the texts.[28] It suffices to note that the themes emphasized by these four clerical chroniclers informed the vast body of medieval literature regarding the First Crusade that followed, and they became the main themes and ideas available to subsequent generations of Latin Christians as they considered crusading. So, they are worth a brief study here as an investigation of what ordinary people took away from the sermons of clerical crusade preachers who spread the word of the expedition throughout Western Christendom in the months following Pope Urban's initial appeal at Clermont.

Fulcher of Chartres (d. ca. 1127) reminds his readers that "the Turks and Arabs" have attacked the Byzantine Empire, occupying territory and winning "seven battles." Churches have been destroyed, the empire devastated and, what is worse, more horrors will follow if those who hear this message do not go to the rescue. "On this account I, or rather the Lord, beseech you as Christ's heralds to publish this everywhere and to persuade all people of whatever rank . . . poor and rich, to carry aid promptly to those Christians and to destroy that vile race." For Fulcher, "Christ commands it." Further, "all who die by the way, whether by land or by sea, or in battle against the pagans, shall have remission of sins," granted by the power of God, with which Urban was invested.[29] He comments that they should give up private wars at home and go to fight "in a proper way against the barbarians."[30]

Robert the Monk (d. 1122) echoes Fulcher's historical introduction, calling the enemy "the people of Persia, an accursed and foreign race, enemies of God," and he provides vivid details of how Christians are being tortured and killed. Further, "they have taken from the Greek empire a tract of land so large that it takes more than two months to walk through it. Whose duty is it to avenge this and recover that

---

28. Persons interested in these accounts of the pope's sermon should start with Jonathan S. C. Riley-Smith, *The First Crusade and the Idea of Crusading* (Philadelphia: University of Pennsylvania Press, [1986] 2009) as well as Penny J. Cole, *The Preaching of the Crusades to the Holy Land, 1095–1270* (Cambridge, MA: Medieval Academy of America, 1991). More recently, three essays, by Arnved Nedkvitne, "Why Did Medieval Norsemen Go on Crusade?," Janus Moller Jensen, "War, Penance and the First Crusade: Dealing with a 'Tyrannical Construct,'" and Sini Kangas, "Deus Vult: Violence and Suffering as a Means of Salvation During the First Crusade," have raised questions about the current interpretation of Urban's intentions. All three are published in a collection by Tuomas M. S. Lehtonen, et al., *Medieval History Writing and Crusading Ideology* (Helsinki: Finnish Literature Society, 2005), 37–50, 51–63, 163–74.

29. On the meaning of the pardon implied by "remission of sin," see the first two chapters, on "Urban's Message," and "The Response of Lay People," in Riley-Smith, *First Crusade* as well as Bull, "Origins," especially 30–33. See also Marcus Graham Bull, *Knightly Piety and the Lay Response to the First Crusade: The Limousin and Gascony, 970–c.1130* (New York: Oxford University Press, [1998] 1993), 166–71.

30. Allen and Amt, *Reader*, 39–40. On the crusade indulgence, see Ane Lise Bysted, "Indulgences, Satisfaction, and Heart's Contrition in Twelfth-Century Crusading Theology," in Lehtonen, *Medieval History Writing*, 85–93, for a recent take on the issue and important bibliography.

land, if not yours?" In Robert's account, Urban, a Frenchman, addresses the audience as "Franks," here meaning the French in particular, and says that their race above all others has been given a military spirit by God. Reminding them of the successful wars of Charlemagne and his successors, who "destroyed Turkish kingdoms and established Christianity in their lands,"[31] he urges them to use their gifts of war in the service of God. Like Fulcher, Robert specifically mentions the remission of sins, but their reward will be more than spiritual. They are to "take that land from that wicked people and make it your own," because their own land in Europe is poor, overpopulated, enclosed by mountains and sea, and can barely yield enough to support them.[32]

Baldric of Dol offers even more history of the East and the conflict with the Turks, emphasizing the shame that is attached to being a knight and doing nothing about this great injustice to other Christians. In his version, Urban accuses his knightly audience of homicide at home and orders them to "either lay down the girdle of such knighthood, or . . . rush as quickly as you can to the defense of the eastern church." The Church at Jerusalem is the source of their faith, and their leader in the fight is Christ himself. "The possessions of the enemy, too, will be yours." Baldric does not mention remission of sins, but he talks extensively of God's reward for labor in His service, including the win-win benefit that they will either despoil the enemy of his possessions and return home victorious or will be killed and earn, thereby, "everlasting glory."[33]

Some of the same themes and elements are picked up in Guibert of Nogent's (d. 1124) account: reverence for the shrines; war in this theater is commanded by God; the wars at home shame Christians who should be fighting God's enemies; and vivid descriptions of the suffering of "the mother of churches." Guibert added, and he was the only one of the four to do so, an apocalyptic note by having Urban state that the time of the Antichrist is nigh.[34] It is clear that the land to be conquered belongs to Christians, by right, and needs to be retaken for the protection of the inhabitants. This was certainly a crucial justification for war.[35]

In each version the message focused on a history of the Holy Land and was accompanied by stories of torture or degradation visited by the enemy on Christian people or holy places. Knighthood is a recurring theme, as is the misuse of power at home that

---

31. A reference to Charlemagne's successful war against the Avars and Otto I's defeat of the Magyars—both a people out of Central Asia's steppe lands, as was the case with the Turks.

32. Allen and Amt, *Reader*, 40–42.

33. Ibid., 42–45.

34. Ibid., 45–47. For a recent view of the apocalyptic elements in some crusade accounts, including Guibert's, see Jay Rubenstein, *Armies of Heaven: The First Crusade and the Quest for Apocalypse* (New York: Basic Books, 2011). For a contrary view, see James Muldoon's essay in this book.

35. On the theories of just war and holy war in the medieval West and their connection to crusading, see Tomaž Mastnak, *Crusading Peace: Christendom, the Muslim World, and Western Political Order* (Berkeley: University of California Press, 2002), especially 59–66, and Frederick H. Russell, *The Just War in the Middle Ages* (Cambridge: Cambridge University Press, 1975).

belonged in God's service abroad.[36] In each case, a spiritual reward is promised. There is also frequent identification with the armies of God in the Old Testament, which might well have made massacre a more acceptable option for the "armies of Christ" sent out by the pope, although the morality of medieval armies on the battlefield was quite different from our own and killing noncombatants and captured enemy soldiers was common-place for all armies, Christian, Muslim, and other.[37] It is likely that these were key points made by Urban and subsequently repeated by preachers across Europe.

The anonymous lay crusader, who composed the *Gesta Francorum* and reported the pope's message from a great distance, is an excellent test case in this regard. The few words he devoted to Urban's message made the following points: Whoever wishes to save his soul should undertake this mission, and if he lacks sufficient funds, God will provide. All who accept this challenge will suffer in the name of Christ but will be rewarded in Heaven.[38] Horror, shame, anger, pity, courage—all the emotions that were expressed in the cry "God wills it," with which the audience reportedly greeted Urban's challenge—were possible only if one believed what the pope said and in his authority to say it. The author of the *Gesta* reported that throughout Gaul, the Franks, when they heard Urban's message, "followed with one accord the footsteps of Christ, by which they had been redeemed from the hand of hell."[39]

It is significant that the lay author of the *Gesta* mentions only the suffering and the heavenly reward that awaited those who "forthwith caused crosses to be sewed on their right shoulders,"[40] and only two of the clerical authors mentioned temporal rewards. Of them, Baldric noted that those who survived *would return home with their spoils*; only Robert mentioned that they would take and make their own the land "flowing with milk and honey" that God had given the children of Israel and which, by implica-tion, was now rightfully land that God intended for the Christian children of the New Covenant.[41] Not even Fulcher of Chartres, who stayed on in the Kingdom of Jerusalem, serving as chaplain to King Baldwin I (r. 1100–1118), and whose account of the First Crusade and its aftermath was written in part to attract settlers from the West to the

---

36. Nedkvitne, "Norsemen," 45–47.

37. For an overview of the theme of destruction of the enemy as enjoined by God, see Susan Niditch, *War in the Hebrew Bible: A Study in the Ethics of Violence* (New York: Oxford University Press, 1993). See also, Andrew Holt, "Crusader and Jihadist Atrocities and Acts of Chivalry," *World History Ency-clopedia*, ed. Alfred J. Andrea, 21 vols. (Santa Barbara, CA: ABC-Clio, 2011), 10:673–74.

38. Peters, *First Crusade*, 26.

39. Ibid. For a recent discussion of Urban's intentions and his audience's perception of his message, see John France, *The Crusades and the Expansion of Catholic Christendom, 1000–1714* (New York: Routledge, 2005), 24–36. France comments that although Christian intellectuals saw Islam as a heresy, "there is no evidence of a widespread hatred of Islam" (31).

40. Peters, *First Crusade*, 26.

41. Allen and Amt, *Crusades*, 41.

crusader kingdom,[42] put into Urban's mouth any mention whatsoever of their obtaining lands in the East should they heed this call.[43]

Arguments from silence are the weakest of arguments and absence of evidence is not evidence of absence, but there is further reason to conclude that Robert the Monk is an unreliable outlier and that Pope Urban never promised the first crusaders lands for their own across the sea. In a collection of texts associated with Urban's close associate, Bishop Lambert of Arras, we find the following indulgence privilege that the pope granted to those undertaking this expedition: "Whoever goes on the journey to free the church of God in Jerusalem out of devotion alone, and not for the gaining of glory or money, can substitute the journey for all penance for sin."[44] Likewise, the pope's letter of September 1096 to the clergy and people of Bologna states:

> If any among you travel not for the desire of the goods of this world, but . . . for the good of their souls and the liberty of the churches [of the East], they will be relieved of the penance for all of their sins, for which they have made a full and perfect confession . . . because they have exposed themselves and their property to danger out of their love of God and their neighbor.[45]

Exposed their property to danger? Whatever did Urban mean, and how did the laity understand this challenge?

Closer in time to the First Crusade and more immediately concerned with the affairs of departing crusaders than the accounts of the pope's sermon are the charters issued to raise funds for the journey or to make arrangements for their property if they failed to return.[46] The two most important studies of such documents in English are by Jonathan

---

42. Fulcher appears to have composed his *Historia Hierosolymitana* (Jerusalem History) in segments and over more than a quarter century from between 1100/1101 to 1127 or 1128. While describing the Kingdom of Jerusalem, he wrote, "For we who were occidentals have now become orientals. . . . We have already forgotten the places of our birth. . . . Those who were poor in the Occident, God makes rich in this land. . . . Therefore why should one return to the Occident who has found the Orient like this? God does not wish those to suffer want who with their crosses dedicated themselves to follow him, nay even to the end." Peters, *First Crusade*, 90–91.

43. Ibid., 39–40. Fulcher does juxtapose "the sorrowful and poor" who remain behind and the "rich" who venture forth, but, despite what he wrote much later about settlers becoming rich in the kingdom (note 42), the context here strongly argues for their being spiritually rich because they are the friends of the Lord, whereas His enemies are sorrowful and spiritually poor.

44. Ibid., 37.

45. Ibid., 44.

46. Giles Constable essentially opened this field of research in his "Medieval Charters as a Source for the History of the Crusades," in *Crusade and Settlement*, ed. Peter Edbury (Cardiff, UK: University College Cardiff Press, 1985), 73–89. The essay is reprinted in revised form in Giles Constable, *Crusaders and Crusading in the Twelfth Century* (Burlington, VT: Ashgate, 2008), 93–116. See also Corliss K. Slack, with translations by Hugh Feiss, *Crusade Charters, 1138–1270* (Tempe: Arizona State University, 2001), which offers photographs, the Latin texts, and English translations of a small collection of charters.

Riley-Smith and Marcus Bull.[47] While songs, poetry, art, letters and other kinds of documents can all be considered evidence for the crusades, arguably, the charters investigated by Bull and Riley-Smith take us closer to the minds of departing crusaders because, unconstrained by literary genres (such as crusade histories and epics), they allow us to filter the financial arrangements of those who joined the earliest expedition through the relatively simple legal format of the charters and the verbiage of the clerical authors who composed and wrote them in Latin.[48]

The vocabulary chosen by those authors might be a barrier to our full understanding of the intentions of a knight who was making the arrangements, but even more so the wording of the charters is evidence of what the Church was preaching about crusading and how the knightly laity perceived and acted on that message. Regardless of the veil imposed by the words chosen by these clerics, the actual arrangements set forth in the charters reflect the realities of the individual's holdings, the constraints imposed on him by his community and family, his relationship to the Church, and the expectations of those closest to him.[49]

Crusade Charters: A Key to Crusaders' "Mentalities"

In his groundbreaking analysis of such charters in 1986, Riley-Smith wrote under the assumption that crusading was a form of armed pilgrimage and compared the documents he examined with similar ones for those departing on a more traditional pilgrimage as an act of penance.[50] He found "a serious and purposeful devotion on the part of would-be crusaders," "a pious desire to arrange for intercessory prayer," sometimes by those whose previous "cruelty" had "astonished" local clerics.[51]

In light of such findings, this raises the question of how earlier scholars came to such vastly different conclusions about the motivations of the first crusaders. In

---

47. Bull, *Knightly*; Riley-Smith, *First Crusade and the Idea of Crusading*.

48. Even when a secular person issued the charter and spoke in the first person, the document was normally composed and written by a cleric at the issuer's direction.

49. There are other issues at stake in using charters as evidence, including provenance, the possibility of forgery, translation of often abbreviated place names, the difficulty of telling when we are looking at a sale disguised as a donation, and the relationships, often fraught with tensions not reflected in the legalese, between the issuers of the documents and those whose intentions are being memorialized. As Riley Smith pointed out, *First Crusade* [1986], 37, a persistent theme is the resolution of often-violent disputes between the crusader and a local church or monastery.

50. Ibid., 27, 30, 37. Not all scholars agree with this identification of crusading with pilgrimage. Paul Chevedden, "The View of the Crusades," 257–329.

51. Riley-Smith, *First Crusade*, [1986], 36–38. Also see p. 39, on the clerical authors of the charters: "It is true that most contemporary commentators, who were, of course, propagandists for the movement, portrayed the crusaders in a highly favourable light as idealists who had renounced worldly things."

part the older view that the first crusaders were mainly motivated by economic gain derived from the popular "younger sons thesis" associated with the work of respected French social historian Georges Duby. In 1977, Duby argued in *The Chivalrous Society* that because, by right of primogeniture, full inheritance went to firstborn sons, many younger second and third sons found themselves in a tough spot, without a chance to inherit their paternal lands. Thus the crusading enterprise provided a means by which these adventuresome additional sons could carve out a place for themselves in the Holy Land.[52] Yet Riley-Smith has highlighted the weakness of this argument by showing that, far from being "an economic safety valve" for landless and impecunious male members of a family, the prospect of any member of a family participating in a crusade resulted in significant financial sacrifices on the part of the family.[53] Moreover, Riley-Smith has shown that such financial sacrifices were usually made to send the head of the family or the eldest son on a crusade, rather than younger sons.

Riley-Smith's arguments have generally been well received by other historians. Indeed, in a 1998 review of Riley-Smith's *The First Crusaders*, Professor William Chester Jordan of Princeton University effectively summed up the view of many current crusade historians of Riley-Smith's research, when he wrote, "Riley-Smith has, I hope, laid to rest for all time the contention that crusaders profited monetarily from the wars. They did not, or at least the vast majority did not. Nor did they say that they expected to profit materially."[54] This is not to say that crusaders expected nothing in the way of an earthly reward. They were well aware that crusading brought with it considerable social capital at home. Crusading families, especially those for whom crusading became a multigenerational tradition in the years after the First Crusade, were highly regarded in their communities.[55] The charters are silent, however, on this all too human expectation of prestige. It is a rare person who openly admits to such desires.

Bull's analysis of the evidence from charters was much more far-reaching than Riley-Smith's but concentrated on only one region of France. Regardless, his findings emphasized all the elements identified by Riley-Smith and added an examination of the tremendous influence of kinship groups, neighbors, and superiors in the recruitment of groups of warriors. That influence reinforced, in his view, the conclusion that a religious culture was the primary motivating factor that drove knightly participation in the First Crusade (rather than economic gain).[56] Indeed, Bull argued that the

---

52. George Duby, *The Chivalrous Society*, trans. Cynthia Posten (Berkeley: University of California Press, 1977), 117–20.

53. Jonathan Riley-Smith, *The First Crusaders: 1095–1131* (Cambridge: Cambridge University Press, 1997), 21.

54. William Chester Jordan, "Review of *The First Crusaders, 1095–1131*," *Church History* 67 (1998): 359–61.

55. Nicholas Paul, *To Follow in Their Footsteps: The Crusades and Family Memory in the High Middle Ages* (Ithaca, NY: Cornell University Press, 2012).

56. Bull, *Knightly Piety*, 283, 285.

preexisting religious values of knights must be considered for a full understanding of their response to a crusade. He pointed out that these lords were well aware of their sinfulness, inasmuch as their status sometimes required sinful behavior in order to maintain their positions in life, but they also respected the consequences of their sins and had long sought the remission of their sins through pilgrimage and acts of public benediction. Thus, when Pope Urban II preached the First Crusade as an armed pilgrimage, it provided knights with an opportunity to continue in their pilgrimage tradition by performing a military act of self-sacrifice pleasing to God.[57]

A third crusade historian, Giles Constable, anticipated and even laid the basis for Riley-Smith's and Bull's work in 1982 with an insightful essay on the financing of crusades in which in pointed to the enormous cost of crusading, the ways in which many crusade lords mortgaged the future and imperiled their heirs' patrimony in order to crusade, and how crusaders did not expect to return richer in the goods of this life.[58]

The Challenge of Understanding Crusader Mentalities

Understanding and contextualizing the crusades is not the same as celebrating them.[59] It is true that however devout many of the participants were, "the crusades confirmed a communal identity comprising aggression, paranoia, nostalgia, wishful thinking and invented history."[60] Nevertheless, our moral outrage at such acts and the ideology that drove them does not excuse us from the hard work of understanding mindsets and worldviews different from our own. To dismiss the very real, if in part (or whole) seriously mistaken, beliefs behind religious warfare is a form of snobbery, or even of cultural bias. It is laudable to resist this impulse when evaluating Muslim and Jewish history. For those writing in the European-Christian tradition, it is equally necessary to be clearheaded about the European past, even if that past includes the cannibalism at Ma`arrat an-Nu'man , with which the Terry Jones series opens.[61]

It is not just dining on the enemy that seems to many to give the lie to a religious motivation for crusading. The Normans, the protectors of the reforming popes,

---

57. Ibid., 177–79.

58. Giles Constable, "The Financing of the Crusades," in *Outremer: Studies in the History of the Crusading Kingdom of Jerusalem Presented to Joshua Prawer*, ed. Benjamin Z. Kedar, Hans Eberhard Mayer, and Raymond C. Smail (Jerusalem: Yad Izhak Ben-Zvi Institute, 1982), 64–88, reprinted in revised and expanded form in Constable, *Crusaders*, 117–41. See also note 46 above.

59. Thus, the Society for the Study of the Crusades and the Latin East holds quadrennial meetings on the anniversaries of crusade events that occurred many centuries earlier. In 2004, for example, when it met in Istanbul, the main conference theme was the Fourth Crusade's capture of Constantinople in 1204. In no way was this academic conference a celebration of that event.

60. Tyerman, *God's War*, xiii.

61. Regarding Ma`arrat an-Nu'man, see Jay Rubenstein, "Cannibals and Crusaders," *French Historical Studies* 31 (2008): 525–52, and this volume's Introduction.

are not inspiring as proofs of the devotional background to the expeditions. Robert Guiscard, Alexius Comnenus' enemy in 1081, died in 1085 as the ruler of southern Italy, which he seized from the Byzantine Empire. His brother Roger (d. 1101) took Sicily from Muslim emirs. His son Bohemond and Bohemond's nephew Tancred, leaders of a Norman contingent in the armies of the First Crusade, took Antioch in 1098 and retained it in the face of Byzantine protests. Another First Crusade leader, Baldwin of Boulogne (d. 1118), first ruled Armenian Christian Edessa, which he had seized in a murderous coup, and then ruled Jerusalem.

As we saw, in Robert's account of the speech at Clermont, Pope Urban had supposedly promised them "a land of milk and honey." As we also saw, the pope probably had made no such allusion or promise, but some crusade leaders—a minority but still an important minority—were happy to drink such milk and eat such honey. Even the pious Raymond of Toulouse, for whom both Pope Urban and Emperor Alexius had a deep respect and affection, ended his days in a campaign to carve out the County of Tripoli, a project completed by his son four years later.

Does all of this make greed the key crusader motivation? First of all, medieval Latin Christians, who were immersed in the historical books of that portion of the Bible that they called the Old Testament, viewed themselves as latter-day Israelites, and like the first Chosen People, they did not see devotion to God and the taking of spoils in a righteous, God-directed war as mutually contradictory acts. Indeed, the great Saladin himself began his career as a Kurdish mercenary captain called Yusuf ibn Ayyub. He, like the First Crusaders, made his career as a soldier of fortune before becoming sultan of Egypt, and like the Europeans, he waged war for God, but he also took the spoils when they fell to him. His followers depended, in fact, on a fair distribution of those spoils. Does that make greed his besetting sin as well? Moreover, the Kingdom of Jerusalem was not, as *Kingdom of Heaven* would have it, indisputably Muslim territory in 1095 or 1187, at least in the minds of European Christians. The point of the sermon accounts was that it belonged to Christians who were called by God to reclaim it.

Alexius Comnenus correctly viewed the lands that the first crusaders proposed to liberate as having been forcibly taken from his Orthodox Christian empire by Muslim armies. For that reason, he had demanded oaths of fidelity from the leaders of the First Crusade in which they pledged to return to him all former imperial lands that they captured. The crusaders initially were true to that oath, agreeing that Nicaea, the capital of the Seljuk Emirate of Rum, which fell to a combined Byzantine and crusader force in the opening stages of the campaign in Anatolia, should be returned to Alexius. And this was done despite the heavy losses that the Westerners had suffered in assaulting the city.

The compact broke down at Antioch. Following a bitter seven and a half-month siege of the city, in which the crusaders lost large numbers through death and desertion, the city fell on June 3, 1098. Although there was strong sentiment within the leadership for returning the city to Alexius, Bohemond of Taranto, who claimed the city for himself by reason of his stratagem that had secured entry into the city, won the day. The fact that many of the crusaders felt that an absent emperor had abandoned them in this epic struggle assured Bohemond's success. Despite the fruitless attempt of Count Raymond of Toulouse to plead Alexius's case, after Antioch, the army's mission of recovering these lands for Christendom did not include returning them to what they saw as the untrustworthy emperor in Constantinople.

In a similar way, Saladin, a Sunni Muslim, established his own family, the Ayyubid, dynasty on the throne of Egypt, which he took from the Shi'a Fatimid dynasty. He used his recent conquest of Egypt and the call to jihad against the Latin states to field an army that would consolidate his control over Syria/Palestine as well. Did any of this make him less pious or less of a committed jihadist? There's no escaping the fact that territory was contested and taken by armies and kept, often in defiance of powers at Rome, Constantinople, Mosul, and Baghdad by leaders on both sides of the conflict in the Holy Land.

A final and compelling reason to conclude that the vast majority of persons who left on the First Crusade had no intention whatsoever of colonizing eastern lands is that most of the surviving veterans, their pilgrimage to the Holy City completed, returned to their homes in the West shortly after the capture of Jerusalem in July 1099, leaving a small minority of Westerners to govern a vast majority of Muslims and Eastern Christians. There were probably not more than 5,000 crusaders, many of them noncombatants, left in the then-three crusader states in late 1099.[62]

Search for a single motivating factor risks simplifying a complex phenomenon to the point of monotonal caricature. Today's historians have begun to put together a multilayered view of the crusade movement that offers a dialogue between the cultures involved about the motivations of Europeans, as well as a careful reconsideration of the evidence. In such new formulations, crusading cannot be dismissed as simply greed, nor can the religious context of the expeditions, on the Christian or the Muslim side, be ignored.[63]

Christopher Tyerman has commented that "few mentalities—enthusiastic for violence, fixed on an afterlife—could be less accessible to modern observers in the Western cultural tradition" than the mindset of the medieval crusader.[64] Perhaps instead of applying images from our recent colonial past to the Middle Ages, or visiting our discomfort with a mix of the religious with the political on hapless crusaders, we should go back to the medieval sources for another look.

---

62. France, *Expansion of Catholic Christendom*, 90.

63. See Nedkvitne, "Norsemen," 47, on the dangers of "monocausal" explanations for historical events.

64. Christopher Tyerman, *The Crusades. A Brief Insight* (New York: Sterling, 2007), 3.

5. Myths of Innocence: The Making of the Children's Crusade

David L. Sheffler

In France, a boy . . . went about singing in his own tongue, Jesus, Lord, repair our loss; restore us thy holy cross. Numberless children ran after him and followed the same tune their captain and chanter did set them. No bolts, no bars, no fear of fathers or love of mothers, could hold them back, but they would go to the Holy Land to work wonders there till their merry music had a sad close, all either perishing on land or drowned by sea. It was done (saith my author) by the instinct of the devil, who, as it were, desired a cordial of children's blood to comfort his weak stomach long cloyed with murdering of men.[1]

Every semester for the better part of a decade, I have begun my courses on the crusades by asking the students to write down three things they know about medieval holy war. For reasons only a historian would understand, I have kept these responses in a disintegrating manila folder at the back of an overstuffed metal filing cabinet. When I'm feeling especially masochistic I pull out the folder and leaf through the pages. The responses range from the banal, "the crusades were against Muslims," to the gruesome, "the crusaders were cannibals." Unsurprisingly, Richard the Lionheart makes the list most years with occasional references to his sexuality, as does violence against the Jews—usually articulated as crusades against the Jews.[2] The Templars, the Assassins, and Frederick Barbarossa also make frequent appearances. But the Children's Crusade, or "Kid Crusade," as one of my students called it, "where they sent a bunch of kids to take over the Holy Land and they died," has made the list every year.

A quick search of Amazon or Google reveals that fascination with the Children's Crusade (a fascination generally unencumbered by facts) is hardly confined to the undergraduates of my midsized public university. Rarely a year goes by without the publication of at least one work bearing the title *Children's Crusade*. And while many of these have nothing to do with the historical Children's Crusade, the potent pairing

---

1. Thomas Fuller, *The Historie of the Holy Warre*, 4th ed. (Cambridge, UK: Thomas Buck, 1651), 152.

2. See Chapter 3 by Daniel P. Franke, "The Crusades and Medieval Anti-Judaism: Cause or Consequence?"

of innocence and violence is somehow irresistible. The range of genres treating the Children's Crusade is staggering: fiction, poetry, popular histories, film, children's literature, and even several musicals.[3] In these depictions, the youthful crusaders become malleable subjects capable of representing an astonishing array of archetypes: bored peasants seeking adventure, idealistic protestors, lower-class revolutionaries, fools, hapless victims of corrupt churchmen, intolerant zealots, religious lunatics, and medieval lost boys, to name just a few.[4]

Despite the diversity of meanings attached to the Children's Crusade, centuries of retelling and remembering has produced a stable, almost canonical product that continues to shape popular literature, and at times even scholarly works. Indeed, the popular narrative occupies such an entrenched position that it has withstood nearly every academic assault. Nowhere is this fact more evident than in the History Channel's *History's Mysteries: The Children's Crusades*. The promotional blurb on the back of the DVD promises that the film will explore:

> the sad fate of some 20,000 children who joined the fight in the 13th century. Using dramatic re-enactments focusing on two 12-year-old boys, this gripping program shows how young French soldiers were promised free transport from Marseilles to the Holy Land, only to be sold into slavery in North Africa, while German children marched to Italy, where their crusade floundered, succumbing to disease and starvation.[5]

All the popular elements of the story are on display. The extraordinary youth of the leaders (precisely twelve years of age), the suspiciously confident head count (20,000), the promise of free transport, the tragic enslavement of the children, and gruesome death. Yet the experts appearing in the film (prominent crusade historians Jonathan Riley-Smith, Jonathan Phillips, Gary Dickson, and Paul Crawford) challenge,

---

3. Elia Wilkinson Peattie, *With Scrip and Staff, The Trumpet of God* (New York: Anson D. F. Randolph, 1891); Walter O'Meara, *The Devil's Cross* (New York: Knopf, 1957); John Wiles, *The March of Innocents* (London: Chatto and Windus, 1964); James Jackson, *Pilgrim: The Greatest Crusade* (London: John Murray, 2008). The world premiere of the antiwar *What a Day for a Miracle*, music by Larry Orenstein and Jeff Alexander, book and lyrics by E. Y. (Yip) Harburg and based on the novel by Henry Myers, *Our Lives Have Just Begun* (New York: Frederick A. Stokes, 1939), was held at the University of Vermont in 1971. *Children's Crusade: An Operatic Musical*, music by Arnold Butcher and lyrics by Amy McGrath, was produced three times between 1975 and 1977. Like the Children's Crusade, both musicals were abject failures, but whereas the Children's Crusade passed into legend, the musicals fell into oblivion.

4. An article appearing in *The Economist* on December 21, 2000 manages to work in most of these, referring to the crusaders of 1212 as bored peasants, deluded fools, and fanatics driven to kill the infidel. "The Children's Crusade: Fairly Holy Innocents," http://www.economist.com/node/457145 (accessed December 29, 2013).

5. *History's Mysteries: The Children's Crusade*, A&E Television Network, 2000, back cover of DVD. A video clip is available at https://www.facebook.com/video/video.php?v=1460887126863 (accessed March 26, 2015).

complicate, or deny every one of these supposed facts. The author of the blurb either did not view the film or, more likely, understood that twelve-year-old European boys and girls sold in African slave markets would outsell the qualified and cautious analysis provided by the experts.

The Popular Narrative

The popular narrative always begins with the twelve-year-old shepherd boy Stephen of Cloyes (both his occupation and age drip with metaphorical possibilities). Having witnessed a new round of impassioned crusade preaching, Stephen burned with a desire to free Jerusalem from the clutches of the infidel. In this state of heightened religious sensitivity, Christ appeared to Stephen and entrusted him with a letter seeking royal support for this new crusade.[6] In the spring of 1212, Stephen traveled to the Abbey of St. Denis outside Paris, where he hoped to receive an audience with the king. Despite Stephen's moving plea and numinous epistle, King Philip II did not endorse Stephen's movement (perhaps the letter from Heaven ploy had already worn thin).

Instead the king ordered this latter-day Peter the Hermit to return home.[7] But the king failed to quell the enthusiasm engendered by Stephen's preaching. Even those children whose parents had placed them under lock and key rushed after the boy shepherd's growing throng. The children eventually made their way to Marseilles, where they hoped to embark for the Holy Land. According to some sources, they expected to cross the sea just as the Israelites of old but, despite their prayers, the sea obstinately refused to part. Seizing on the opportunity, two unscrupulous traders agreed to provide passage to the Holy Land but instead sold the children as slaves in Africa.

Meanwhile, to the north and east, another twelve-year-old boy (if you aren't skeptical by now you should be) preached a nearly identical message.[8] The innocence of children, which Jesus had favorably compared with the Kingdom of Heaven (Mt 19:14), would succeed where corrupt adults had failed. Nicholas of Cologne, as he is remembered in the sources, promised to lead the children to the Holy Land and convert the infidel to Christianity. Having gathered thousands of followers from the cities and towns of the Rhineland and Low Countries, Nicholas set out over the Alps to Genoa.

---

6. More cynical authors imagine a sly imposter, perhaps a disguised priest seeking to exploit Stephen's evident religious enthusiasm that aroused the masses. George Zabriskie Gray, *The Children's Crusade: A History*, with a forward by Thomas Powers (New York: William Morrow, 1972), 42. A Kindle edition of the 1870 original version of Gray's work is also available.

7. Regarding Peter the Hermit, see Chapter 2, "Mad Men on Crusade: Religious Madness and the Origins of the First Crusade" by James M. Muldoon.

8. One source reports that he was a boy younger than ten. Oskar Holder-Egger, ed. *Sicardi Episcopi Cremonensis Cronica*, in *Monumenta Germaniae Historica Scriptores*, 31: 180–81. http://www.dmgh.de/de/fs1/object/display/bsb00000783_00030.html?sortIndex=010:050:0031:010:00:00 (accessed December 31, 2013); see also Gray, *Children's Crusade*, 59.

Gustave Doré, *The Children's Crusade*. A nineteenth-century romanticized portrayal of the French segment of this movement. Photo source: Wikimedia.

The chronicles recount the trials of the journey in lurid detail. Boys and girls alike suffered bodily exploitation, the older men and women who traveled with the crusaders gave themselves over to every vice, few of the girls returned home with the flower of their virtue intact. Worst of all, just as at Marseilles, the sea remained unmoved by their entreaties. Some disillusioned child crusaders stayed on in Genoa, some were sold to Saracen pirates, while others continued the journey south to Pisa and on to Rome, where they supposedly met with Pope Innocent III, who reputedly commended them for their piety and crusade zeal that put adults to shame but ordered them to return home. As the crusade disbanded, a small remnant trickled home to mockery and derision. A small band continued on to the port city of Brindisi in southern Italy, but they never made it to the Holy Land from there. One former crusader who had been sold in the East returned to western shores after eighteen years in slavery. Through him we learn that the children were sold as far away as Baghdad and that eighteen had been martyred for their refusal to abjure their Christian faith.[9]

9. *Chronica Alberici monachi trium Fontium*, Paul Scheffer-Boichorst ed., in *Monumenta Germaniae Historica Scriptoris*, 23: 893. http://www.dmgh.de/de/fs1/object/goToPage/bsb00000886.html?pageNo=893&sortIndex=010%3A050%3A0023%3A010%3A00%3A00 (accessed December 31, 2013).

Such stories are simply too good to be easily abandoned. Not only do they indulge us with exotic medieval otherness, they can be made to speak to a range of contemporary concerns and anxieties. As a result, this patchwork of stories, like so many literary Legos, has been assembled and reassembled countless times. The 2006 Dutch film *Kruistocht in spijkerbroek* (Crusade in Jeans, also known as Crusade: A March through Time) provides a case in point.[10] Using a transparent time travel conceit, the viewer enters the thirteenth century through the eyes of a twenty-first-century Dutch teenager.

The chasm between the modern teenager's lack of faith and the naïve piety of the crusader children appears in sharp relief. But, as with nearly all modern screenplay representations of the medieval Church, the religious hierarchy is cynical and manipulative. Nicholas, the sincere, if somewhat dreamy and indecisive leader of the crusade fares better. Although for much of the film he is the unwitting dupe of the greedy priest Anselmus, who encouraged the enthusiasm of the children for the sole purpose of selling them into slavery, Nicholas ultimately emerges to save many of the crusaders from his mentor's clutches. While the film, as far as I know, is the first to introduce the odd specter of roving bands of pagan slavers in the Alpine passes, the rest of the story merely reiterates what has become the standard telling of the crusade.

Historians and the Construction of the Popular Narrative

These popular understandings of the Children's Crusade have roots that reach back at least to Enlightenment thinkers. Voltaire and the Encyclopedists saw the crusades as a manifestation of the worst aspects of human barbarism, a *maladie épidémique* that infected Europe and constituted the very definition of cruelty.[11] In *Une Histoire des croisades* (A History of the Crusades), Voltaire sums up his assessment: "This epidemic spread also to the children, led by school masters and monks, thousands abandoned their homes and their parents . . . their leaders sold some to the Muslims. The rest died of misery."[12] For such writers there was nothing to admire—the Church and the leaders of the crusade basely manipulated the sensibilities of the children, who themselves were at best ignorant dupes and at worst intolerant and intolerable zealots.

Writing in 1870, the Episcopalian theologian and amateur historian George Zabriskie Gray crafted a version of the crusade that balanced the sharply anti-Catholic

10. The film, loosely based on the novel *Crusade in Jeans* (New York: Scribner, 1975) by Thea Beckman, is available on DVD, and can be viewed at https://www.youtube.com/watch?v=IQ1iYpLt2hY (accessed August 20, 2014).

11. Gary Dickson, *The Children's Crusade: Medieval history, Modern Mythistory* (New York: Palgrave Macmillan, 2008), 171–72. See also Louis de Jaucourt, "Cruauté," in *L'Encyclopedia Diderot et d'Alembert*, http://alembert.fr/index.php?option=com_content&id=755287079 (accessed December 27, 2013).

12. Voltaire, *Micromegas avec une histoire des croisades et un nouveau plan d l'histoire de l'esprit humain* (Berlin: 1753), 103. See also Dickson, *Children's Crusade*, 171–72.

CHURCH OF THE NEW INNOCENTS.

An imaginative image of the supposed ruins of the Church of the New Innocents, frontispiece of the 1870 edition of George Zabriskie Gray's *The Children's Crusade*. As Gray tells the story, for which there is no credible evidence, Pope Gregory IX (r. 1227–1241) ordered that a memorial church be constructed on the island of San Pietro near Sardinia, where many of the children had perished in the wrecks of two ships. The uncorrupted bodies of these "martyrs" were exhumed and placed in the church, which became a popular place of pilgrimage for three centuries. Thereafter, for reasons unknown, the cult of the New Innocents diminished and eventually the church was abandoned and fell into ruin. Photo source: Wikimedia.

rhetoric of the Encyclopedists with a sincere admiration for the simple, misguided piety of the children (*pueri*).[13] On the one hand, Gray describes Pope Innocent III as "Vicar of the Prince of War,"[14] guilty of promoting "one of the greatest crimes upon the pages of history."[15] Lest the reader miss his point, Gray launches into an almost formulaic rant against the "profane farce" that characterized many of the practices of the medieval Church in France. If such things could occur, Gray continues, "in the most Christian land of Europe . . . what must have been the religious teaching of a clergy, so degraded and so defiant of all things sacred!"[16] On the other hand Gray admired or, at the very least, sympathized with the children.

They were the new holy innocents; like the murdered Innocents of Bethlehem, they had fallen victim to a corrupt regime. And when the putative Church of the New Innocents, which Gray believed had been constructed and consecrated in their honor, supposedly fell into disrepair, Gray's sentimental Victorian imagination saw these medieval children slumbering "in their neglected and deserted tomb; but the little birds that found there a nest and a home sang over them sweeter, purer

13. Dickson, *Children's Crusade*, 181–83, 188–89.

14. Gray, *The Children's Crusade*, 29.

15. Ibid., 31.

16. Ibid., 22.

requiems than ever had been chanted by forgotten priests."[17] That such a church probably never existed is one of those inconvenient points raised by killjoy historians to ruin a good story.[18] As one historian put it succinctly, "Gray does not even pretend to be an historian; his work exhibits his vivid imagination but very few facts."[19]

Gray's portrait of the Children's Crusade has proven remarkably adaptable. In the late 1960s and early 1970s, as headlines compared Vietnam to the Children's Crusade and young campaigners for Eugene McCarthy flocked under the banner of the Children's Crusade, Gray's work was reissued.[20] The journalist Thomas Powers, who wrote the forward for the re-edition, was unaware (or unconcerned) that the book had long been rejected by scholars, asserting that "nothing has been learned in the last century which alters the story Gray told in 1870." For Powers the well-intentioned but ill-fated crusades constituted an apt parallel to the American youth movements of the 1960s. "In both cases the young set off with an unshakable faith in the rightness of the their cause. . . . And in both cases they knew little of the past." Like their medieval predecessors, Powers informs us, "young Americans paid a high a high price for their idealism. They were not thanked for pointing out the injustice in America. . . . Children who ran away from home looking for a new way of life in rural communes, or in the hippie ghettoes of New York and San Francisco, often found a brutal world of drugs, disease, and violence."[21]

Although generally without the overt anti-Catholicism of Gray and the Encyclopedists, more recent work on the Children's Crusade continues to reflect their influence. Steven Runciman, whose three-volume *A History of the Crusades* is still in print more than sixty years after its initial publication, leaves little doubt as to where he stands. His treatment of the Children's Crusade follows a similar vein, corrupt churchmen leading pious, deluded children. The French leader of the crusade, Stephen of Cloyes was "an hysterical boy . . . infected with the idea that he too could become a preacher."[22] Runciman's telling of the events echoes Gray in nearly every detail: from the unfounded assertion that the crusaders were to meet at Vendôme to the claim that the leaders of the bands carried a copy of the French royal oriflamme

---

17. Ibid., 165.

18. There is no credible evidence that such a church ever existed. See Norman P. Zacour, "The Children's Crusade," in *A History of the Crusades*, 2nd ed., ed. Kenneth M. Setton et al., 6 vols. (Madison: University of Wisconsin Press, 1969–1989), 2:325–42, at 337–38, http://digital.library.wisc.edu/1711.dl/History.HistCrusades (accessed August 20, 2014).

19. Joseph E. Hansbery, "The Children's Crusade," *Catholic Historical Review* 24 (1938): 30–38 at 30, n.1.

20. Among many examples, see Henry Kamm, "Conflict Near the Ho Chi Minh Trail is Often a Children's Crusade," *New York Times*, March, 9, 1970, 3.

21. Thomas Powers, Forward to Gray, *Children's Crusade*, 8.

22. Steven Runciman, *A History of the Crusades*, 3 vols. (Cambridge: Cambridge University Press, 1951–1954), 3:139–40.

as a symbol for the movement.[23] Despite many obvious problems with Runciman's narrative, the continued popularity of his work has ensured that this image of the Children's Crusade remains dominant.

Deconstructing the Popular Narrative

Runciman's version was already passé among specialists when it first appeared in 1954. That it continues to have influence today testifies to the enduring beauty of Runciman's prose and his gift for a good story well told.[24] As early as 1914, Dana C. Munro problematized aspects of the popular narrative by pointing out the conflicting nature of the surviving evidence. Munro called earlier historians, especially George Zabriskie Gray and even the eminent Reinhold Röhricht, to task for their uncritical acceptance of clearly legendary aspects of their sources.[25]

Munro's stricture was known to but not sufficiently heeded by Joseph Hansbery, who in 1938 launched an assault on Gray's narrative by attempting to reconstruct the story through a reconciliation of all of the printed medieval sources available to him. Unfortunately, by accepting these sources at face value, he was not able to strip away the many myths that pervade them.[26] In the early 1960s, Norman Zacour poked further holes in many of the most cherished details of the popular narrative.[27] In the 1970s, Peter Raedts went so far as to deny that the participants were children in the modern sense at all but rather poor landless peasants. Thus, rather than being an indicator of age, the classification *pueri* signified economic and social status.[28] Gary Dickson has convincingly countered Raedts's claim by pointing out that although the chroniclers never denied that these *pueri* came from a number of social-economic backgrounds, including poor peasants, and that the marchers included some older members, they are clear on the point that the vast majority of the participants were young.[29]

---

23. Ibid., 140–41. Dickson, *Children's Crusade*, 189, has pointed out that Runciman's depiction of the crusade lacks any real foundation in the sources. In fact, although he cites D. C. Munro, Reinhold Röhricht, and Paul Alphandéry, the real source for his version of events seems to be Gray.

24. Dickson, *Children's Crusade*, 189. Nonspecialists continue to cite Runciman for the details of the crusade. Even a historian as careful as Shulasmith Shahar reproduces Runciman's garbled version in her *Childhood in the Middle Ages* (London: Routledge, 1990), 250.

25. Dana C. Munro, "The Children's Crusade," *The American Historical Review*, 19 (1914): 517–24, at 517–18; Reinhold Röhricht, "Der Kinderkreuzzug" [The Children's Crusade], *Historische Zeitschrift* 36 (1876): 1–8.

26. Hansbery, "Children's Crusade," 30–38, passim. See note 19 above.

27. Zacour, "Children's Crusade," 325–42, passim. For Zacour the crusade was the result of a kind of mass hysteria sparked by social and economic tensions combined with the sustained excitement of crusade preaching. Ibid., 327–28.

28. Peter Raedts, "The Children's Crusade of 1212," *Journal of Medieval History* 3 (1977): 295–97.

29. Dickson, *Children's Crusade*, 33–35.

Until the appearance of Dickson's analysis, crusade historians were reticent to speak too confidently about the Children's Crusade or to go into any great detail on it. Norman Housley, *Fighting for the Cross: Crusading to the Holy Land*, dispensed with the children in four noncontiguous sentences.[30] In *The Crusades: c. 1071–c. 1291*, the distinguished French crusade historian, Jean Richard accepted the historicity of the Children's Crusade and noted that its emphasis on recovery of the True Cross lost at the Battle of Hattin in 1187 "allows us to class the movement as a crusade." At the same time, he acknowledged that its origins and chronology were unclear, and his use of scare quotation marks around the term "children" shows his doubt that these *pueri*, whom he characterizes as "young people," were actually children.[31]

In the first two editions of his influential *A History of the Crusades*, Jonathan Riley-Smith treated the Children's Crusade in a manner that indicated that, while he accepted as fact the rise of spontaneous movements in France and the Rhineland among "children," some of whom actually traveled to Italy, the details escaped him, and he did not even accord these movements the title of "crusade," although he noted that Pope Innocent dispensed from their vows those who had reached Rome, "although their vows were not technically valid anyway"[32]

In the current third edition of the book, however, he acknowledges that Dickson has "convincingly established the course of events," and devotes four paragraphs of detail to the crusade but notes that this mass movement (largely among adolescents who were joined by adults) was one that so fired imaginations that within thirty years of its appearance it was being heavily mythologized. Moreover, because Riley-Smith is a leading crusade Pluralist, and Pluralists maintain that papal authority was a necessary condition for a true crusade, he characterizes this movement as an "upheaval" that was one of the "so-called popular crusades" and does not count it as a real crusade[33]

In his 2004, *Fighting for Christendom: Holy War and the Crusades*, Christopher Tyerman accepted the Rhenish movement "apparently led by a boy called Nicholas of Cologne," as a "holy war of the spirit" but larded his short account of what he termed "the so-called Children's Crusade" with modifiers that indicated his uncertainty over the details. He further saw the movement in northern France led by Stephen of Cloyes as "a series of penitential and revivalist processions" that voiced "vague appeals for moral reform" and gave no clear evidence of any intention to liberate Jerusalem.[34] Yet, in his more recent *God's War:*

---

30. Norman Housley, *Fighting for the Cross: Crusading to the Holy Land* (New Haven, CT: Yale University Press, 2008), 15, 30, 36, 200.

31. Jean Richard, *The Crusades c. 1071–c. 1291* (Cambridge: Cambridge University Press, 1999), 288–89.

32. Jonathan Riley-Smith, *A History of the Crusade*, (New Haven, CT: Yale University Press, 1987), 141; 2nd ed. (2005), 171–72.

33. Jonathan Riley-Smith, *A History of the Crusade*, 3rd ed. (London: Bloomsbury, 2014), 196–97.

34. Christopher Tyerman, *Fighting for Christendom: Holy War and the Crusades* (Oxford: Oxford University Press, 2004), 65–66.

A New History of the Crusades, Tyerman, inspired and informed by the work of Dickson and Raedts, dedicates a full four pages, with detail, to the topic (even as he acknowledges that the records are confusing and have been clouded by "later lurid romantic fantasies"). As is the case with Riley-Smith, Tyerman, also a leading Pluralist, treats both the French and German-Flemish movements as examples of the popular dimension of crusading.[35]

Despite Dickson's ability to accord primacy to children (or, at least, young people) in the Children's Crusade by virtue of his careful analysis of the surviving accounts of this phenomenon and despite all that he has done to put this crusade into the mainstream of the crusade narrative, the facts of the Children's Crusade are still disputed.

Constructing a New Narrative

The durability and broad consistency of the popular narrative is even more remarkable in light of the complexity and inconsistency of the sources themselves. The sources comprise some fifty references from across Latin Christendom, many composed decades after the events they purport to describe.[36] Frequently, they are no more than a single sentence "in that same year a certain *infans* less than ten years old came with an infinite number of poor from Germany claiming that without a ship they would cross the sea and retake Jerusalem,"[37] or a short playful verse, "in the year 1212 children with children hurried to protect the holy places."[38] (It's more playful in Latin.)

As William MacLehose has noted, despite their relative wealth in numbers, the sources agree on only two things: "that children were thought to be involved and

---

35. Christopher Tyerman, *God's War: A New History of the Crusades* (Cambridge, MA: Belknap Press of Harvard University Press, 2006), 607–11. Yet, in *Fighting for Christendom*, 34, Tyerman slightly skewers those medieval elites and modern historians who have undervalued these movements when he notes, "The Peasants' (1096), Children's (1212), and Shepherds' (1251, 1320) Crusades speak for themselves, socially pigeon-holed by historians' (and contemporary) snobbery."

36. See the assessment of William MacLehose, *A Tender Age: Cultural Anxieties over the Child in the Twelfth and Thirteenth Centuries* (New York: Columbia University Press, 2008), 175. See Also Dickson, *Children's Crusade*, 9–14.

37. "Sicardi Epicopi Cremonensis Chronica," Oskar Holder-Egger, ed., in *Monumenta Germaniae Historica Scriptores (in folio)*, 31, 180–81: "Eodem anno quidam minus X annorum infans cum infinita multitudine pauperum venit de Teutonia asserens sine nave transiturum mare et Ierusalem recuperaturum." http://www.dmgh.de/de/fs1/object/goToPage/bsb00000783.html?pageNo=181& sortIndex=010%3A050%3A0031%3A010%3A00%3A00 (accessed December 31, 2013).

38. "Annales Thuringici Breves," Oskar Holder-Egger, ed., in *Monumenta Germaniae Historica Scriptores (in folio)* 24, 41: "Anno milleno bis centeno duodeno cum pueris pueri currunt loca sancta tueri." http://www.dmgh.de/de/fs1/object/display/bsb00000866_00052.html?sortIndex=01 0%3A050%3A0024%3A010%3A00%3A00 (accessed December 31, 2013).

that religious motivations supposedly lay behind the movement."[39] Moreover, the chroniclers themselves, who were almost exclusively clerics, were often more interested in imparting moral lessons than accurately describing historical events. They warn against disobedience, the rashness of youth, and the dangers of popular piety, and they assert the superiority of the Christian faith and the authority of the Church's hierarchy. The historical events are hardly the point.

Despite these facts, historians continue to attempt to construct a single authoritative narrative that knits together these unruly sources. Dickson's recent effort is especially noteworthy for its careful scholarship. But any coherent reconstruction must almost arbitrarily ignore or explain away contradictions. And the contradictions are legion. How old were the leaders? Ten? Twelve? Or simply youthful? When did they embark? 1209? 1212? 1213?[40] How old were their followers?[41] Were they exclusively poor or did they include members of the nobility?[42] Where were they headed? To Marseilles? Genoa? Pisa? Rome? Vienne?[43] Was Nicholas

---

39. William MacLehose, *Tender Age*, 179.

40. The preponderance of sources cites 1212 but a significant number indicate 1213 and at least one dates the pilgrimage to 1209. "Annales s. Medardi Suessionensibus," ed. Georg Waitz, in *Monumenta Germaniae Historica Scriptores*, 26: 521. http://www.dmgh.de/de/fs1/object/goToPage/bsb00000864.html?pageNo=521&sortIndex=010%3A050%3A0026%3A010%3A00%3A00 (accessed December 31, 2013): "1209 . . . Innumera multitudo infantium et puerorum . . . absque licentia et assensu parentum, exeuntes, dicebant, se causa sancte cruces querende iter ultra mare arripuisse" (An innumerable multitude of infants and children, without parental consent went forth; they say they took the journey across the sea for the sake of the cross).

41. The lack of clarity regarding age is evident in the following passages regarding the German elements of the crusade: *MGH SS* 17, 84 *Annales Spirensis* http://www.dmgh.de/de/fs1/object/goToPage/bsb00000842.html?pageNo=84&sortIndex=010%3A050%3A0017%3A010%3A00%3A00 (accessed December 31, 2013): "facta est magna peregrinacio tam masculorum quam puellarum, tam senum quam iuvenum, set tantum de plebe" (There was a great pilgrimage of both male and female both old and young, but only from the lowest levels of society). *Annales Placentini Guelfi*, *MGH SS* 18, 426, http://www.dmgh.de/de/fs1/object/display/bsb00000888_00440.html?sortIndex=010%3A050%3A0018%3A010%3A00%3A00 (accessed December 31, 2013): "quidam puer Theothonicus signo cruces signatus qui vocabatur Nicholaus, cum magna et indefinita multitudine Theothonicorum puerorum et infantium lactantium, mulierum et puellarum, signo crucis Domini signatorum per Placentiam transitum fecerunt ultra mare profisci festinantes" (A certain German boy called Nicholas, who had been signed with the cross, together with a great multitude of German children, infants and nursing babes, women and girls, and crusaders passed through Piacenza hurrying to cross the sea).

42. Jacobi der Voragine *Chronicon*, ed. L. A. Muratori, Rerum Italicarum Scriptores, 9, no. 45: "multi autem inter eos erant filij nobilium, quos ipsi etiam cum nutricibus destinaverunt" (Moreover there were among them many sons of the nobility together with their nurses).

43. The chronicler of Ebersheim informs us that the crusaders came "to Vienne which is on the sea [it is no where near the sea], and there after having boarded ships they were seized by pirates and sold to the Saracens." *MGH SS* 23, 450.

killed? Did he finally make it to the Holy Land?[44] Did the child crusaders even have leaders?[45]

Given such inconsistencies, some historians have begun to ask very different questions. MacLehose, for example, uses the accounts to explore medieval conceptions of childhood. From this perspective the specifics of the Children's Crusade no longer occupy center stage. Instead he focuses on the chroniclers' use of the crusade to discuss broader anxieties about the vulnerability and innocence of children.[46] Even Dickson, although he attempts to construct a plausible history of the event itself, explores the process of mythmaking (or, as he calls it, the mythistoricizing of the *pueri*).[47] Viewed in this way, the contradictions themselves become the focus of inquiry revealing the chroniclers' ambivalence toward the child crusaders. But more importantly they also reveal broader anxieties about popular piety, the innocence of children, the source of religious inspiration, and the crusading movement itself.

The reported age and makeup of the participants in the Children's Crusade offers an especially powerful example of the potential of this line of inquiry. As noted above, the chroniclers provide a wide range of potential ages, from babes in arms to the cusp of adulthood and beyond. But rather than simply record the age of the crusaders, the chroniclers frequently employ age symbolically. Jesus himself was said to be twelve when he briefly abandoned his family during a pilgrimage to Jerusalem. Here the chroniclers could draw both on Jesus' ultimate obedience (something lacking in the youthful crusaders) but also the youthful wisdom of the child Christ.

Not coincidentally, the Franciscan chronicler Salimbene draws the most explicit connections between the crusaders and the twelve-year-old Jesus. Saint Francis after

---

44. *Cotinutio Admuntensis, MGH SS* 9, 592, http://www.dmgh.de/de/fs1/object/goToPage/bsb00000841.html?pageNo=592&sortIndex=010%3A050%3A0009%3A010%3A00%3A00 (accessed December 31, 2013): "Facta est expeditio puerorum utriusque sexus instinctu diabolico, et preterea virorum et mulierum provectorum, quorum dux erat Nicolaus quidem puer de Colonia; qui mortui et venditi sunt in locis diversis. Post non multum temporis in pregrinatione sancte cruces prefatus dux transfretavit, et aput Akirs et in obsidione Damiate, ad duos fere annos strennue militavit et tandem incolumis remeavit" (An expedition, inspired by the devil, was made by children of both sexes, as well as men and women, the leader of these was a certain boy Nicholas of Cologne. These died or were sold in diverse places. Not long after this the aforementioned leader crossed the sea to Acre and fought bravely during the siege of Acre for nearly two years before he finally returned home unharmed); *MGH SS* 24, 399: "Venditi enim erant gentilibus a patre Nicholai, et sic demonum maleficio atrracti; propter quod et puer ipse periit" (They were sold as slaves by the father of Nicholas, and thus they were drawn by the wickedness of the demons, for this reason the boy perished).

45. *Annales Stadenses, MGH SS* 16, 355: "Circa idem tempus pueri sine rectore, sine duce, de universis omnium regionum villis et civitatibus versus transmarinas partes avidis gressibus cucurrerunt" (Around that same time, children with no director or leader hurried from every region, village, and city to cross the sea).

46. MacLehose, *Tender Age*, 178–79.

47. Dickson, *Children's Crusade*, 132.

all was also a runaway.[48] In fact Salimbene says nothing negative about the youthful crusaders, noting only that they declared "with a unanimous heart and with one voice that they would cross the sea on dry land and recover Jerusalem through the power of God. But nearly all vanished."[49] The chronicler of Piacenza also connects the crusader to Christ in his description of some of the crusaders, whom he describes as a great multitude of children and *infantium lactantium* (of suckling infants).[50] The chronicler selected these words, not because they reflect the true age of the crusaders but because they call to mind Christ's words in Matthew 21 (itself a quotation from the Psalms) "out of the mouths of infants and sucklings you have prepared praise for yourself."[51]

Elsewhere and for other medieval authors the participation of children symbolized the breakdown of both the social and natural order. Albert of Stade focuses on the chaos of the Children's Crusade and the dangerous zeal of the participants. The leaderless mob broke free of all parental control and "eagerly rushed to cross the sea," casting aside all reason, order, and rational thought. In Albert's version, the children seem to have fallen under some sort of spell so that "when asked the reason for their journey, they said they did not know." As if this subversion of social order wasn't enough, "around that same time naked women traveled through the villages and towns saying nothing."[52]

Such extraordinary disruptions extended even to the natural world: fish, frogs, butterflies, and birds set out in the same manner as the children. What is more, a large number of dogs gathered near Monshymer, divided themselves into two groups, and fought ferociously. Like the children, nearly all of them were killed and few ever returned home.[53] Despite the importance of these events to the chronicler himself (he devotes more than three quarters of his account to them), they are excised from most popular and scholarly accounts—as if the exclusion of the miraculous somehow makes the account more historical instead of simply impoverishing it by denying its cultural context.

These prodigious events could also reveal the baleful power of the Devil and heresy as far as some contemporaries were concerned. Henry of Heimburg reports that in

---

48. Ibid., 134–35.

49. Salimbene de Adam, *MGH SS* 32, 30: "unanimi corde et una voce dicentium se per siccum maria transituros et terram sanctam Ierusalem in Dei potentia recuperaturos; sed demum quasi evanuit universa."

50. *Annales Placentini Guelfi*, *MGH SS* 18, 426.

51. Matthew 21:16 and Luke 8:2: "ex ore infantium et lactantium perfecisti laudem propter inimicos tuos et destruas inimicum et ultorem."

52. Albert of Stade, *Annales de Stadenses*, *MGH SS* 16, 355. http://www.dmgh.de/de/fs1/object/goToPage/bsb00000943.html?pageNo=355&sortIndex=010%3A050%3A0016%3A010%3A00%3A00 (accessed December 31, 2013).

53. Annales S. Medardi, 521.

the year 1212 a "multitude of little children were sold by heretics to the Saracens."[54] The chroniclers of Admont and Ebersheim wrote that the children were inspired by the Devil.[55] Whereas the Trier chronicler discerned the influence of the Devil on Nicholas's father, who not only encouraged his son to seduce the children but later sold them to the Saracens. Ever the moralist, the chronicler metes out swift justice on Nicholas's father "because of this, his son died and his father was cruelly murdered in Cologne."[56]

The moralizing of the chroniclers is perhaps most evident in the stories surrounding the end of the crusade. The failure of the crusade, the sale of the children into slavery, the physical violation of the children, and the death of many all highlight the dangers of uncontrolled popular religious enthusiasm. However, not all the accounts condemn the children. Several elicit sympathy for their fate or offer the children as a model for the adults. Alberic of Trois Fointaines reports with satisfaction that Iron Hugo and William the Pig, the alleged traitors who sold the children into slavery, died ignominious deaths by hanging (a form of death that would bring to mind the suicide of Judas who had betrayed Jesus). Alberic even recasts the children as the early fourth-century Eighteen Martyrs of Saragossa, telling his readers that eighteen of the children were killed in Baghdad "through diverse types of martyrdom" for their refusal to abandon their faith.[57]

So what really happened? Similar in some respects to the later Shepherds' Crusades of 1251 and 1320, the *pueri* of 1212 represented a popular movement. Or perhaps better, several popular movements, which Gary Dickson has termed "crusade revivals."[58] The French *pueri*, who may or may not have directly influenced the German-Flemish crusaders, appear to have had both religious and political motives

54. Henry of Heimburg, *Annales*, in *Monumenta Germaniae Historica Scriptores*, 17, 714: http://www.dmgh.de/de/fs1/object/goToPage/bsb00000842.html?pageNo=714&sortIndex=010%3A050%3A0017%3A010%3A00%3A00 (accessed December 31, 2013): "1212 Multitudo infancium ab hereticis traditur Saracenis."

55. *Continuatio Admuntensis*, in *Monumenta Germaniae Historica Scriptores*, 9, 592. http://www.dmgh.de/de/fs1/object/goToPage/bsb00000841.html?pageNo=592&sortIndex=010%3A050%3A0009%3A010%3A00%3A00 (accessed December 31, 2013): "Facta est expedition puerorum utriusque sexus instinctu diabolico"; *Chronicon Eberheimense* in *Monumenta Germaniae Historica Scriptores*, 23, 450. http://www.dmgh.de/de/fs1/object/goToPage/bsb00000886.html?pageNo=450&sortIndex=010%3A050%3A0023%3A010%3A00%3A0 (accessed December 31, 2013).

56. *Gesta Treverorum Continuata* in *Monumenta Germaniae Historica Scriptores* 24, 398. http://www.dmgh.de/de/fs1/object/goToPage/bsb00000866.html?pageNo=398&sortIndex=010%3A050%3A0024%3A010%3A00%3A00 (accessed December 31, 2013): "propter quod et puer ipse periit, et pater eius Colonie mala morte peremptus est."

57. *Chronica Albrici monachi Trium Fontium*, in *Monumenta Germaniae Historica Scriptores* 23, 893. http://www.dmgh.de/de/fs1/object/goToPage/bsb00000886.html?pageNo=893&sortIndex=010%3A050%3A0023%3A010%3A00%3A00 (accessed December 31, 2013). The account is redolent of the story of the eighteen martyrs of Saragossa still celebrated as saints in the thirteenth century.

58. Dickson, *Children's Crusade*, 128–30.

with the desire to influence the king clearly evident from the start. The movements also reflected an implicit critique of the Church hierarchy. If the Church could not redeem Jerusalem, the *pueri* could. Whoever the *pueri* were, contemporary accounts are nearly unanimous in noting their youthfulness. Nearly all of the accounts connect the movement with a desire to reclaim Jerusalem, and all agree that they did not succeed in their objective. Beyond this, however, they agree on precious little.

The tensions within and between these accounts reflects the clear ambivalence felt by the authors themselves and the often contradictory meanings they wished to draw from the events. For many of the authors, nearly all clerics, the movement challenged the appropriate order of Christendom. At the same time, the youth and piety of the crusaders fit neatly into medieval conceptions of the special calling and purity of children and elicited sympathy even in the most critical authors. These medieval authors did not fail to represent the historical reality of the Children's Crusade because they were bad historians. They failed because they were good moralists. Whatever the facts of Children's Crusade, for contemporaries it was an irresistible opportunity to critique the social, religious, and political realities of their day and to assert essential truths about the world in which they lived. In that regard very little has changed.

6. Templars and Masons: An Origin Myth

Jace Stuckey

The lunatic is easily recognized. He is a moron who doesn't know the ropes. The moron proves his thesis; he has a logic, however, twisted it may be. The lunatic, on the other hand, doesn't concern himself at all with logic; he works by short circuits. For him, everything proves everything else. The lunatic is all idée fixe, and whatever he comes across confirms his lunacy. You can tell him by the liberties that he takes with common sense, by flashes of inspiration, and by the fact that sooner or later he brings up the Templars.

. . . There are lunatics who don't bring up the Templars, but those who do are the most insidious. At first they seem normal, then all of the sudden. . . .[1]

The words of Umberto Eco's fictional character Belbo, one of the three neurotic editors at Garamond Press in Milan, which specializes in hermetic and occult works, are emblematic of the widespread fantasies concerning Templar conspiracies. In the novel *Foucault's Pendulum,* the three editors concoct a plan to create an imaginary secret history that connects various myths and legends with reality—a plan that works all too well. "The fundamental axiom," states Casaubon, another of the three editors, is that "the Templars have something to do with everything." The third editor, Diotallevi, quickly responds, "That goes without saying."[2] Some twenty years after Eco first published *Foucault's Pendulum,* "the Plan" as well as Eco's explicit criticism of conspiracy theories concerning the Templars have become the epitome of life imitating art.

In the first decade of the twenty-first century perhaps no other aspect of the history of the medieval crusades has become more attractive to modern enthusiasts than the rise and fall of the Poor Fellow-Knights of Christ and the Temple of Solomon, popularly known as the Knights Templar, or Templars.[3] However, at the same time

---

1. Umberto Eco, *Foucault's Pendulum* (San Diego: Harcourt Brace Jovanovich, Inc., 1989), 67. See also Malcolm Barber, *The New Knighthood: A History of the Order of the Temple* (Cambridge: Cambridge University Press, 2000), 332–34.

2. Eco, *Foucault's Pendulum,* 375.

3. An indication of the continuing popular interest in the Templars is the catalog, *The Knights Templar: From the Days of Jerusalem to the Commanderies of Champagne* (Paris: Somogy éditions d'art, 2012) accompanying the exhibition *Templiers. Une Histoire, nostre trésor* (The Templars: A History, Our Treasure) held in Troyes, France, June 16 through October 31, 2012. Lavishly illustrated essays on aspects of Templar history by twenty-two eminent French scholars (and Malcolm Barber, the

there has been no topic more misunderstood or more misused than the Templars. A close second might be the Assassins,[4] and imagine the myths that abound when someone claims that the Templars and Assassins shared an occult bond.[5] Assassins aside, from fiction writers to conspiracy theorists, the Knights Templar have come to play a key role in the modern imagination of the medieval world, and they have been the subjects of numerous myths, chief among which is their putative connection to the Freemasons.[6]

A Brief History of the Templars

The foundation and history of the Knights Templar is not as mysterious or sinister as modern conspiracy theorists would have us believe. The Knights Templar owed their origins to the precarious situation that developed in the Holy Land during and after the First Crusade (1096–1099). In the immediate wake of the conquests of the crusader armies, leaders established the Western-style Latin Kingdom of Jerusalem, the Principality of Antioch, and the County of Edessa. Shortly later, in 1109, the Frankish armies added the County of Tripoli. However, following the conquest of Jerusalem in 1099, most of the surviving crusaders returned to Europe, leaving the four small Latin Christian territories undermanned and largely isolated in a hostile region.[7]

The Templars, who were created to partially fill that vacuum by providing security to Christian pilgrims in the Holy Land, received papal recognition in 1129 at the Council of Troyes and were declared a "military order," a new creation—a religious order dedicated to defending Christians and their territories in the Holy Land by force of arms. According to contemporary sources, this was the "ninth year" of

---

lone English historian) accompany the annotated images of the forty-four items or sets of items in the exhibition.

4. See Farhad Daftary, *The Assassin Legends: Myths of the Isma`ilis* (London: I. B. Tauris & Co., 1994).

5. James Wasserman, a member of the Ordo Templi Orientis (Order of the Eastern Temple), which acknowledges a modern foundation but claims to draw some of its occult traditions from the Knights Templar, has composed a number of books that purport to be nonfictional accounts of the Templars and their secrets. In *The Templars and the Assassins: The Militia of Heaven* (Rochester, VT: Inner Traditions, 2001), he posits the thesis that at some time in the medieval past the Templars and Assassins cross-pollinated to create a new occult sect. See note 51 below for more on this supposed Templar-Assassin connection.

6. See Sean Martin, *The Knights Templar: The Histories and Myths of the Legendary Order* (New York: Avalon Publishing, 2004), 11–13 and 127–45; Ghislain Brunel, "Myth and Legends," in *Knights Templar: From the Days of Jerusalem*, 180–85; Helen Nicholson, "Conclusion: The Templar Myth" in *The Knights Templar: A New History* (Stroud, UK: Sutton Publishing, 2001), 238–46.

7. Regarding the issue of whether or not most or even many of the participants in the First Crusade intended from the start to establish overseas colonies in the Holy Land, see Corliss Slack's chapter "The Quest for Gain: Were the First Crusaders Protocolonists?"

the Order's foundation, and Malcolm Barber has concluded that the "official date of foundation . . . must fall between January 14, and September 13, 1120."[8] Their name stems from the place of the original headquarters in Jerusalem at the Al-Aqsa Mosque, believed by Christians to have been on the original site of Solomon's Temple.[9]

The concept was novel, and the idea of a "militarized religious order" provoked some initial resistance but became widely accepted by the mid-twelfth century, although the Templars never lacked critics throughout their almost two centuries of existence as a military order. Notwithstanding criticism, the Templars eventually gained significant recognition, thanks in part to support from charismatic and zealous proponents such as Saint Bernard of Clairvaux (1090/91–1153), who wrote *De laude novae militiae* (In Praise of the New Knighthood) in support of the new order, claiming that these new knights committed not homicide but *malicide* (the killing of evil) when they killed enemies of the Faith in combat.[10]

The Templars were granted ecclesiastical privileges by the pope, gained extensive lands in the Holy Land and Western Europe, built large castles and fortresses in both regions, and eventually became involved in banking as a direct consequence of their crusading mission and their need to transfer funds from Europe to the Middle East.[11] They set up a sophisticated system whereby pilgrims could make deposits in a Templar house in Europe and then collect their funds later in the Holy Land. They also lent out funds, especially to crusaders, and in the course of the thirteenth century became an important element in Western Europe's financial markets.[12]

From a military standpoint, by the Second Crusade (1147–1149), the Templars were already playing a prominent role throughout the Holy Land and in northern Spain and inspired the formation of other knightly orders in both areas. They would continue to be an influential military force throughout the twelfth and thirteenth centuries. However, much of the modern infatuation with the Templars begins with the end of the Order and particularly with the dramatic events of the investigation into and dissolution of the Order in the fourteenth century.

In the early fourteenth century, the Templars found themselves at odds with the powerful and unpredictable French king Philip IV (r. 1285–1314). As a result, many

---

8. Barber, *New Knighthood*, 9. See also Helen Nicholson and David Nicole, *God's Warriors: Crusaders, Saracens, and the Battle for Jerusalem* (Oxford: Osprey Publishing, 2005), 140–75; Helen Nicholson, *The Knights Templar, 1120–1312* (Oxford: Osprey Publishing, 2004), 8; Nicholson, *The Knights Templar: A New History*, 17–46, which presents an extended overview of Templar origins.

9. Barber, *New Knighthood*, 7.

10. Bernard of Clairvaux, "In Praise of the New Knighthood," trans. Conrad Greenia in *The Works of Bernard of Clairvaux*, Treatises III (Kalamazoo, MI: Cistercian Publications, 1977), 115–67, at 134. The first five of the thirteen chapters of this treatise are newly translated in Malcolm Barber and Keith Bate, eds. and trans., *The Templars: Selected Sources Translated and Annotated* (Manchester, UK: Manchester University Press, 2002), 215–27.

11. Barber, *The Trial of the Templars* (Cambridge: Cambridge University Press, 2006), 1.

12. Barber, *New Knighthood*, 267–79.

members of the Order were arrested and put on trial throughout Europe for heresy, idolatry, and multiple other crimes. It is possible that Philip, who was quite pious, did indeed see the Templars as an order that had been infected with various heretical beliefs and sacrilegious practices. However, Philip also required significant revenue to finance his wars, and this was likely a major motivating factor for targeting a group whose holdings, if confiscated, would bring in immense wealth.

As already noted, there are many popular myths associated with the Knights Templar. One myth is that, following the mass arrest of members all over Europe on Friday the 13th 1307, the Order and all or most of its members were found guilty. In fact, the investigation extended for a long period of time, but the Order and most of its members were not found guilty of the charges, which included that they denied Christ,

A Templar in Paradise. King Kalakua (r. 1874–1891) of Hawai'i, the kingdom's last reigning king, was a 32nd Degree Mason. Here he wears several Templar crosses as part of his Masonic regalia. In 2003, his Knights Templar sword was returned to the 'Iolani Palace in Honolulu. Photo source: Wikimedia.

defiled crucifixes, engaged in homosexual practices, and worshipped idols,[13] although Jonathan Riley-Smith has suggested that some of the charges of "unusual" practices might actually have had merit.[14]

Ultimately, Pope Clement V concluded that the charges were not proven, even though several Templars confessed after being tortured. However, enough damage had been done to their reputation to justify putting an end to the Order at the Council of Vienne, March 1312.[15] Most of the few who were found guilty spent time in prison as their punishment, but there were two exceptions. In a dramatic climax to the story of the Knights Templar, the aged Grand Master Jacques de Molay recanted his confession

---

13. Malcolm Barber, *The Trial of the Templars* (Cambridge: Cambridge University Press, 1978), 178–93. See also Helen Nicholson, *Knights Templar: A New History*, 11–13 and Barber, *New Knighthood*, 298–313.

14. Jonathan Riley-Smith, "Were The Templars Guilty?" in *The Medieval Crusade*, ed. Susan Ridyard (Woodbridge, UK: Boydell Press, 2004), 107–24.

15. The pope's bull suppressing the order is available in Malcolm Barber and Keith Bate, eds. and trans., *The Templars: Selected Sources Translated and Annotated* (Manchester, UK: Manchester University Press, 2002), 309–18.

and was burned to death as a lapsed heretic, along with Geoffrey of Charney, precep-
tor (commander) of Normandy, in March of 1314. A popular story that arose from
this event is that Molay prophesized that his persecutors would answer for their crimes
within a year and a day. King Philip IV and Pope Clement V were both dead within
a year. Clement died from a nagging sickness that he had been dealing with for some
time, while Philip fell victim to a hunting accident.

The Origins of Templar Myths

At this point, the Order of the Temple faded from the scene. Most of its land and
much of its wealth went to the Order of Saint John of the Hospital (the Hospitalers),
although some military orders in Iberia profited from this windfall as well. Some
knights spent time in prison and some roamed Europe and beyond as adventurers,
but most were either pensioned off and allowed to live out their lives in other religious houses or permitted to join various other military orders, such as the Order
of Christ in Portugal, founded in 1319 in order to absorb the displaced Templars of
that region.[16] This prosaic reality has subsequently been transformed into the romantic myth of the "crypto-Templars"—a view among some conspiracy theorists that
somehow the Templars remained active as Templars even after the Order's official
suppression but "hidden" within various other organizations and institutions. There is
absolutely no evidence to support such a notion, but the very lack of evidence is proof
enough for some that a conspiracy of silence was and is at work.

A lack of sources, in this instance a *supposed* lack of sources, is the focal point of
another Templar myth. The idea that there are not a lot of sources left by the Templars
is a commonly held but mistaken assumption. In this miasma of ignorance, since very
little is presumably known about the Templars, their history is open to wide speculation and gossip and is a haven in which conspiracy theories thrive. Although it is difficult to gage what constitutes a "lack of sources" when considering the Middle Ages
and its extant documentary sources, this is not an accurate view of the field. It is true
that the Templars' central archive was lost in the sixteenth century when the Ottoman
Turks took the island of Cyprus, the site of former Templar headquarters.[17] But, relatively speaking, there is a plethora of sources concerning their foundation, military
activities, land acquisitions, and a rather abundant collection concerning the trial
proceedings that led to the Order's eventual demise.[18] For the person who does not

16. Nicholson, *Knights Templar, 1120–1312*, 14–15. See also Barber, *New Knighthood*, 310, where
he points out that shortly before the Order of Christ was founded in Portugal, the Aragonese
king, James II, created in 1317 the Order of Montesa, which received former Templar holdings in
Valencia. So the possibilities for former Templars were diverse.

17. Barber, *New Knighthood*, 8–12.

18. Barber, *Trial of the Templars*, 122–53; 193–248. Perhaps the most intriguing source is the so-
called *Chinon Chart* discovered by Barbara Frale in the Vatican archives. This source indicates that

read medieval Latin, Malcolm Barber and Keith Bate have collected, translated into English, and annotated a large anthology of selected sources relating to the Templars from the Order's origins to its demise.[19]

Beyond that, the most common myth is the identification of the Order as a secret society. The Templars were not a secret society and should never be categorized as such.[20] The Rule of the Templars was written in Latin in 1129; clauses were added in French, and it was eventually translated into French in its entirety. As already noted, Bernard of Clairvaux, a Cistercian abbot, the leading churchman of his day, and a fervent supporter of crusading and the Templars, lent the new order credibility, and from the beginning, its leaders were able to recruit significant numbers from within a network of contacts throughout France.

Many of the earliest members were from the French and Provençal noble and knightly classes, and some of their earliest landholdings in Europe were in the same rather populous regions. Additionally, the Templars attracted recruits from throughout Latin Christendom, and their convents, fortresses, and churches were scattered throughout Western Europe and the Eastern Mediterranean. Two of their prominent locations were in the hearts of Paris and London. So, there was certainly no secretive element to their early development or subsequent growth.

Of course, the Order did have its secrets, but this was not unique to it or the period and primarily involved military information. No fighting force—and the Templars were an elite military organization as well as a religious order—can afford to allow potential and real enemies to discern its strength and plans of operation. Also, church and secular leaders often used Templar convents and fortresses as safe repositories for their prized goods, including documents, and they expected a high level of discretion regarding those items that they had entrusted to the knights. Additionally, Templars were often employed by popes, kings, and others as emissaries on sensitive diplomatic missions and were likewise expected to be closemouthed about their duties.[21]

That noted, it also seems likely that, as is often the case with elite military units, the Templars had unique bonding practices that were closed to outsiders, and during their protracted trial in the early fourteenth century, one of the most credible charges brought against them was that they swore all initiates to secrecy regarding the ritual by which they were received into the Order.[22] However, none of this rises to the level

---

the Templar leaders appeared before the papal curia in 1308 and that the pope granted them absolution. Prior to this discovery, only indirect knowledge of these events existed. Barbara Frale, "The Chinon Chart: Papal Absolution to the Last Templar, Master Jacques de Molay," *Journal of Medieval History* 30 (2004): 109–34.

19. See note 15.

20. Nicholson, *Knights Templar, 1120–1312*, 13–14.

21. Nicholson, "Most Trustworthy Servants: In the Service of European Kings" in *Knights Templar: A New History*, 160–80.

22. Clement V's bull of suppression of the Order in Barber and Bate, *Templars*, 317.

of its being a secret society, but identification of the Templars as a closed community that jealously guarded ancient mysteries is by far one of the most enduring myths to make it into the modern perception of the Order.

Central to this misunderstanding of the Templars, which rises out of a popular infatuation with mystery, is the idea that the occult knowledge preserved by the Templars as well as their guiding spirit, esoteric rituals, and various roles in society were passed on to and preserved by modern Freemasons. This notion, often referred to as "Templarism," became an important part of the origin myth associated with modern Freemasonry in Britain and especially on the continent in the eighteenth century.

Templars and Freemasons

Many fraternal organizations from this period, which contemporary German and English intellectuals termed "the Enlightenment," used ancient symbols and adopted heritages in order to give themselves a noble lineage, but many knew that these connections were symbolic and mythical rather than historical. Nevertheless, for all the supposed rationalism of the so-called Enlightenment, interest in Rosicrucians, secret orders, magic, esotericism, and alchemy spread to all parts of Europe and was particularly prominent in aristocratic circles.[23] Indeed, for a society whose intellectual elite often exhibited considerable contempt for what they viewed as the religious fanaticism and general backwardness of the supposed medieval "Gothic" world (a term of disdain coined in the early sixteenth century), there seems to have been an unusual fascination and comfort among the Freemasons with adopting a crusading order as a vital part of their origin myth.

It is possible and likely that the eighteenth-century image of the Middle Ages mirrored today's popular views, which range from the overly negative image of an uncivilized backwardness that bred superstition, intolerance, religious warfare, and the Inquisition on the one hand, to an idealistic interpretation of chivalry, romance, and knighthood on the other.[24] This latter view certainly helped to foster interest in supposed Masonic-Templar connections. Additionally, the increased interest in genealogy and the more or less contemporaneous rise of Romanticism and nationalism also inspired an increased interest in origins and foundations.

It is important to note that knowledge of and interest in the Templars existed prior to their imaginative revival by the Masons. They were the subject of numerous

---

23. The Rosicrucians, officially the Ancient Mystical Order of the Rose (or Rosy) Cross (AMORC), is a secret society that first appeared in early seventeenth-century Protestant Germany and claims to possess esoteric truths that date back to its presumed origins in antiquity. See Frances Yates, *The Rosicrucian Enlightenment* (London: Routledge, 1972).

24. Marcus Bull, *Thinking Medieval, An Introduction to the Study of the Middle Ages* (New York: Palgrave Macmillan, 2005), 7–41.

writings of the late Renaissance and Early Modern period.[25] Nevertheless, the modern revival of interest in the Templars and medieval knighthood can be traced to the early eighteenth century with the rise of Speculative Freemasonry.[26] This was a fraternal organization dedicated to upholding the laws of the Supreme Being and performing public acts of charity while maintaining secret rites and signs within the brotherhood.

On the surface, a historical connection between the Templars and Freemasons would seem impossible because the former ended in the early fourteenth century and the latter, as we know it, formally began in the eighteenth century with the formation of the aforementioned Grand Lodge in London in 1717. However, some scholars contend that a convincing case can be made for placing the roots of modern Freemasons somewhat earlier—in the late sixteenth century.[27] Even so, at the very least, more than two centuries separated the collapse of one organization and the inception of the other. Of course, the historical disconnection between Templars and Masons did not stop some of the early members from supposing links to ancient and medieval orders, and it has not stopped modern conspiracy theorists from wholeheartedly proclaiming them and perpetuating the myth through modern novels, pseudohistories, films, and faux documentaries.

One of the earliest sources to discuss Masonic history is the *Constitutions of the Freemasons* by James Anderson (1679–1739).[28] Anderson, an ordained minister of the Church of Scotland and master and grand warden of the Grand Lodge of London and Westminster, was commissioned by the Grand Lodge in 1721 to record the constitution, history, charges, orders, regulations, and the usages of the "Right Worshipful Fraternity of Accepted Freemasons."[29] Although historians believe that others played a role in the compilation, Anderson's name is the one associated with the *Constitutions.*

---

25. See Partner's discussion in *Murdered Magicians*, 96–99. Some works available to interested persons in this era were Elias Ashmole, *Institutions, Laws and Ceremonies of the Most Noble Order of the Garter* (1672); Pierre Dupuy, *Histoire de l'Ordre Militaire des Templiers ou Chevaliers du Temple de Jérusalem* [History of the Military Order of the Templars or Knights of the Temple of Jerusalem] (1654); Cornelius H. Agrippa, *De occulta philosophia libri tres* [Three Books on Occult Philosophy] (Cologne, 1533); M. Del-Rio, *Disquisitionum magicarum libri sex* [Six Books of Magical Inquiry] (Cologne, 1679); Pierre Dupuy, *Traitez concernant l'histoire de France* [A Treatise on the History of France] (Paris, 1700); Thomas Fuller, *History of the Holy War* (1639).

26. Malcolm Barber, *The New Knighthood*, 317–18. For similar refutations of the Templar myth by Freemasons, see W. J. C. Crawley, "The Templar Legends in Freemasonry," *Ars Quator Coronatum* 26 (1913): 45–70 and William E. Parker, "Jacques DeMolay, The Knights Templar, and Freemasonry": http://www.greyfriars51.fsnet.co.uk/the_knights_templar_and_freemasonry.htm (accessed March 30, 2014).

27. David Stevenson, *The Origins of Freemasonry: Scotland's Century 1590–1710* (Cambridge: Cambridge University Press, 1988).

28. James Anderson, *The Constitutions of the Freemasons, 1723* (London: Bernard Quaritch Limited, 1923), 46.

29. Ibid., 7.

The completed work first appeared in print in 1723, but the first American edition was printed by Benjamin Franklin, the grandmaster of Pennsylvania in 1734.[30] The section concerning the history of the order begins with the creation of the world, Adam, and other early Old Testament characters. Anderson writes:

> Adam our first Parent, created after the image of God, the great Architect of the Universe, must have had the Liberal Sciences, particularly Geometry, written on his Heart; for ever since the Fall, we find the Principles of it in the Hearts of his Offspring, and which, in process of time, have been drawn forth into a convenient Method of Propositions, by observing the Laws of Proportion taken from Mechanism: So that as the Mechanical Arts gave Occasion to the Learned to reduce the Elements of Geometry into Method, this noble Science thus reduc'd is the Foundation of all those Arts, (Particularly of Masonry and Architecture) and the Rule by which they are conducted and perform'd."[31]

He emphasizes that the early principles of geometry and masonry were essentially part of humanity's pursuits from the beginning and continued to be passed on to subsequent generations. Overall, it reads like a short history of the development of architecture and, what Anderson calls the ancient lodges. The term "lodges" is often used and discussed with regularity and their existence is assumed and claimed in one form or another.

Naturally, there is a great deal of emphasis on the construction of Solomon's Temple and the specifics of that architectural achievement. It is, in a way, held up as a model for the Order. Anderson further writes:

> But Dagon's Temple, and the finest structures of Tyre and Sidon, could not be compared with the ETERNAL God's Temple at Jerusalem, begun and finish'd, to the Amazement of all the World, in the short space of seven years and six months, by the wisest Man and most glorious King of Israel, the Prince of Peace and Architecture, SOLOMON (the Son of David, who was refused that Honour for being a Man of Blood) by divine Direction, without the Noise of Work-men's Tools, through there were employ'd about it no less than 3600 Princes, or Master-Masons, to conduct the Work according to Solomon's Directions.[32]

Despite what we might expect, very little attention is given to the Middle Ages. There is some analysis of Gothic architecture, but little else. Gothic cathedrals became

---

30. *The Constitutions of the Free-Masons (1734) An Online Edition* (Lincoln: University of Nebraska-Lincoln, 2006), http://digitalcommons.unl.edu/cgi/viewcontent.cgi?article=1028&context=library science (accessed October 29, 2014).

31. Anderson, *Constitutions*, 7–8.

32. Ibid., 13–14.

the new form of architecture, and the term "Gothic" itself seems to encompass virtually everything that was constructed in the Middle Ages. The narrative at one point proceeds quickly from a one-paragraph discussion of William the Conquer and the Norman influence in the late eleventh century to King Edward III (r. 1312–1377)—essentially skipping the more than two centuries when the major crusades occurred and the Templars were founded and flourished. In fact, there is no mention of the Knights Templar or any other medieval religious order or even the crusades, although he does note at the end of his historical survey, "Nay, if it were expedient, it could be made appear, that from this *ancient Fraternity* [Masonry],the Societies or Orders of the *Warlike* KNIGHTS, and of the *Religious* too, in process of time, did borrow many solemn Usages."[33]

The role that medieval people played in this history seems to be relegated simply as a link with the ancient past. However, this was written in England where interest in knighthood and the revival of chivalry were not initially central concerns of the Masons.[34]

During the 1720s and 1730s Masonic lodges sprang up all over Britain and the continent. It was during this period, once the movement spread to the continent, especially in France and Germany, that the appearance of medieval knightly ancestors became a central feature of Masonic lore and gained popularity. In the two decades that followed the publication of Anderson's *Constitutions*, the knightly orders of the crusading era went from being almost entirely absent from Masonic historical writing to becoming the critical link to the rites, wisdom, and knowledge that became a staple of Masonic tradition. The establishment of an origin myth and plausible connections to the medieval past were intended to give the Masons a greater sense of legitimacy and permanence. In addition, the particular connection to the Templars would help solidify the identity of the Masons as a Knightly Order with all the idealized and romanticized notions that this carried with it. This would be increasingly important in the nineteenth and twentieth centuries, when idealized images of medieval chivalry reached their apex.[35]

The specific connections between medieval crusaders and the Masons appears to have been born in the speeches of Andrew Michael Ramsay (1696–1743), in which he essentially turned many of the original members of the professional corporations of "free masons" into persecuted knights who went into hiding as a result of their continued post-medieval suppression by the Church.[36] Ramsay was a Scots baronet, a knight of the Military and Hospitaler Order of Saint Lazarus of Jerusalem, an order

---

33. Ibid., 46.

34. Margaret C. Jacob, *The Radical Enlightenment: Pantheists, Freemasons, and Republicans* (London: George Allen, 1981), 109–37.

35. Bull, *Thinking Medieval*, 19–41.

36. Richard Barber, *The Holy Grail: Imagination and Belief* (Cambridge, MA: Harvard University Press, 2004), 306–9.

that originated in the twelfth-century Latin Kingdom of Jerusalem, a devotee of mysticism and natural religion, and a Catholic Jacobite living in France. The Masonic movement in France was just getting started in the 1730s and Ramsay's influence was considerable.[37] By the outbreak of the Revolution in 1789 there were more than six hundred lodges in Paris alone. France clearly embraced the new fraternal organization, whose membership included nobles, priests, brothers of the king, and many of the most prominent figures of the Enlightenment.

Ramsay speculated that crusaders were both stonemasons and knightly warriors and referred to the crusaders as "our ancestors." In a speech to Freemasons in Paris in 1737, Ramsay stated:

> At the time of the Crusades in Palestine, many princes, lords, and citizens associated themselves, and vowed to restore the Temple of the Christians in the Holy Land, and to employ themselves in bringing back their architecture to its first institution. They agreed upon several ancient signs and symbolic words drawn from the well of religion in order to recognize themselves amongst the heathen and Saracens. These signs and words were only communicated to those who promised solemnly, and even sometimes at the foot of the altar, never to reveal them. . . . Sometime afterwards our Order formed an intimate union with the Knights of St. John of Jerusalem [the Hospitalers]. From this time our Lodges took the name of Lodges of St. John. This union was made after the example set by the Israelites when they erected the second Temple, who whilst they handled the trowel and mortar with one hand, in the other held the sword and buckler. Our Order therefore must not be considered a revival of the Bacchanals, votaries of Bacchus, drunken revelers, but as an Order founded in remote antiquity, and renewed in the Holy Land by our ancestors in order to recall the memory of the most sublime truths amidst the pleasures of society.[38]

Several important connections are established in this short passage. The emphasis on architecture (i.e., the Temple of the Christians, better known as the Church of the Holy Sepulcher) is initially emphasized, the secret signs and words that would become a part of regular Masonic practices are present, and the idealized noble virtues that medieval knighthood would come to represent for many in the eighteenth and nineteenth centuries are clearly reflected in the speech. The medieval "parentage," rather than being a nominal link with the ancient past as it was in Anderson's work, now came to represent

37. Partner, *Murdered Magicians*, 102–4.

38. Text from the *Discourse Pronounced at the Reception of Freemasons by Monsieur de Ramsay, Grand Orator of the Order*, www.frenchfreemasonry.org/english/the-documents/masonic-historical-documents/chevalier-ramsay-s-oration-1736 (accessed October 29, 2014). See also Jean Palou, *La Franc-Maçonnerie* (Paris: Payot, 1964); G. A. Schiffmann, *Andreas Michael Ramsay* (Leipzig, 1878); and G. D. Henderson, *Chevalier Ramsay* (London: Thomas Nelson and Sons, 1952).

something much more important and romantic. From this point forward, the language of eighteenth- and nineteenth-century writers reflected the increasing importance and centrality of a religious Order of Chivalry in Masonic history.

In Ramsay's version of Masonic history, the Masons had an ancient history, but the critical period was the crusades when the military-religious orders were most prevalent.[39] Ramsay placed an emphasis here because this is where the Masons' knightly chivalric identity was established. This is when the recognizable Masonic identity of the eighteenth century could be projected backward onto medieval Europe with some sense of certainty. This was perhaps an easier link for eighteenth-century men to make rather than the ancient biblical world of Solomon and other Old Testament characters, which was disconnected geographically as well as by about three millennia. Any connection to the "master masons" of Solomon's time must have seemed abstract and distant. On the other hand, French and the German lands were once held by the military orders and were the heart of medieval chivalric development.[40]

However, Ramsay's history was too general, and it did not connect the Masons with the Templars but rather with the Knights of St. John of Jerusalem (popularly known as the Hospitalers). His knighthood in the much smaller and less distinguished Order of Saint Lazarus might have impelled him to connect the Freemasons with this greater and far better known hospitaler-military order, but this assertion was potentially problematic because the Hospitalers still existed as the Knights of Malta and could dispute any historical connection with the Masons. Of course, no such problem existed with the Templars.[41]

The transition to the Templars came in Germany, where the first Masonic lodge was founded in Hamburg in 1733. Membership here also initially included a high concentration of nobility and royalty. Historians have suggested that to some extent the egalitarian emphasis of Freemasonry in Britain and France was less prevalent in Germany, and instead a society dominated by older social and political divisions continued. As a result, the knightly origin and character of the Templars and its connection to nobility proved more attractive.

A number of myths developed and circulated in Germany by 1760.[42] Perhaps the most prominent of these new versions of Masonic history was that of Baron Karl Gotthelf von Hund (1722–1776). A wealthy German landowner whose influence on the Templar-Mason origin myth was profound, he was the creator of the *Rite of Strict Observance* sometime after 1764. This established the Knight Templar and the Military Order of the Temple as prominent grades (or degrees) within the rite, and in the Yorkist Rite, the Order of the Temple became the highest of its Chivalric Orders.

---

39. Peter Partner, *The Knights Templar and Their Myth* (Rochester, VT: Destiny Books, 1990), 103–8.

40. Edward Burman, *The Templars: Knights of God* (Rochester, VT: Destiny Books, 1986), 178–80.

41. Partner, *Murdered Magicians*, 105.

42. Ibid., 110.

Hund himself might have actually been initiated into a Templar degree as early as 1743.[43] He also established many new Orders and lodges throughout Europe. During the height of his influence, he had extensive contacts from Britain to Italy and as far to the east as Russia. A perceived connection can also be found in America at the lodge of St. Andrew's Royal Arch Chapter in Massachusetts.[44] A source from August of 1769 mentions the Templars, stating that "William Davis was accepted and accordingly made by receiving the four steps; that of Excellent, Super Excellent, Royal Arch, and Knight Templar"[45]

Hund's outright obsession with Templarism led him to construct an elaborate myth that connected the Templars to the Masons and to call the lodges a "restoration of the Templars."[46] According to Hund, after the dissolution of the Templars and the execution of the last grand master, Jacques de Molay, eight Templars fled France to Ireland. They then traveled to Scotland before reorganizing the Order there. As a result, Scotland became the new center of the Templar-Masonic lodges. The irony is that the Templars were never numerous in Scotland, even at the height of their power. However, it was Hund's story that became the preferred narrative among the versions of Templar-Mason connections. The *Ancient and Accepted Scottish Rite,* created in the eighteenth century, eventually became the largest Masonic association in terms of number of initiates and likely played an important role in keeping Scotland at the center of the Templar-Mason origin myth.[47]

During this same period, the mid to latter part of the eighteenth century, myths about the Templars and Masons multiplied exponentially, with different versions and conspiracies appearing in Germany and across the continent. It would be almost impossible to outline all the parallel developments and various tangents. Part of the reason for this phenomenon stems from the enormously complex structure of late eighteenth-century Speculative Freemasonry and its fragmentation into competing orders and separate systems. However, the basic premise of virtually all of the myths is the idea that some Templars survived the dissolution of the Order and that the grand master, Molay, managed to pass on the secret knowledge or do something to

---

43. Henrik Bogdan, *Western Esotericism and Rituals of Initiation* (New York: State University of New York Press, 2007), 96–106.

44. There was a lodge established in 1733 in Boston, Massachusetts and in Charleston, South Carolina by 1735.

45. Edward Batley, "Lessing's Templars and the Reform of German Freemasonry," *German Life and Letters* 52 (1999): 297–313.

46. Partner, *The Knights Templar and Their Myth*, 117–20. One story has a French prisoner during the Seven Years War work with a German pastor to construct a Templar connection. In another version, a Scottish nobleman, working under the assumed name of George Frederick Johnson, wrote that he had knowledge and access to the Templar secrets. There were others who claimed previous knowledge of the Templar Order, such as Johann August von Stark and C. G. Marschall von Bieberstein, who set up rival Templar rites and pursued renewed interest in potential connections with the occult.

47. One of the highest degrees of the Scottish Rite is the Knight Commander of the Temple.

ensure the survival of the Order before his public execution. The Templars relocated to remote places such as Scotland and stayed largely underground until the eighteenth century, when they reemerged in the Masonic lodges.

With the connection between the Templars and the Masons well established in legend, if not fact, many supporters and critics turned their attention to speculation on exactly what was being passed on and why it was so important, which coincidentally is where much popular interest remains today.

Templar "Secret Knowledge"

From the 1760s forward, the elaborate myths that connected the Templars to the Masons were given an added element. The Templars became the "guardians" of secret esoteric knowledge and great hordes of treasure. Additionally, specific famous relics, such as the Shroud of Turin, the head of Saint John the Baptist, and the Holy Grail, were speculated to be among Templar possessions.[48] Of course, the idea that the Templars had great hordes of treasure might actually stem from medieval stories of the tremendous wealth that Templar houses acquired in the twelfth and thirteenth centuries.

As already suggested, when King Philip IV ordered the arrest of the Templars in 1307, he clearly saw an opportunity to confiscate some of this money. However, although some monarchs were able to seize some of that wealth, the sources indicate that most of the lands and wealth eventually passed to the Order of the Hospital and various military orders in the Iberian Peninsula. In fact, the settlement of much of the property and wealth was well established with the papal bull *Ad providam* issued in May of 1312 by Clement V.[49]

Once the conspiracy theories gained credence, none of the inconvenient facts that separated the Templars and Masons proved strong enough to untether the mythical bond that had been created. There are a number of aspects about the Templars that were attractive to the early leaders of Freemasons. First, there was the supposed noble and chivalric background of medieval knights, and their elaborate genealogies gave the Masons a long pedigree. Second, the perception of secrecy and legendary history of the Templars was seized upon and used as a plausible background for Masonic origins, since actual proof of any connection was part of the secret rites. Last, perhaps the perceived persecution by the Church seemed a perfect fit for Masonic tradition.

The image of the suppression of the Templars by the combined forces of the Church and the French king was an ideal parallel to the modern Masons, who were often viewed as a threat to the traditional roles of the Church and monarchies. This

---

48. Thus, in the film *Indiana Jones and the Last Crusade* (1989), the Holy Grail is guarded by an immortal Templar. Even Walt Disney got into the act. In "Uncle Scrooge and the Crown of the Crusader Kings," Scrooge McDuck, Donald Duck, and his nephews discover under Castle McDuck in Scotland the Templars' treasure, which contains, among other items, the Holy Grail and the Ark of the Covenant: *Knights Templar: From the Days of Jerusalem*, 208–9.

49. Barber, *New Knighthood*, 304; a translation of the bull is in Barber and Bate, *Templars*, 318–22.

became especially relevant when the Masons were linked with supposed roles in the various revolutionary uprisings of the eighteenth century and following.

Templars, Freemasons, and Revolution

One reason the Templar myth proved to have such durability in the eighteenth and nineteenth centuries is that the connections were claimed by both critics and supporters of the Masons.[50] The revolution in France no doubt played some role in this phenomenon. Inspired by the public execution of King Louis XVI, Louis Cadet de Gassicourt in his *Le Tombeau de Jacques Molay* (The Tomb of Jacques Molay, 1796) argued that the Templars were created by the "Old Man of the mountain."[51] The reference is to Hasan ibn al-Sabbah, the founder of a secret order of the Ismaili sect of Islam (ca. 1090), or Assassins as they were known in the West. Their members were devoted followers of Hasan who used terror and assassination as political tools. Their eighteenth-century successors were supposed to be anti-French anarchists, who incited revolutionary uprisings, including the Jacobin conspirators whose role in the French Revolution and the Terror was emphasized.

On the other side and in horrified reaction to the Terror, the Jesuit Augustin de Barruel subsequently published his *Mémoires pour servir à l'histoire du Jacobinisme* (Memoirs Regarding the History of Jacobinism), which linked the Jacobins with both the Masons and anti-Christianity. He also traced the anti-Christian conspiracies to the third century with the foundation of Manichaeism.[52] This proved attractive for conspiracy theorists, because it linked both contemporary and ancient groups to the Masons. Ultimately, he linked the Manichaeans, Cathars,[53] Templars, and Jacobin Masons into a convenient chronology of anti-royal and anti-Church conspirators.[54]

---

50. Barber, *New Knighthood*, 317–23.

51. Charles Louis Cadet de Gassicourt, *Le Tombeau de Jacques Molai, ou, Le secret des conspirateurs, à ceux qui veulent tout savoir; oeuvre posthume* (Paris, 1792). See also Partner, *The Knights Templar and Their Myth*, 130.

52. Augustin de Barruel, *Mémoires pour servir à l'histoire du Jacobinisme* (London, 1797–1798). See the discussion in Partner, *The Knights Templar*, 131–33. See also Robert Darnton, *Mesmerism and the End of the Enlightenment in France* (Cambridge, MA: Harvard University Press, 1968). Manichaeism, a dualistic faith that arose in what is today Iraq in the third century CE, styled itself the Religion of Light and preached a universal message that perceived life as a cosmic struggle between the forces of Light and Darkness. It was a syncretic religion that incorporated Gnostic (note 55), Zoroastrian, Buddhist, Hindu, Jewish, and Christian elements.

53. Twelfth- and thirteenth-century dualist "heretics" in Languedoc. See Malcolm Barber, *The Cathars: Dualist Heretics in Languedoc in the High Middle Ages* (London: Longman, 2000). Notes 52 and 55 provide an explanation of dualism.

54. See Augustin de Barruel, *Memoirs Illustrating the History of Jacobinism*, translated from the French (London, 1797–1798), and Partner, *Knights Templar*, 131.

The connection of the Masons to the Templars had a kind of reciprocal effect on the Templars. Since the Templars were now a part of the chain of development within Masonic history and tradition, by default they became connected to various antisocial and anti-Church groups deemed as outsiders and heretics in the Middle Ages. These sometimes included the Gnostics,[55] Manicheans, Waldensians,[56] and Cathars.

Templars, Freemasons, and Romanticism

The nineteenth century saw both the expansion and institutionalization of the connection. There were no longer any vague references to the medieval order, but rather elaborate genealogies and histories that further entrenched the myths. The Scottish connections continued to be the most popular narrative. Many of the idealized notions of the Middle Ages that are current today are products of the nineteenth century.

Romanticized notions of knighthood and chivalry were especially prevalent, such as those of Sir Walter Scott's *Ivanhoe (1819)* and *The Talisman (1825),* which feature Templars as major characters.[57] Scott, initiated as a Mason himself in 1801, is often rightly credited with helping to increase the popular interest in chivalry and the history of the Middle Ages.[58] Ironically this Masonic father of the European historical novel portrayed the two chief Templar characters in these two stories (both grand masters of the Order) as rapacious, conniving, and morally compromised. Both die as a consequence of their sins and passions.

In nineteenth-century America, the presumed chivalric character of the medieval knight was seized upon by various Masonic groups. The former Confederate brigadier general Albert Pike penned the treatise *Morals and Dogma of the Ancient and Accepted Scottish Rite of Freemasonry,* first published 1871 and had many subsequent editions. Not surprisingly, the Templars figure prominently in Pike's history of the Masons. Pike's chivalric masonry was particularly prominent in the American South after the Civil War (1861–1865).

Pike's narrative history of the Masons discusses the role of Templars and other predecessors in a section titled "Prince of Jerusalem." Concerning the Templars, Pike focuses on a description of the arrest, persecution, and dissolution of the Order.

---

55. The Gnostics were dualists (believers in two mutually hostile divine beings or entities—the forces of Light and Darkness, Spirit and Matter) who flourished during the several centuries on either side of the beginning of the Common Era and who further believed that the key to salvation is a secret *gnosis* (knowledge) that reveals the spark of divinity within one's foul body.

56. Also known as the Poor Men of Lyons, an evangelical, anticlerical movement that was declared a heresy by the late twelfth-century papacy.

57. Bull, *Thinking Medieval*, 29–41.

58. Barber, *New Knighthood*, 323–30; Marcus Bull, *Thinking Medieval*, 25–41.

Subscribing to the myth that, prior to his death, Molay set up lodges of Masonry, Pike wrote:

> The end of the drama is well known, and how Jacques de Molai and his fellows perished in the flames. But before his execution, the Chief of the doomed Order organized and instituted what afterward came to be called the Occult, Hermetic, or Scottish Masonry. In the gloom of his prison, the Grand Master created four Metropolitan Lodges, at Naples for the East, at Edinburgh for the West, at Stockholm for the North, and at Paris for the South.[59]

Pike goes on to discuss the movement of the Order underground, claiming:

> The Order disappeared at once. Its estates and wealth were confiscated, and it seemed to have

Albert Pike as Master Mason. Photo source: Wikimedia.

ceased to exist. Nevertheless it lived, under other names and governed by unknown Chiefs, revealing itself only to those who, in passing through a series of Degrees, had proven themselves worthy to be entrusted with the dangerous Secret.[60]

The secret foundation of Lodges just prior to Molay's execution became commonplace for the Masonic historical narrative, and it is still the preferred narrative of modern conspiracy theorists. Additionally, reminiscent of Gassicourt, Pike calls attention to a revenge element in his work emphasizing a Masonic connection with the death of Philip IV's royal successor Louis XVI, who went to the guillotine in January of 1793, and "thenceforward the Army of the Temple was to direct all its efforts against the Pope."[61]

The Templars in the Twentieth and Twenty-First Centuries

Notwithstanding the remnants of chivalric masonry that could be found in the South and regardless of such institutions as De Molay International, which was founded in Missouri in 1919 as an international fraternity for boys and young men ages 12–21, significant interest in medieval orders such as the Templars was largely and noticeably

---

59. Albert Pike, *Morals and Dogma of the Ancient and Accepted Scottish Rite of Freemasonry* (Charleston, 1871), 820.

60. Ibid., 821.

61. Ibid., 824.

absent for much of the twentieth century. Indeed, for much of the second half of the twentieth century, there seemed to be a decrease in interest in both the Templars and their supposed association with Masons. In the early 1970s, J. M. Roberts confidently wrote of the mythologies of secret societies that "the intellectual tone of our society is against them, it prefers other mythologies."[62]

Now, however, it appears that society has again changed its tone, inasmuch as recently these myths have been revived and expanded. Part of the reason for this stems from the preponderance of popular re-enactors and many modern neo-Templar groups, such as the Daughters of Tsion.[63] More important was the 2003 publication of *The Da Vinci Code*,[64] which sparked much of the current interest in Templar and Masonic lore. The Templars are not the main focus of the book, but they are an important part of Brown's storyline. In Brown's version of the history of the Knights Templar, the Order's "true" goal is revealed. The Templars were not a military order tasked with protecting pilgrims and helping to maintain Christian control of the Holy Land; their true mission was to retrieve the secret documents of the Priory of Sion from beneath the ruins of the Temple.

These are the very documents that prove the sacred bloodline of Christ and Mary Magdalene lives on—the crux of Brown's narrative as well as of its equally ahistorical progenitor of the mid-1980s *Holy Blood, Holy Grail*.[65] These documents and this knowledge were preserved by the Templars in the face of brutal oppression by the Church and eventually were passed on to various other groups, including the modern Freemasons. In a similar vein, *The Templar Revelation: The Secret Guardians of the True Identity of Christ (1997)*,[66] provided Brown with a number of pseudohistorical elements that he included in his novel, including a portrayal of the Templars as an occult body of heretics that was part of an unbroken, two-thousand-year-old tradition, which included the Freemasons. Like most recent books of this type, the authors of these three meretricious works of bizarre fiction present the Templar-Mason connection as an established historical "fact."

The Da Vinci Code phenomenon spawned a cottage industry of new Templar pseudohistories and conspiracy theories. Recent titles include *Pirates and the Lost Templar*

---

62. Roberts, *The Mythology of the Secret Societies* (New York: Macmillan Publishing, 1972), 2.

63. Esoteric Interfaith Church, New Order of the Knights Templar and The Daughters of Tsion, http://www.northernway.org/school/templars.html (accessed February 15, 2014). See also note 76.

64. Dan Brown, *The Da Vinci Code: A Novel* (New York: Doubleday, 2003).

65. Michael Baigent, Richard Leigh, and Henry Lincoln, *Holy Blood, Holy Grail* (New York: Delacorte, 1982).

66. Lynn Picknett and Clive Prince, *The Templar Revelation: The Secret Guardians of the True Identity of Christ* (New York: Simon and Schuster, 1998). In the same vein, their equally ahistorical *The Sion Revelation: The Truth about the Guardians of Christ's Sacred Bloodline* (New York: Simon and Schuster, 2006), continues this fabrication.

Fleet: The Secret Naval War between the Knights Templar and the Vatican[67] and *The Templar Papers: Ancient Mysteries, Secret Societies, and the Holy Grail.*[68] Generally, these types of book fall into one of two categories, and many of these books, or at the very least the conspiracy theories in them, have a significant following among the general public. First there are the outright pseudohistories and faux documentaries, both of which, despite appearances, are little more than works of fantasy and bizarre conspiracy theories. William Mann's *The Knights Templar in the New World: How Henry Sinclair Brought the Grail to Acadia* is typical of the kind of pseudohistory frequently found on the market.[69] Mann, who is the grandnephew of a supreme grandmaster of the Knights Templar in Canada, weaves together an elaborate mythology and chronology of Templar history that defies all logic.

Then there are books that are often touted as works of fiction, such as *The Da Vinci Code,* but that term "fiction" purportedly concerns only the book's storyline, not the claimed "historical backdrop" in which it takes place. Such books of "novelized history" that revolve around Templar conspiracies include Steve Berry's novel *The Templar Legacy*[70] as well Raymond Khoury's *The Last Templar,* which was on the *New York Times* best seller list for twenty-two weeks and was made into a television miniseries.[71] One of the most egregious is Grigor Fedan's *The Templars, Two Kings and a Pope.* Fedan claims his novel is based on new research into the last twenty-five years of the Templars and their subsequent underground existence, but it is only rehashed conspiracy theories.[72] Whether they connect the Templars directly with the Freemasons or not, all of these books perpetuate the myth of the survival after 1314 of crypto-Templars who preserved the secrets and mission of the Order, which in turn feeds the continued belief of many people in a direct and unbroken Templar-Freemason connection.

Popular reviews of these books are a good place to demonstrate how ingrained many of these myths are in our culture. They often get very positive reviews that rave about the "factual basis" of the arguments as well as their author's supposed meticulous and original research. Consider Grigor Fedan's *The Templars, Two Kings and a*

67. David Hatcher Childress, *Pirates and the Lost Templar Fleet: The Secret Naval War between the Knights Templar and the Vatican* (Kempton, IL: Adventures Unlimited Press, 2003).

68. Oddvar Olsen, *The Templar Papers: Ancient Mysteries, Secret Societies, and the Holy Grail* (Franklin Lakes, NJ: New Page Books, 2006).

69. William Mann, *The Knights Templar in the New World: How Henry Sinclair Brought the Grail to Acadia* (Rochester, VT: Destiny Books, [1999] 2004).

70. Steve Berry, *The Templar Legacy: A Novel* (New York: Ballantine Books, 2006).

71. Raymond Khoury, *The Last Templar* (New York: Dutton, 2005). See also its sequel, *The Templar Salvation* (New York: Dutton, 2010).

72. Grigor Fedan, *The Templars, Two Kings and a Pope* (n.p.: Hafiz Publishers, 2009). See Grigor Fedan, Knights Templar, History, Mystery, http://grigorfedan.com/main/Modern_Day_Knights_Templar_The_Masons (accessed March 28, 2014).

Pope. One Amazon.com reviewer noted, "Any Freemason who has been involved in the 'higher' degrees (Scottish or York Rite) will find this very interesting, as it deals with some of the foundations of our orders." Another wrote:

> I can give nothing but praise to the author and the book that he created from an enormous vault of facts. This book does what books seldom do, which is to place correctly the facts of actual circumstances at the reader's fingertips, to open the door to the mind and expose him/her to knowledge seldom presented. If you have an interest in the Knights Templar, Gnosis, or the Esoteric in general, then this is the book for you. Truth is stranger than fiction at times, and it is about time that the truth of the Templars was presented to the public.[73]

These theories have a kind of currency or "street credit" among the general population, which for various reasons is suspicious of academic historians. It will continue to be difficult to persuade a society that has been continuously inundated in the popular media with myth, legend, and conspiracy of every sort that such stories and theories, while entertaining, have no credible supporting evidence. Once again, one of Eco's characters, Signor Garamond, makes the point so poignantly when he says, "I realize that these people will gobble up anything that's hermetic . . . anything that says the opposite of what they read in their books at school."[74] Much to the dismay of professional historians and scholars, he is right.

These books and theories are indeed popular and have empowered the authors and legitimated conspiracy theories. As such, conspiracy theorists are often dismissive of traditional academia and scholarship. Richard Barber aptly points out this attitude in claims made by the authors of *Holy Blood and Holy Grail.* They contend that not only is an interdisciplinary approach necessary, but drawing connections between people and places largely disconnected by space and time, such as the third and twelfth or the seventh and eighteenth centuries, is not only permitted but necessary. In addition, "it is not sufficient to confine oneself exclusively to facts."[75] This is a remarkable statement, but strangely one that often goes unchallenged. Barber argues that this freedom from facts gives them carte blanche to invent or suppose connections in the absence of actual evidence and to call such inventions proven or conclusive.

---

73. http://www.amazon.com/THE-TEMPLARS-TWO-KINGS-POPE/dp/061526431X (accessed March 30, 2014). Another list of favorable reviews, some by Masons, is at http://books.google.es/books-?id=hpEyEJOLmGoC&pg=PA1&lpg=PA1&dq=The+Templars,+Two+Kings+and+a+Pope,+review&source=bl&ots=ypyDblSQJM&sig=6ap3r8EHGPlTcnY6ZbwzCudW_QA&hl=es&sa=X&ei=eko4U9HBM4PJ0AXel4D4Cg&ved=0CIABEOgBMAk#v=onepage&q=The%20Templars%2C%20Two%20Kings%20and%20a%20Pope%2C%20review&f=false (accessed March 30, 2014).
74. Eco, *Foucault's Pendulum*, 261. See also Barber, *New Knighthood*, 330–33.
75. Barber, *Holy Grail*, 30. Taken from Michael Baigent, Richard Leigh, and Henry Lincoln, *The Holy Blood and the Holy Grail* (London: Delacorte Press, 1982), 273.

For conspiracy theorists, there is virtually nothing new in the world—at least nothing important that does not have an ancient antecedent. There are no historical disconnections or dead ends. There are always ways around these—when contemporary sources do not exist or contradict the theory, they are simply dismissed. Everything has a direct or indirect connection with something formed in the distant past under enigmatic circumstances, and the survival of the conspired-against group often depends on extraordinary episodes of persecution and escape. It is often claimed that movements or organizations were forced underground for long periods of time as a result of persecution. It takes a willing suspension of reality to make these kinds of connections between Templars and Masons but one that has continued since the eighteenth century.

The historical basis of what started as an attempt to give the Masons a romantic mythology—a story that was intended to be more romantic and idealistic than historical—has been lost on most modern audiences, including many members of the Freemasons themselves. Indeed, some other, more recently founded fraternal orders use the terminology of the Templars and actually call themselves Templars by name, such as the Ancient Gnostic Order of Knights of the Temple of Solomon.[76] However, historically the modern revival of the Templar tradition does not have any direct historical connection to the medieval order.

The overwhelming popularity of these myths has put historians into a minority position, forcing them to defend a less mysterious, less secretive, and ultimately less popular version of Templar and Masonic history. However, it is critical to give voice to this position since, and this is one of the more ironic twists of the story, the actual history of the Knights Templar is much more intriguing than its many myths.

---

76. Http://www.ancientgnosticknightstemplar.org/ (accessed March 30, 2014; not available March 26, 2015). Lists of neo-Templar organizations are at http://www.neotemplar.info/index.ahtml and http://www.neotemplar.info/country_47.ahtml?NKLN=47 (accessed March 30, 2014).

7. ISLAM AND THE CRUSADES: A NINE HUNDRED-YEAR-LONG GRIEVANCE?

Mona Hammad and Edward Peters

The Crusades are almost forgotten in the West but not closer to the lands in which the fighting took place. Anyone who doubts that need only recall the fanfare with which in 1987 Muslims in Egypt, Syria, Jordan and Iraq celebrated the 800th anniversary of the victory that led to the Muslim reconquest of Jerusalem, or consider the leading role Islamic groups have played in mass demonstrations against the war [First Gulf War] in the streets of Cairo, Damascus and Amman. The historical conflict between Islam and the Christian West, in other words, is still a powerful rallying symbol among many Muslims.[1]

When read in conjunction with the title under which they appeared, "Long Memories of the Crusades Overshadow the Future," these words, part of an editorial in the *Sydney Morning Herald* that appeared only hours before coalition forces secured Baghdad in the Second Gulf War, can only be understood to mean one thing: a centuries-long Muslim memory of the crusades fuels today's hostility toward the West on the part of many Muslims. Four years earlier, John Esposito, a professor of International Affairs and Islamic Studies at Georgetown University, had written in a similar vein:

> Few events had a more shattering or long-lasting effect on Muslim-Christian relations than the Crusades. . . . For Muslims, the memory of the Crusades lives on as the clearest example of militant Christianity, an earlier harbinger of the aggression and imperialism of the Christian West, a vivid reminder of Christianity's early hostility toward Islam. If many regard Islam as a religion of the sword, Muslims down through the ages have spoken of the West's Crusader mentality and ambitions. Therefore, for Muslim-Christian relations, it is less a case of what actually happened in the Crusades than how they are remembered.[2]

The question is: Are they correct?

---

1. "Long memories of the Crusades overshadow the future," *Sydney Morning Herald*, April 12, 2003, http://www.smh.com.au/articles/2003/04/11/1049567875704.html (accessed May 2, 2014).

2. John L. Esposito, *The Islamic Threat: Myth or Reality?* 3rd ed. (New York: Oxford University Press, 1999), 37–38. In a like mode, John Trumpbour has written, "The Crusades left a lasting impression on the Muslim world. The brutality of their campaigns, particularly in comparison with the noble reputation of Saladin, continues to color Muslim perceptions of the Christian West." John Trumpbour, "Crusades," in *The Oxford Encyclopedia of the Islamic World*, ed. John L. Esposito et al., 6 vols. (New York: Oxford University Press, 2009), 2:9–14 at 12, col. 2.

The Thesis of This Chapter

The crusades took place in several complex pasts, and their history has an even more complex present. In the West they have been understood and explained in ways that are both favorable and hostile but always as a substantial part of European history and culture. In the Islamic world they have been described largely by selective reliance on the language and ideas of hostile Western historical criticism but not, until recently, as a major component of Islamic history. To complicate matters, at the extremes of both Western and Muslim interpretations of the crusades are popular cultural and political attitudes that remove them entirely from history—in the West by dismissing them (usually linking them to "the Inquisition") as episodes of primitive barbarism and bigotry, and in some parts of the Islamic world by a kind of fictionalized political theology. Here is an example of the latter:

> Soon after 11 September [2001] Osama bin Laden extended the term Crusaders to include Australians in East Timor. His rhetoric distorted history and geography. But it struck a chord with Southeast Asian Islamists. Imam Samudra, the operational chief of the October, 2002 Bali bombings screamed out "Crusaders!" when confronted by his victims' relatives.[3]

There are doctrines at work in such attitudes that have nothing to do with history and everything to do with a contemporary designation of some aspects of the present in terms of a radical ideology that instrumentalizes the past. It has distorted the historical character of "crusades" and related terms more than any earlier definition. This chapter proposes to consider how such a process came about and how a wide range of interpretations of the crusades remains active in both the West and the Islamicate. In this essay the term "the West" designates the broad culture of Europe and the Americas from approximately the sixteenth century on. The less familiar term "Islamicate" designates the broad culture of distinctively Islamic societies, including ethnic differences as well as cultural and political components that extend beyond religion in its narrowest sense.

---

3. Umej Bhatia, "The War on Terrorism: A Crusade?" *Institute of Defence and Strategic Studies Commentaries* 22 (2004): 1, http://www.researchgate.net/publication/38443034_War_on_terrorism__a_crusade (accessed March 26, 2015). See also the next note. The attack took place on October 12, 2002. On Samudra's rationale of the attack, see Muhammad Haniff Hassan, "Imam Samudra's Justification for Bali Bombing," *Studies in Conflict and Terrorism* 30 (2007): 1033–56. Ironically, there is an actual Australian cricket team called the Crusaders. The authors are grateful to Benjamin Z. Kedar, Roger Allen, Konrad Hirschler, and Paul M. Cobb for very helpful advice.

History as Constructed Memory

Every belief system asserts an absolute past, one that is not quite history as that term is academically understood today (although it is usually made to appear to be history) but a past that is a component of the system itself—its constructed memory. Its purpose is to account for the emergence and identity of—and to legitimate—a belief system, to identify the greatest threats to its existence, to celebrate its past triumphs, and to account for its present perceived condition. It is essentially dogma rather than history, or rather dogma asserted to be history. Some aspects of the past seem to serve this purpose more effectively than others and to do so at particular times, usually periods of anxiety or triumphalism. On occasion, a single belief system may entertain conflicting visions of the dogmatic past that reflect not conflicting histories but the polemical instrumentalizing of this past, in order to deal with conflicting ideas in the present. The crusades are part of both the present-day Western and the Islamicate pasts. But they have served very different understandings between them and sometimes very different purposes within each.[4] Within this context, the critical study of history must somehow manage to keep its distance from extreme ideological positions, no matter how difficult that can often be.

Western "Memories" of the Crusades

From the Western academic perspective, the crusades were originally a series of militarized and (for their participants) devotional-penitential campaigns that commenced in the late eleventh century and originally were directed at the recovery and strategic protection of the Holy Land.[5] They occurred during a remote and variously under-

---

4. A number of aspects of dogmatic pasts are considered in recent historical research on collective memory. For the purposes of this essay, the brief discussion in Umej Bhatia, *The Crusades in Modern Muslim Memory*, Rajaratnam School of International Studies Monograph No. 12 (Singapore, 2008), 7–26, 59–65, citing Maurice Halbwachs, *On Collective Memory*, ed. and trans. Lewis A. Coser (Chicago: Chicago University Press, 1992), and Jacques Le Goff, *History and Memory*, trans. Steven Randall and Elizabeth Claman (New York: Columbia University Press, 1992), is largely sufficient. Bhatia discusses public figures and political theorists rather than academics. His appendix, "The Crusades Continue," 89–92, consists of a contemporary and quite distorted version of crusade history from a British Salafist website, *Mission Islam* (http://www.missionislam.com). In addition, for the topic of this essay, see Bernard Lewis, *History Remembered, Recovered, Invented* (New York: Simon and Schuster, 1987).

5. As noted in the Introduction to this book, both the beginning and end of the crusades remain matters of scholarly debate, as does their definition. Our focus here is on the Holy Land crusades and the establishment of crusader states in what was called *Outremer*, the land beyond the sea. These crusades and crusader states are virtually the only aspect of crusade historiography in Arabic today. The most extensive recent survey of this perspective is that of John Tolan, Gilles Veinstein, and Henry Laurens, *Europe and the Islamic World*, trans. Jane Marie Todd, with foreword by John L. Esposito (Princeton, NJ: Princeton University Press, 2013), for the Middle Ages, 12–107.

stood period called the Middle Ages (itself a frequently changing and debated intellectual construct), which has been condemned by some historians as a distant age of barbarism and religious bigotry and celebrated by others as the beginning of a distinct and dynamic European culture.[6] Likewise, as noted in the Introduction, the medieval crusades might be regarded as examples of either greed-inspired, intolerant, and unprovoked aggression of the worst kind, which manifested itself in inhumane acts of cruelty, or else as instances of high idealism, religious or not, and great dedication to an admirable moral cause in the face of religious and political hostility. Thus, the "Western view" of both the Middle Ages and the crusades has often consisted of two quite distinct and polarized perspectives, a fault line within a single belief system.

Whatever one thinks of these questions, it is a mistake to assume that Europeans began to consider Islam only with the launching of the crusades. They had formed an image of Islam centuries before, and that image changed little over time, partly as a result of the crusades, and in many circles it has lasted till the present.[7] More-

---

6. A brief and wise overview is that of Timothy Reuter, "Medieval: Another Tyrannous Construct?" reprinted in Reuter, *Medieval Polities and Modern Mentalities*, ed. Janet L. Nelson (Cambridge: Cambridge University Press, 2006), 19–37. For early European history and its nationalistic future, see Patrick Geary, *The Myth of Nations: The Medieval Origins of Europe* (Princeton, NJ: Princeton University Press, 2002). Most recently, Michael Mitterauer, *Why Europe? The Medieval Origins of its Special Path*, trans. Gerald Chapple (Chicago: University of Chicago Press, 2010).

7. Two brief general surveys are Norman Housley, "The Crusades and Islam," *Medieval Encounters* 13 (2007): 189–208 and Jonathan Phillips, "The Call of the Crusades," *History Today* 59 (2009), http://www.historytoday.com/jonathan-phillips/call-crusades (accessed May 5, 2014). See also J. W. Fück, "Islam as an Historical Problem in European Historiography since 1800," in *Historians of the Middle East*, ed. P. M. Holt and Bernard Lewis (London: Oxford University Press, 1962), and Shirin A. Kahnmohadi, *In Light of Another's Word: European Ethnography in the Middle Ages* (Philadelphia: University of Pennsylvania Press, 2013). One of the best shorter studies remains that of Jonathan Riley-Smith, "Islam and the Crusades in History and Imagination, 8 November 1898–11 September 2001," *Crusades* 2 (2003): 151–67. Riley-Smith has expanded his earlier studies in *The Crusades, Christianity, and Islam* (New York: Columbia University Press, 2008). For early Christian attitudes, see Albert Hourani, *Islam in European Thought* (Cambridge: Cambridge University Press, 1991); Angeliki Laiou and Roy Parviz Mottahedeh, eds., *The Crusades from the Perspective of Byzantium and the Muslim World* (Washington, D.C.: Dumbarton Oaks, 2001); John V. Tolan, *Saracens: Islam in the Medieval European Imagination* (New York: Columbia University Press, 2002); and Jean Flori, *L'Islam et la fin des temps: L'Interprétation prophétique des invasions musulmanes dans la chrétienté médiévale* [Islam and End Times: Prophetic Interpretations of the Muslim Invasions in Medieval Christendom] (Paris: Seuil, 2007). For a more recent work, see Jacob Lassner, *Jews, Christians, and the Abode of Islam: Modern Scholarship and Medieval Realities* (Chicago: University of Chicago Press, 2012), particularly on the relatively humble status of history in the Muslim organization of knowledge. General histories in the Muslim world largely consisted of chronicles of cities and regions, histories of dynasties within regions, personal memoirs, and biographies of great Muslim (usually Arab) heroes. Where any of these touched on historical crusades, the crusades occupied a peripheral place. For Islam itself, see James Howard-Johnston, *Witnesses to a World Crisis: Historians and Histories of the Middle East in the Seventh Century* (Oxford, Oxford University Press, 2012). Nor did criticism of crusades begin only in the sixteenth century. See Elizabeth Siberry, *Criticism of*

over, by the end of the eighteenth century in Europe, the crusades had long since been fought, lost, and largely forgotten, except for the cynicism and scorn heaped upon their memory and motives by both Protestant and some Roman Catholic religious critics and skeptical Enlightenment philosophical historians such as Hume and Gibbon, who roundly condemned them and those who had launched them. Enlightenment skepticism and secular anticrusade polemic were succeeded in the nineteenth century by different and more crusade-favorable myths.

Romantic idealism, nationalism, and a Catholic revival all rejected Enlightenment criticism and appropriated crusade history as an essential and admirable component of European identity and history. Regardless of these revisionist movements, the Enlightenment view that the crusades had been launched out of financial and territorial greed rather than from religious motives and were marked by savagery and brutality survived among a significant body of nineteenth-century skeptics who attributed such impulses and qualities to medieval Europeans in general.[8] But such polarized opinions have been considerably reduced in the twentieth-century West in the corridors of serious scholarship, even though many of these notions survive in the tendentiousness of uninformed journalism, much confessional and political discourse of a similar kind, lazy schoolbooks, political thriller novels, pseudoethical movies, and therefore much popular opinion, often reflected in social media.[9] In this sense,

Crusading, 1095–1274 (Oxford: Oxford University Press, 1985); Christopher Tyerman, *The Debate on the Crusades* (Manchester and New York: Manchester University Press, 2011), 7–36. The entire problem (and the theme of this book) is the subject of a perceptive essay by Paul Crawford, "Four Myths about the Crusades," *The Intercollegiate Review* 46 (2011): 13–22.

8. See James M. Muldoon, "Mad Men on Crusade: Religious Madness and the Origins of the First Crusade" and Corliss Slack, "The Quest for Gain: Were the First Crusaders Proto-Colonists?" in this book.

9. In September and November 2001, one current (George W. Bush) and one former (William J. Clinton) American president made public statements about crusades in the wake of the events of September 11th. Their statements, different as they were, revealed that neither president had the vaguest idea of what the historical crusades had been. Clinton's consisted of a postmodern anachronism, for a correction of which see Benjamin Z. Kedar, "The Jerusalem Massacre of July 1099 in the Western Historiography of the Crusades," *Crusades* 3 (2004): 15–75 and Jay Carter Rubenstein, "Cannibals and Crusaders," *French Historical Studies* 31 (2008): 525–52. Bush's use of the term appeared to be based on a general secularized idea of a moral conflict, although in the months following, the presidents of both France and Germany criticized Bush for interpreting the Middle East in an evangelical, Christian, apocalyptic context, for which see Garry Wills, "With God on His Side," *New York Times Magazine*, March 30, 2003, http://www.nytimes.com/2003/03/30/magazine/30THEOCRACY.html (accessed May 5, 2014). On June 2, 1944 Dwight Eisenhower told allied troops just before the Normandy invasion that they were engaged on "a great Crusade," and he later titled his memoirs of World War II *Crusade in Europe*, although it is doubtful that Eisenhower knew much about what the crusades had been. His usage reflected a mid-twentieth-century secular understanding. The first U.S. government war film was titled *Pershing's Crusaders* (1918), https://www.youtube.com/watch?v=aKq2n3qazWI (accessed March 27, 2015) and may have influenced Eisenhower's usage. Coincidentally, the British Department of Information film on World War I *The New Crusaders: With the British Forces on the Palestinian Front*, was released in March of the same year.

common Western historical notions of crusades are no more based on the results of scholarly research than are most of those of the Islamicate.

Since the sixteenth century the historical sources of the crusades have slowly been discovered, retrieved, edited, printed, critically interpreted, translated into modern vernacular languages, and studied in the West according to the principles of an increasingly rigorous historical scholarship created by much learned debate and critical polemic. Crusade studies in the West, largely but not exclusively in the United Kingdom and the United States, are considered an essential part of medieval studies and are supported by many colleges and universities, extensive library collections, a number of regional research centers, a professional inter-national scholarly association, the Society for the Study of the Crusades and the Latin East (SSCLE), which holds quadrennial international conferences and pub-lishes *Crusades*, since 2003 the journal of that society, and the resources of the Internet, such as JSTOR.

Other professional associations, such as the Medieval Academy of America, also support crusade studies, and annual international scholarly conferences usually have sessions devoted to crusade research. Both general historical and specialized scholarly journals also accommodate crusade studies. Put briefly, the modern trans-formation of crusade studies in the West has been conducted without the West's having any longer a religious or cultural stake in their nature or outcome. But only relatively recently have most crusade scholars paid attention to Islamicate literature and thought.[10]

---

10. On the development of a critical historical method for crusade history and its relation to disin-terested historical research generally, see Tyerman, *Debate*, 125–54, 182–215. Until the mid-nine-teenth century the utter lack of Western interest in Islamic sources for the crusades or most other historical issues is indicated in the discussion of crusade sources and crusade histories in Heinrich von Sybel's 1841 study of the subject, parts of which, with material from his Munich lectures of 1858 are conveniently available in Heinrich von Sybel, *The History and Literature of the Crusades*, trans. Lady Duff Gordon (London, 1861; 2nd ed. 1881; rpt. 1905), especially his discussion of the sources on 239–72, where he notes "Oriental sources" twice, once in an instance when they had not been used and then in a discussion of Friedrich Wilken's history, *Geschichte der Kreuzzüge nach morgenländischen und abendländischen Berichten* [History of the Crusades according to Eastern and Western Accounts], 7 vols. (Leipzig, 1807–1832), which did use "Oriental authorities with good results," but without specifying what these were, and nothing more. On Wilken's great history, see Tyerman, *Debate*, 127–40. Between 1841 and 1906, the great French publishing project *Recueil des Historiens des Croisades* [Collection of Crusade Historians] published sixteen folio volumes of crusade sources in Latin, Greek, Armenian, and Arabic. The sources in Arabic were unreliably edited and little used by Western historians. On the history of the development of Western scholarship on Arabic sources and Islam, see Robert Irwin, *Dangerous Knowledge: Orientalism and Its Discontents* (Woodstock, NY: Overlook Press, 2006) and the earlier study by Maxime Rodinson, "The Western Image and Western Studies of Islam," in *The Legacy of Islam*, 2nd ed., ed. Joseph Schacht and Clifford Edmund Bosworth (Oxford: Oxford University Press, 1979).

Early Islamic Views of the Crusades

In the Islamicate itself, whose religious, geographical, ethnic, and historical range now may be said to extend from Morocco to China, Indonesia, and the Philippines, as well as more recently to Muslim communities in the Americas and Western Europe, interest in the crusades has been relatively recent and of different kinds. Before the late nineteenth century, when Muslim thinkers considered Europe at all they rarely paid much attention to the crusades, focusing largely on various regions of the *Dar al-Islam*—or Abode of Islam—and the conventional topics of Arabic historical writing.[11]

From the many local chronicle accounts of crusade history written in Arabic from the twelfth to the sixteenth centuries, the crusades, taken together, consisted of random momentary and largely local episodes in what was otherwise a much longer, larger, and until the early twentieth century, triumphalist history.[12] The European "Franks" (*Firanj, Faranj,* or *Ifranj*) had, after all, been barbarians and infidels who had managed to wrest control of parts of Syria and Palestine and to invade Egypt several times (largely because of divided and rival Muslim powers, as Arabic chroniclers regularly attested). They had been eventually and inevitably defeated in the Levant by Muslim forces led by such pious leaders as Nur ad-Din, Saladin, and Baybars, and the infidels had gone away.[13] The departure of the European Christians from the Holy Land seemed to have justified the Muslim principle of *al-sabr*, patience in the face of temporarily irresistible opposition and confidence in eventual success (Qur'an, Surah 12 Yusuf 17–18).

Muslim observers did not originally regard the crusades as something separate and distinct from other conflicts with the Franks, nor did they initially single out the crusaders from the long series of infidel enemies whom they fought from time to time. The chroniclers report in detail the smallest skirmishes between Muslims and Frankish troops, but they have little to say about the internal affairs of the Frankish states in the Levant and even less about their lands in Western Europe. With one or two minor exceptions, Muslim historians made no attempt to trace the invaders back to

---

11. Bernard Lewis, *The Muslim Discovery of Europe* (New York: W.W. Norton, 1982); Nabil I. Matar, *Europe through Arab Eyes, 1578–1727* (New York: Columbia University Press, 2009), and above, note 7. A parallel instance is the Islamic world's reading of Darwin: Marwa Elshakry, *Reading Darwin in Arabic, 1860–1950* (Chicago: University of Chicago Press, 2013).

12. The most thorough recent study is Carole Hillenbrand, *The Crusades: Islamic Perspectives* (New York: Routledge, 2000). See also Paul M. Cobb, *The Race for Paradise: An Islamic History of the Crusades* (New York: Oxford University Press, 2014). On the forms of genres in Arabic literature, see Konrad Hirschler, *The Written Word in the Medieval Arabic Lands* (Edinburgh: Edinburgh University Press, 2012).

13. Nur ad-Din and Baybars were Turks, and Saladin was a Kurd. Subsequent Arabic historiography has tended to subordinate their ethnicity to either their Muslim faith or a process of implicit Arabization. There is little historiography in Arabic on the Christian conquests in Iberia and Sicily save for a number of elegiac poems.

their countries of origin or to the mighty yet invisible movement that had launched them across the Mediterranean.[14]

Medieval Arab historians also seldom distinguished between different ethnic groups of crusaders (much as Western Christians used the name "Saracens" [Latin *saraceni*] for all Muslim peoples). They called the Europeans *Firanj*, "Franks," or *Rum*, "Romans," the Arabic term for the Byzantine Greeks, already found in earlier Arabic sources. Many authors initially regarded the invasion of the Franks merely as a variant of recurrent Byzantine assaults. Most twelfth- and thirteenth-century Arab authors do not show particular hatred or animosity, religious or otherwise, toward the crusaders, although hostile epithets, such as "May God curse them" (*la'anahumallah*) are often used conventionally after mentioning the Franks. As Joseph Drory notes, "The predominant attitude is one of grief over the casualties and sorrow for the damages inflicted by the Franks, as by any other invaders, on human beings, property or religious monuments." The crusaders' conquests of Islamic territories, including Jerusalem, were described much like natural disasters and "were not regarded as national traumas, nor as major threats against which all Muslims should defend themselves."[15]

In any case, the memory of crusades paled before the disaster of the Mongol invasions of the thirteenth century and their murder of the last Abbasid caliph. The immense

---

14. One exception was the Damascus scholar Ali ibn Tahir al-Sulami (1039–1106), whose *Kitab al-jihad* argued that the events of 1095–1099 were part of a comprehensive Christian effort (which he termed a jihad) against the Muslims. Paul E. Chevedden, "The Islamic View and the Christian View of the Crusades: A New Synthesis," *History* 93 (2008): 181–200, has made a case for al-Sulami's substantial influence on later Arab historiography, but the subject remains open to investigation, since the exclusively religious understanding of jihad in a crusade context did not emerge until the second half of the twelfth century. Roy Parviz Mottahedeh and Ridwan al-Sayyid, "The Idea of Jihad in Islam before the Crusades," in *The Crusades*, ed. Laiou and Mottahedeh, 23–29. The literature on jihad is endless. See Gilles Kepel, Jihad: *The Trail of Political Islam* (London: I. B. Tauris, 2002) and Michael Bonner, *Jihad in Islamic History: Doctrines and Practice* (Princeton, NJ: Princeton University Press, 2006). Important early studies and Arabic texts in translation are in Emmanuel Sivan, *L'Islam et la croisade* (Paris: Libraire d'amerique et d'orient, 1968) and Francesco Gabrieli, *Arab Historians of the Crusades* (Berkeley: University of California Press, 1969) and more recently Joseph Drory, "Early Muslim Reflections on the Crusaders," *Jerusalem Studies in Arabic and Islam* 25 (2001): 92–101 and Bernard Lewis, "The Use by Muslim Historians of Non-Muslim Sources," in *Historians of the Middle East*, ed. Holt and Lewis; see also Emmanuel Sivan, "Modern Arabic Historiography of the Crusades," in Emmanuel Sivan, *Interpretations of Islam: Past and Present* (Princeton, NJ; Darwin Press, 1985), 1–43; Françoise Micheau, "Les Croisades vues par les historiens arabes d'hier et d'aujourd'hui," [The Crusades as Seen by Arab Historians in the Past and Present], *Res Orientales* 6 (1994); *Itinéraires d'Orient. Hommage à Claude Cahen*, 169–185; Franco Cardini, *Europe and Islam* (Oxford: Blackwell, 2001); Edward Peters, "The *Firanj* Are Coming—Again," *Orbis* (winter 2004): 3–17; Cobb, *Race*, passim; Jean Flori, *Guerre sainte, jihad, croisade: Violence et religion dans le christianisme et l' islam* [Holy War, Jihad and Crusade: Violence and Religion in Christendom and Islam] (Paris: Seuil, 2004), reprinted ed. with a new preface and an introduction.

15. Drory, "Reflections," 94; John M. Chamberlin V, *Imagining Defeat: An Arabic Historiography of the Crusades* (Monterey, CA: Ft. Belvoir Naval Postgraduate School, 2007), 9–19.

destruction they caused, their sacking of Baghdad in 1258, and their defeat in 1260 by the Turkish Mamluks of Egypt far outshone the crusaders' capture of Jerusalem and the Mamluk capture of Acre in 1291 and remained sufficiently compelling that the Palestinian newspaper *Al-Quds* compared the fall of Baghdad in April 2003 to its conquest by the Mongols, the greatest imaginable historical disaster for Islam.[16]

By the fourteenth century the Islamic world was placed squarely on course for the successive later triumphs of the Mamluks and then the Safavids in Persia and the Ottoman Empire from the fourteenth century to the end of the seventeenth. The crusades receded into a vast and now largely Ottoman-dominated and -defined past.[17] They reemerged in the wake of European colonial policies and the attempts to create national governments in the territorial remains of the now-dissolved Ottoman Empire after 1919. Conflicting pasts within belief systems and conflicting pasts between belief systems constitute the background for the emergence of Arabic modernity, a period in which various pasts played new and ultimately more dangerous roles.

A Nineteenth-Century Turning Point: European Nationalism, Colonialism, and the Crusades

As European attitudes toward and understanding of the crusades (and often the Middle Ages with them) shifted from the religious criticism and reciprocal polemic of the several confessional sides and political interests of the Reformation to the more secular and largely negative criticism of the Enlightenment, and finally toward Romantic nationalism and the resurgent historical polemics between Catholicism and Protestantism, other political circumstances gave a new historical prominence to

---

16. "A Nation at War: Global Viewpoints; Commentary Divided on Fall of Baghdad," http://www.nytimes.com/2003/04/13/world/a-nation-at-war-global-viewpoints-commentary-divided-on-fall-of-baghdad.html (accessed May 4, 2014). For the fall of Acre, see Donald P. Little, "The Fall of 'Akkā in 690/1291: The Muslim Version," in *Studies in Islamic History and Civilization in Honour of Professor David Ayalon*, ed. M. Sharon (Jerusalem: Cana Ltd., 1986), 159–81.

17. Hillenbrand, *Islamic Perspectives*; Bhatia, *Modern Muslim Memory*. The scholarly study of modern Arabic political thought continues especially in the work of Emmanuel Sivan, *Radical Islam: Medieval Theology and Modern Politics* (New Haven, CT: Yale University Press, 1990), *Mythes politiques arabes* (Paris: Fayard, 1995), "Muslim Representations of the Crusades," in *Verso Gerusalemme: Il convengo internazionale nel IX centenario della 1 croiciata (1099–1999) (Bari, 11–13 gennaio 1999)* (Naples: M. Congedo, 1999), 125–33, and his essays collected in his *Interpretations of Islam: Past and Present* (Princeton, NJ: Darwin Press, 1985); Jonathan Riley-Smith, *The Crusades, Christianity, and Islam*, chapter 4, "Crusading and Islam," and now the perceptive and important study by Abbès Zouache, "Écrire l'histoire des croisades, aujourd'hui, en Orient et Occident," [Writing the History of the Crusades Today in the East and West] in *Construire la Méditerranée, penser les transferts culturelles. Aspects historiographiques et perspectives de recherche*, ed. Rania Abdellatif, Yassir Benhima, Daniel König, Elisabeth Ruchaud, Ateliers des Deutschen Historischen Instituts Paris, Vol. 8 (Munich, Germany: Oldenbourg Verlag, 2012), 121–47, with substantial further bibliography.

the crusades.[18] Whereas until the early nineteenth century, crusades had been largely considered by Western scholars as pan-European and Catholic, in the course of the nineteenth century they came to be considered as part of national histories (and contemporary national identities with their own dogmatic pasts) and often, but not exclusively, as religious phenomena.

With the immensely popular crusade histories by the French journalist and royalist propagandist Joseph-François Michaud (1767–1839) and the French invasion of Algeria in 1830, followed by the later French and British assertions of the right to protect Christians in the Levant (and the considerable impact upon local government and law in the exercise of that right), French diplomacy in the Muslim Middle Eastern soon took on a religious dimension that colored French (and later British and German) colonialism for the rest of the century.[19] Michaud's work helped inspire

---

18. Tyerman, *Debate*, 37–135. Benedict R. Anderson, *Imagined Communities: Reflections on the Origin and Spread of Nationalism* (London: Verso, 1983; rev. ed. London, 2006); Eric J. Hobsbawm, *Nations and Nationalism since 1780: Programme, Myth, Reality* (Cambridge: Cambridge University Press, 1990); Joep Leerssen, *National Thought in Europe: A Cultural History* (Amsterdam: Amsterdam University Press, 2006). On nineteenth-century nationalism in France and the resuscitated idea of crusade in the service of empire, see Ronni Ellenblum, *Crusader Castles and Modern Histories* (Cambridge: Cambridge University Press, 2007), chapter 2, and Geary, *The Myth of Nations*.

19. Joseph F. Michaud, *Histoire des croisades* [History of the Crusades], 6 vols. (Paris, 1812–1822), 7th ed. by J. L. A. Huillard-Bréholles, 4 vols. (Paris, 1849). Michaud also published a four-volume collection of original sources in French translation, *Bibliothèque des croisades* [Crusade Library] (1829), the correspondence of his journey to the Middle East in seven volumes (1833–1835), and a posthumous and patriotic brief account for young people. Michaud was influenced by the royalist, conservative, and strongly Catholic Chateaubriand, whose *La Génie du christianisme* [The Genius of Christianity] had appeared in 1802. Chateaubriand had also visited the Holy Land and been made a knight of the Holy Sepulcher, an honorific title much coveted in the nineteenth century. See Tyerman, *Debate*, 101–21, 141–52. Ironically, Michaud's seat 29 in the French Academy has been held since 2011 by the Lebanese-born Christian Francophone journalist and author of several books on crusades and the modern Middle East, Amin Maalouf, whose study *The Crusades through Arab Eyes* (London: Al Saqi Books, 1984) is one of the earliest attempts to address the subject evenhandedly. The nineteenth-century European nationalist search for historical heroes often turned up crusaders. In France, the crusader king and later saint Louis IX served this purpose (Adam Knobler, "Saint Louis and French Political Culture," in *Medievalism in Europe II*, ed. Leslie J. Workman and Kathleen Verduin, Studies in Medievalism VIII [Cambridge, UK: D. S. Brewer, 1996], 156–74), as did Godefroid de Bouillon (Godfrey of Bouillon) in nineteenth-century Belgium. The versatile figure of Frederick Barbarossa often served a comparable purpose in Germany, particularly with the history by Hans Prutz, *Kaiser Friedrich I*, 3 vols. (Danzig, 1871–1874). Prutz (1843–1929) succeeded Wilken as the leading German historian of crusades, especially with his work on the Templars and his *Kulturgeschichte der Kreuzzüge* [A Cultural History of the Crusades] (Berlin, 1883). In England, the case of Richard the Lionheart is an example. See John Gillingham, "Some Legends of Richard the Lionheart: Their Development and Their Influence," in *Richard Coeur de Lion in History and Myth*, ed. Janet L. Nelson (London: Centre for Late Antique and Medieval Studies, King's College, 1992), 52–69. Richard is commemorated in the equestrian statue at Westminster by Carlo Marochetti installed in 1860. Godfrey of Bouillion was commemorated in the twelfth-century *Liber Floridus* and in the large and heroic

Louis-Philippe's decision in 1843 to convert the abandoned palace at Versailles into a grand museum of French history, including the Salles des Croisades, five large rooms of commissioned historical paintings and coats of arms (some of them authentic) of crusading families.[20]

In addition, the development of source criticism and source publication in the nineteenth century soon outstripped even the herculean labors of Michaud. Published between 1841 and 1906, the *Receuil des historiens des Croisades* (Collection of the Historians of the Crusades), a massive collection of thousands of documents in Latin, Greek, Arabic, Armenian, and Old French relating to the crusades, was the most ambitious of these. The private wealth and the forty thousand-volume private library of Comte Paul Riant (1836–1888) enabled him to establish the Société de l'Orient Latin (Society of the Latin East) in 1875, which printed two volumes of *Archives de l'Orient Latin* between 1881 and 1884, and then the twelve-volume *Revue de l'Orient Latin* between 1893 and 1911. That is, in France alone a veritable flood of scholarly and popular crusade materials appeared in print and often, as elsewhere, in modern vernacular translation and in a broad range of media, both scholarly and popular. All of this was occurring while France extended its colonial presence into North Africa, Syria, and Lebanon, asserting its right to protect local Christians and contending with British and Russian ambitions to do the same, the latter on behalf of Orthodox Christians.

Although the precise relation between any of these individual scholars and scholarly projects and French colonial policy has yet to be studied in detail, it is clear that the imagery and ideas of the crusades entered nineteenth-century European consciousness on a number of levels and in dramatic and inescapable ways.[21] Today, however, Western historians have largely ended the discussion as far as both colonialism and economic advantage in the modern world might in any sense echo or continue

---

equestrian statue made in 1848 by Louis-Eugène Simonis, now on the Place Royale in Brussels. For Muslim memory, besides the works cited below, see Umej Bhatia (note 4, above) and Matar, *Europe through Arab Eyes*. In 1993 a very large equestrian statue of Saladin, accompanied by representatives of simple Muslim faith and popular resistance to crusaders (and two prominent defeated crusaders at Hattin), made by Abdallah al-Sayed and located in front of the citadel, was dedicated in Damascus. The iconography of this group indicates the historical argument that successful Muslim resistance to the Franks was accomplished by popular military enthusiasm and the simple Muslim faith of Sufism.

20. Francis Haskell, *History and Its Images: Art and the Interpretation of the Past* (New Haven, CT: Yale University Press, 1993), 281–82; Siberry, *The New Crusaders*, 51–53, 208–11; Giles Constable, "Medieval Charters as Sources for the History of the Crusades," revised in *Crusaders and Crusading in the Twelfth Century*, 93–116.

21. The point has been made by Christopher de Bellaigue, "Where Edward Said Was Wrong [review of Robert Irwin, "Dangerous Knowledge: Orientalism and Its Discontents"]," *Times Literary Supplement*, May 17, 2006, and above, note 7. One exception is Kim Munholland, "Michaud's *History of the Crusades* and the French Crusade in Algeria under Louis-Philippe," in *The Popularization of Images: Visual Culture under the July Monarchy*, ed. Petra ten-Doeschate Chu and Gabriel P. Weisberg (Princeton, NJ: Princeton University Press, 1994), 144–65.

the crusades, rather than their being wholly original nineteenth-century enterprises.[22] But the extent to which Arab historians have used hostile Western secularist criticism of the crusades suggests that they have a bearing on the contemporary Islamicate's understanding of its crusade past.

A Nineteenth-Century Turning Point: The Renaissance of Arabic Literature

In the course of the nineteenth century, European cultural influence helped institute the *Nahda*, or renaissance, of Arabic literature. Arabic history, along with nearly all other literature, science, and technology, gradually and selectively adopted Western topics and methods and was strongly influenced by what were initially hostile Western norms and points of view. This influence and adaptation occurred at different rates in different parts of the Arabic world and among different social strata. One of the most productive areas in this respect was Maronite Christian Syria. Until the mid-nineteenth century there had been no specific term in Arabic for the crusades. The Arabic phrase for the crusades, *al-hurub al-salibiyyah* (Wars of the Cross), was coined by Maronite Christian Arab translators of French crusade histories, notably in 1865 in a work attributed to an otherwise unidentified M. Monrond, and probably translated by the Melkite patriarch of Jerusalem, Maximos III Mazloum.[23] From that point, crusades became an object of distinct and separate interpretation in the Arabic-speaking world. Furthermore, European diplomacy enhanced both the acceptance and rejection of European ideas in the Islamicate.

22. James M. Powell, "Crusading: 1099–1999" reprinted in Powell, *The Crusades, the Kingdom of Sicily, and the Mediterranean* (Aldershot, UK: Ashgate, 2007), I.

23. M. Monrond, *Tarikh al-hurub al-muqaddasa fi l'Mashriq al-mad`uwa Harb al-Salih* [A History of the Holy Wars in the East, Otherwise Called the Wars of the Cross] (Jerusalem, 1865). The patriarch himself is quite plausibly suggested as the translator by Chamberlin in *Imagining Defeat*, 21–32, and the French author identified as the popular nineteenth-century writer Maxime de Montrond. Chamberlin's discussion of Franco-Maronite relations in this context is highly informative. There is a list of subsequent histories written in Arabic that generally follow the hostile Western model of crusade criticism in Chevedden, "The Islamic View and the Christian View of the Crusades," 183, note 5 and Bhatia, *Crusades in Modern Muslim Memory*. The most recent study of this Arabic translation of Montrond's French original *La Guerre saintes d'Outre Mer, ou tableau des croisades retracé d'apres les chroniques contemporaines* [The Holy Wars of *Outremer*, or a Picture of the Crusades drawn from Contemporary Chronicles] (1840) is Iris Shagir and Nitzan Amitai-Preiss, "Michaud, Montrond, Mazloum and the First History of the Crusades in Arabic," *Al-Masaq: Islam and the Medieval Mediterranean* 24, no. 3 (2012): 309–12, http://dx.doi.org/10.1080/09503110.2012.72 7660 (accessed August 18, 2014).

The End of a Century and New Influences on the Islamic Vision of the Crusades

At the end of the century new circumstances brought the crusading past into even greater prominence. The years 1898–1899 signaled a significant turn in the Islamicate's and West's understanding of the historical nature of the crusades. In 1898 on a grand tour of the Middle East, Kaiser Wilhelm II, himself a cultural and diplomatic product of one particular strand of European thought on the subject, costumed as an elegant, imperial pilgrim, triumphantly entered Jerusalem on a white horse through a specially made gate in the city wall and visited the holy places. In the Syrian city of Damascus, he paid public tribute to the memory of Saladin, commissioning a restoration of Saladin's tomb and a memorial wreath to be placed upon it, a key moment in the process by which the memory of the Kurd Saladin was revived and revised as that of an Arab and Muslim hero.[24] The kaiser's visit was part of a longer-range German effort to expand its diplomatic influence and to thwart Anglo-French interests in the Middle East and Asia. It can also be seen to serve as a landmark in the process by which German diplomatic and cultural influence played a prominent but inconsistent role in the Islamic world before, during, and after World War I.[25]

---

24. On the Kaiser's visit and its attendant rituals as well as the formation of the Saladin legend, see Anne-Marie Eddé, *Saladin*, trans. Jane Marie Todd (Cambridge, MA: Belknap Press, 2011), especially 1–10, 492–502; Werner Ende, "Wer ist ein Glaubensheld, wer ist ein Ketzer? Konkurrierende Geschichtsbilder in der modernen Literatur islamischer Länder" [Who Is a Believer, Who Is a Heretic? Concurrent Historical Pictures in Modern Islamic Lands] *Die Welt des Islams* [The World of Islam] new series 23–24 (1984): 70–94; Eitan Bar-Yosef, "The Last Crusade? British Propaganda and the Palestine Campaign, 1917–1918," *Journal of Contemporary History* 36 (2001): 87–109 (revised and expanded version in Bar-Yosef, *The Holy Land in English Culture, 1799–1917: Palestine and the Question of Orientalism* [Oxford: Clarendon Press, 2005], 247–94); Hillenbrand, *Islamic Perspectives*, 592–600; Elizabeth Siberry, *The New Crusaders: Images of the Crusades in the Nineteenth and Twentieth Centuries* (Aldershot, UK: Ashgate, 2000), and above, note 15. For the broad historiographical background, see Christopher Tyerman, *The Invention of the Crusades* (Toronto, Canada: University of Toronto Press, 1998), 90–126; Tyerman, *Debate*, passim; Giles Constable, "The Historiography of the Crusades," revised in Constable, *Crusaders and Crusading in the Twelfth Century*, (Farnham, UK: Ashgate, 2008), 3–43. For an articulate contrary voice that criticizes the notion that Western admiration for Saladin was a significant influence on Arabs and Muslims, see Diana Abouali, "Saladin's Legacy in the Middle East before the Nineteenth Century," *Crusades* 10 (2011): 175–85.

25. The nature and extent of such influence is a much disputed subject, dating back at least to the polemical study by the great Dutch Arabist Christiaan Snouck Hurgronje, *The Holy War "Made in Germany"* (New York: G. P. Putnam's, 1915) and novels like John Buchan's politically fanciful propaganda piece *Greenmantle* (1916). On the latter genre, see Reeva Spector Simon, *Spies and Holy Wars: The Middle East in Twentieth-Century Crime Fiction* (Austin: University of Texas Press, 2010), with additional examples in Robert Irwin's review, "Delhi Dreadful," *Times Literary Supplement*, May 19, 26, 2011, 3–4. The important question of German influence on Arab attitudes toward Jews in the nineteenth and twentieth centuries has been widely debated. One of the clearest and least polemical studies is that of Gilbert Achcar, *The Arabs and the Holocaust: The Arab-Israeli War*

A mural in Baghdad depicting Saddam Hussein in the company of two other conquerors from Iraq, the Babylonian emperor Nebuchadnezzer and Saladin. Hussein also emphasized that both he and Saladin were natives of the city of Tikrit. Photo source: Wikimedia.

In 1899 two important historical works were published by Muslim scholars, both of which dealt with the crusades and represented different historical traditions. Syed Ameer Ali, a learned Shi'a jurist in British India, published *A Short History of the Saracens*, which contained a brief account of the crusades derived from heavily critical European accounts by Gibbon, Mills, Michaud, and other writers to his own day.[26] The second work, the first specifically dealing with the crusades to be written in Arabic and to use both Arabic sources and Western scholarship, was that of the Egyptian writer Sayyid Ali al-Hariri, *Kitab al-akhbar fi al-hurub al salibiyyah* (The Great Book of the Wars of the Cross). In his history, Al-Hariri praised the Ottoman caliph and sultan Abdulhamid II (r. 1876–1909): "The sovereigns of Europe nowadays attack our Sublime Empire in a manner bearing a great resemblance to the deeds of those people [the crusaders] in bygone times. Our most glorious sultan, Abdulhamid II, has

---

of Narratives, trans. G. M. Goshgarian (New York: Metropolitan Books, 2010). The great virtue of Achcar's work is its long chronological range (from 1933 to the present) and his ability to consider the differences among several distinct varieties of Arab and Muslim thought on the subject and the varying significance of recent Jewish history in each, particularly the case of Muhammad Amin al-Husseini, the Grand Mufti of Jerusalem (131–59). For the volume and character of Nazi-Arabic propaganda, see Jeffrey Herf, *Nazi Propaganda for the Arab World* (New Haven, CT: Yale University Press, 2009). Herf does not mention the crusades in this propaganda war until the postwar polemics of the Muslim Brotherhood and al-Qutb, 258. Further, see Meir Litvak and Esther Webman, *From Empathy to Denial: Arab Responses to the Holocaust* (New York: Columbia University Press, 2009).

26. Syed Ameer Ali, *A Short History of the Saracens* (London: Macmillan, 1900 [1899]), 320 ff., bibliography 629–30.

rightly remarked that Europe is now carrying out a crusade against us in the form of a political campaign."[27]

As Al-Hariri indicates, the Arabic term for crusade (and crusaders, *as-salibyyu,* "followers of the cross") and its purpose in characterizing the policies of contemporary European powers in the Eastern Mediterranean and elsewhere was circulating in the Ottoman world well before 1898, and its use was by no means restricted to Abdulhamid II. Virtually every major power in Abdulhamid's world used the term "crusade" in various senses in regard to its own diplomatic, colonizing, and military enterprises. These included France, Spain (where, ironically, Abdulhamid II had been made a knight of the Golden Fleece in 1880), Greece (in the *Megale Idea,* or "Grand Idea" of Eleftherios Venizelos and other pan-Hellenic nationalists, to recreate the Byzantine Empire with its Christian capital at Constantinople), Russia (where the word *krestosonets,* "crossbearer," formerly designating a liturgical participant or a pilgrim, now acquired the Western meaning of religious combatant), Britain, Bulgaria, and even Ethiopia.[28] To add yet another example, on April 5, 1848, General Giovanni Durando, commanding a papal army sent north to prevent an Austrian invasion of the Papal States, issued a proclamation stating that his force constituted a crusade against foreigners. Pope Pius IX, however, was not pleased with the gesture that called for a papal crusade against Austria, a Catholic nation, and the designation was quietly dropped.

That Abdulhamid II used the term defensively about the Ottoman Empire should come as no surprise. He was simply echoing contemporary geopolitical rhetoric that had acquired in the mid to late nineteenth century a distinct, but not predominantly religious tone and in that semantic fog was applying it defensively to the Ottoman Empire. Even though Abdulhamid II had also been advised by the widely traveled Persian journalist and publicist of pan-Islamism Sayyid Jemal-ad-Din al-Afghani (1836–1897) to the effect that representing himself as caliph and the empire as an

---

27. Cairo, 1899. There is a discussion and partial translation in Chamberlin, *Imagining Defeat,* 28–31. An abbreviated Turkish translation of Michaud's *Histoire des Croisades* had appeared around 1870, and it elicited a history of Saladin and other earlier heroes now appropriated by the Ottomans; the *Evraq-I perishan* [Scattered Leaves] by the young Ottoman intellectual Namik Kemal. Kemal was highly critical of Michaud's hostile characterization of Saladin and helped inaugurate the long career of Saladin as an Ottoman and later a modern Arab and Muslim hero. For late Ottoman historiography generally, see Ercüment Kuran, "Ottoman Historiography of the Tanzimat Period" in *Historians of the Middle East,* ed. Holt and Lewis, 421–29. Most Muslim scholarship on the subject, however, has been written in Arabic.

28. Adam Knobler, "Holy Wars, Empires, and the Portability of the Past: The Modern Uses of Medieval Crusades," *Comparative Studies in Society and History* 48 (2006): 293–325, for France, see 295–97. On the then-contemporary circulation of the terms and their meaning in France, there is an exhaustive discussion in Ellenblum, *Crusader Castles and Modern Histories,* chapters 1–3; Munholland, "Michaud's *History*"; and William E. Watson, *Tricolor and Crescent: France and the Islamic World* (Westport, CT: Praeger, 2003).

Islamic power would garner greater support among Muslims worldwide, the advice was not always accepted.[29] Nor should it be surprising that when, on November 11, 1914, Abdulhamid's brother and successor, Mehmed V (r. 1909–1918), proclaimed a political jihad as the Ottoman Empire entered World War I as an ally of Germany, there was relatively little Muslim response.[30]

The Allies' Dismemberment of the Ottoman Empire

The circulation of terms and images of crusading as various groups of nineteenth-century European thinkers understood and used them can easily be seen, not only in romantic, nationalist, and colonialist vocabularies and Muslim responses to them but also in diplomacy since the Crimean War, whose own strongly religious dimension (although Britain and France were allied with the Ottoman Empire against Russia)

---

29. Nikki R. Keddie, "The Pan-Islamic Appeal: Afghani and Abdulhamid II," *Middle Eastern Studies* 3 (1966): 46–67; Keddie, *Sayyid Jamal ad-Din "al-Afghani": A Political Biography* (Berkeley, University of California Press, 1972); Keddie, *An Islamic Response to Imperialism: The Political and Religious Writings of Sayyid Jamal ad-Din "al-Afghani"* (Berkeley: University of California Press, 2003). See also Albert Hourani, *Arabic Thought in the Liberal Age, 1789–1939* (London: Oxford University Press, 1962, reprinted Cambridge: Cambridge University Press, 1983); Jacob M. Landau, *The Politics of Pan-Islam: Ideology and Organization* (Oxford: Oxford University Press, 1990) and Azmi Ozcan, *Pan-Islamism: Indian Muslims, the Ottomans and Britain (1877–1924)* (Leiden, Netherlands: Brill, 1997). The account written by the American publicist and eugenicist Lothrop Stoddard, *The New World of Islam* (New York: C. Scribner's Sons, 1921), 45–97, was one of the earliest English-language accounts of the pan-Islamic movement after that of Snouck Hurgronje. Stoddard, who greatly admired ethnic Arabs and Wahabi Islam, despised other Muslims, including Shi'as, and all other races besides his own Caucasian, as indicated in his *The Rising Tide of Color against White World Supremacy* (New York: Scribner, 1920) and his *The Revolt Against Civilization: The Menace of the Underman* (New York, 1922). He also argued that twentieth-century atrocities continued those of the crusades. For a recent work on al-Afghani, see Pankaj Mishra, *From the Ruins of Empire: The Revolt Against the West and the Remaking of Asia* (London: Allen Lane, 2012).

30. Kemal H. Karpat, *The Politicization of Islam* (Oxford: Oxford University Press, 2001). The call to jihad was not common on the part of the Ottoman sultans. In 1827 the sultan had proclaimed it against unbelievers on the occasion of the battle of Navarino Bay. R. C. Anderson, *Naval Wars in the Levant 1559–1853* (Liverpool, UK: University Press, 1951), 492–93, 523–36, cited in David Abulafia, *The Great Sea: A Human History of the Mediterranean* (Oxford: Oxford University Press, 2011), 539. Further references are in the major study by Michael Cook, *Ancient Religions, Modern Politics: The Islamic Case in Comparative* Perspective (Princeton, NJ: Princeton University Press, 2014), 218–34. The target of the 1914 jihad was "the oppressive entity that bears the name 'Triple Entente' . . . whose national pride takes extreme pleasure in the subjection of thousands of Muslims." Henry Laurens notes, "Because the Ottoman Empire belonged to the Central Powers, it could not make any reference to a Christian enemy, which was in keeping both with nineteenth-century reformist thought and with the increasingly national character of the war." Laurens, in John Victor Tolan, Gilles Veinsteiner, Henry Laurens, et al., *Europe and the Islamic World: A History* (Princeton, NJ: Princeton University Press, 2013), 361.

has recently been asserted by Orlando Figes.[31] That diplomacy was greatly strained by the entry of the Ottoman Empire into World War I on the side of Germany in 1914 and the resulting Middle Eastern theater of the war, the so-called sideshow.[32] It is evident in the D-Notice (Defence Notice)—an official request not to publish something in the interest of national security—issued to the press by a section of the British Department of Information on November 15, 1917 (within two weeks of the Balfour Declaration concerning British support for a Jewish homeland) that referred to "the undesirability of publishing any article paragraph or picture suggesting that military operations against Turkey are in any sense a Holy War, a modern Crusade, or have anything whatsoever to do with religious questions."[33]

The subdued formal entry of General Edmund Allenby into Jerusalem, on December 11, 1917, wearing a field khaki uniform and on foot, was not only a rebuke to the grand entry of the Kaiser in 1898 but also perfectly consistent with the instructions of the D-Notice a month earlier. But British communications media routinely ignored the D-Notice. Crusade language in its triumphalist form had become too attractive and expected.[34] Few realized that it could also become lethal.

---

31. Orlando Figes, *The Crimean War: A History* (New York: Metropolitan Books, 2012). See also Bernard Lewis, *The Emergence of Modern Turkey* (London: Oxford University Press, 1968); Caroline Finkel, *Osman's Dream: The Story of the Ottoman Empire 1300–1923* (New York: Basic Books, 2006), 354, 488–99, 529. On the image of the Turk in the literature of crusading, see Margaret Meserve, *Empires of Islam in Renaissance Historical Thought* (Cambridge, MA: Harvard University Press, 2008); Christopher Tyerman, "Holy War, Roman Popes, and Christian Soldiers: Some Early Modern Views on Medieval Christendom," in *The Medieval Church: Universities, Heresy, and the Religious Life: Essays in Honour of Gordon Leff*, ed. Peter Biller and R. B. Dobson (Woodbridge, UK: Boydell, 1999), 293–307, with extensive bibliographical references; and Tyerman, *Debate*, 37–66, 208–11; Géraud Poumarède, *Pour en finir avec la croisade: Mythes et réalités de la lutte contre les Turcs aux XVIe et XVIIe siècles* [To Complete the Crusade: Myths and Realities in the Struggle against the Turks in the Sixteenth and Seventeenth Centuries] (Paris: Presses universitaires de France, 2004) and Nancy Bisaha, *Creating East and West: Renaissance Humanists and the Ottoman Turks* (Philadelphia: University of Pennsylvania Press, 2004), both cited in Housley, "The Crusades and Islam." The image had been formed in the course of sixteenth-century European debates about the legitimacy of war and the place of the past amid contemporary religious and political conflicts. Robert Schwoebel, *The Shadow of the Crescent: The Renaissance Image of the Turk, 1452–1517* (New York: St Martin's Press, 1967); Kenneth M. Setton, *Western Hostility to Islam and Prophecies of Turkish Doom* (Philadelphia: American Philosophical Society, 1992).

32. E.g., the ominous titles of the study by Anthony Bruce, *The Last Crusade: The Palestine Campaign in the First World War* (London: John Murray, 2002) and that of Eitan Bar-Yosef, "The Last Crusade?" above, note 24.

33. The full text appears in Bar-Yosef, "The Last Crusade?" 87. Needless to say, the press and other media paid very little attention to the D-Notice. The British army was particularly sensitive to the Islamic beliefs of many of its troops in Palestine and especially India and elsewhere in the East.

34. For example, F. H. Cooper, *Khaki Crusaders: With the South African Artillery in Egypt and Palestine* (Cape Town, South Africa: Central News Agency, 1919).

The Allied victory and the subsequent peace conferences at Versailles and elsewhere completed the dismemberment of the Ottoman Empire and also raised the questions of pan-Islamism and Arab nationalism, as well as other diplomatic issues across the Middle East.[35] Here, too, crusades came into at least rhetorical play. At one point during the peace conference at Versailles, Stephen Pichon, the French foreign minister, spoke at length and with great certainty about France's long involvement in Syria since the crusades, until Emir Feisal, the son of Sharif Hussein of the Hejaz (who had launched the Arab revolt in Arabia in June 1916), is said to have asked (through his translator, T. E. Lawrence), "Pardon me, Monsieur Pichon, but which of us won the Crusades?"[36] The subsequent creation of mandates out of former Ottoman possessions in Syria, Mesopotamia, and Palestine and the anticipation of their independence was one more factor leading to an Arab sense of identity and national aspirations.

"The Last Crusade" Celebrating the capture of Jerusalem from Ottoman forces by Field Marshal Sir Edmund Allenby on December 9, 1917, *Punch*, a British magazine of humor and satire, depicted King Richard the Lionheart gazing down on the city he had been unable to regain and declaiming "My dream comes true."

But Mandate Palestine, also known as the Holy Land, was probably the most complex of these factors, because it was not simply another part of the dismembered Ottoman Empire but an appealing and incendiary focus for Jewish, Zionist, and Arab interests. Palestine had an initially fluctuating, but increasingly large Jewish population since the Russian discriminatory laws of 1882, and it became a growing center of friction not only because of steady Jewish immigration into this Promised Land but, conversely, because of stiff British interdiction of immigration, especially after anti-Semitic events in Nazi Germany in 1933 and 1935. The increasingly violent character of conflicting local communities was also aggravated in part by the shifting and deceptive character of Anglo-French diplomacy and its inimical influence on both Jews and Arabs.[37] In November 1936, the Peel Commission even argued (unsuccessfully) for separate Arab and Jewish mandate territories in Mandate Palestine. The

35. David Fromkin, *A Peace to End All Peace: The Fall of the Ottoman Empire and the Creation of the Modern Middle East* (New York: H. Holt, 2001); James Barr, *A Line in the Sand: The Anglo-French Struggle for the Middle East, 1914–1948* (New York: W. W. Norton, 2012), especially 41–65.

36. Bhatia, *The Crusades*, 14, citing B. H. L. Hart, *Lawrence of Arabia* (London, 1989), 315. The retort is also attributed to Lawrence himself in a brief discussion with Georges Clemenceau by Arnold Toynbee, in his *Acquaintances* (Oxford: Oxford University Press, 1967), 187–88. See the discussion in Barr, *A Line in the Sand*, 65–68, and Peters, "The *Firanj* Are Coming—Again."

37. Barr, *A Line in the Sand*, 155–62; Henry Laurens in Tolan, Veinsteiner, Laurens, *Europe and the Islamic World*, 350–53, 359–83.

language of crusading then came to play a new, irregular, and more dangerous role in the peace process and later.[38]

The Crusades from the Perspectives of Arab Nationalism and Radical Pan-Islamism

The Islamicate's understanding of crusades in the late nineteenth and early twentieth centuries, approximately until the Versailles agreements, consisted chiefly of resentment against the current diplomatic and economic intrusion of Western European powers into the Mediterranean and Middle Eastern worlds. The initial wave of pan-Islamism did not possess the means to create Arab and Muslim states at the time, although it did witness the emergence of several pan-Islamic, antinational revival movements such as Salafism in India and Egypt, which preaches a fundamentalist interpretation of the Qu'ran and a literal following of the practices of the earliest Muslims.

Arab nationalism could also add to it an increasingly hostile degree of religious and cultural friction, no longer against the original local Jewish rural communities but against a larger and more politically aware Jewish presence that represented political Zionism, and by extension against the West in general. Zionism, in the context of an increasingly large Jewish immigration, mostly from Europe, inspired a number of Jewish thinkers as well as Arab opponents to regard it as yet another instance of Western colonialism, peopled largely by Eastern Europeans, and now analogous, in terms of both geography and Arab scholars' interests in the region, to the crusades as an earlier movement of the same kind.[39]

The deteriorating relations between Arabs and Jews in the midst of the collapse of the British Palestine Mandate reached a flash point with the declaration of Israeli independence in 1948. The deliberate imprecision of the Balfour Declaration of 1917[40] and subsequent reinterpretations of it by Britain as well as by Jews and Arabs had made it possible for different peoples affected by it to interpret it in different ways. Those European immigrant Zionists who urged militancy in *Eretz Israel* (the Land of

---

38. For an extreme example, see Adam Knobler, "Crusading for the Messiah: Jews as Instruments of Christian Anti-Islamic Holy War," *Tolerance and Intolerance: Social Conflict in the Age of the Crusades*, ed. in Michael Gervers and James M. Powell (Syracuse, NY: Syracuse University Press, 2001), 83–89.

39. See Corliss Slack's chapter in this book, "The Quest for Gain: Were the First Crusaders Proto-Colonists?"

40. "His Majesty's Government view with favour the establishment in Palestine of a national home for the Jewish people, and will use their best endeavours to facilitate the achievement of this object, it being clearly understood that nothing shall be done which may prejudice the civil and religious rights of existing non-Jewish communities in Palestine, or the rights and political status enjoyed by Jews in any other country," http://history1900s.about.com/cs/holocaust/p/balfourdeclare.htm (accessed May 6, 2014).

Israel) also began to use the terminology of crusade and colonialism about themselves. So did their opponents. As early as the eve of World War I some Arab political leaders had also referred to what were initially European Jewish agricultural settlements as a parallel with earlier crusader states. The policies of the Zionist movement in Israel came to be regarded by Arab and some Israeli thinkers as designs to avoid the fate of the earlier colonists—the crusaders.[41] Several different kinds of Jewish thought came to focus on Mandate Palestine variously as a Jewish religious state, a democratic Euro-pean-type state, or a socialist state, and each of these had consequences in interpreting the place of the crusades, if any, in state formation and identity.[42]

From the perspective of much of the Islamicate, the new state of Israel, located precisely in former crusader territories and peopled by European and some American Jews, had been imposed upon Mandate Palestine by European powers, which cen-turies earlier had launched crusades. In some radical Arabic thought, this was also a new colony, since it was now claimed that Jews had never lived in the area before and had originally come to Eastern Europe from Khazaria, a Central Asian khanate whose leaders converted to Judaism in the ninth century. The land was thus authentically and from the beginning only Arab land, successively invaded and polluted by hostile Western powers, first during (and in some narratives far earlier than) the crusades, and now by Zionists, the new crusaders. Hence the identification of Zionism with "crusaderism." Even contemporary Western-sponsored scholarly conferences, such as the quadrennial meetings of the Society for the Study of the Crusades and the Latin East, could be interpreted as collaborations with Zionist scholars and venues for a Zionist message.[43] The United States was first included among the new crusaders in

41. Benjamin Z. Kedar, "Il motivo della crociata nel pensiero politico israeliano" [The Crusade Motif in Israeli Political Thought] in *Verso Gerusalemme*, 135–50 (above, note 12); Sophia Menache, "Israeli Historians of the Crusades and Their Main Areas of Research, 1946–2008," *Storia della Storiografia* 53 (2008): 3–24; Baruch Kimmerling, "Academic History Caught in the Cross-Fire: The Case of Israeli-Jewish Historiography," *History and Memory* 7 (1995): 41–65, at 56; David Ohana, "Are Israelis the New Crusaders?" *Palestine-Israel Journal of Politics, Economics and Culture* 13 (2006), http://www.pij.org/details.php?id=865 (accessed May 4, 2014).

42. Michael Stanislawski, *Zionism and the Fin de Siècle: Cosmopolitanism and Nationalism from Nordau to Jabotinsky* (Berkeley: University of California Press, 2002). Jabotinsky had proclaimed Zionism as a colonizing venture, echoing the terminology of nineteenth- and early twentieth-cen-tury British and French propagandists, crusade historians, and diplomats. Yosef Gorni, *Zionism and the Arabs, 1882–1948: A Study of Ideology* (Oxford, UK: Clarendon Press, 1987).

43. Ziad J. Asali, "Zionist Studies of the Crusader Movement," *Arab Studies Quarterly* 14 (1992): 45–60. Asali, not a historian himself, points out that there were very few Middle Eastern scholars represented at the conference in Syracuse that he attended in 1990, although the society has been making a continuing effort to attract more members from the Islamic world. In his address to the scholars meeting with the SSCLE in Jerusalem in 1987, the president of Israel, Chaim Herzog, warned against facile and false analogies in which the crusader states are compared with the nation of Israel. Some attendees at the conference who identified themselves as crusade historians were

some of the polemic of the Muslim Brotherhood in Egypt during the 1950s and later in Libyan anti-American propaganda.

Various movements of Arab nationalism vigorously promoted Arab identity and cohesion, not only by writing histories in Arabic and emphasizing Arab preeminence in Islamic history but also by asserting an Arabic popular resistance to the regimes of the crusader states and the centrality of Egypt in that effort.[44] They also claimed (borrowing from a group of earlier and entirely discredited Western arguments on the subject) that Europeans had appropriated so much Arabic science and learning (and with it earlier Greek learning as well) through the crusades that the process led to the end of "feudalism" and hastened the arrival of the Renaissance and modernity as well as later forms of European domination in the Islamic world. Such assertions put history to a strenuous test, one that forces it to fail unless it becomes capable on both sides of directly addressing the full range of historical circumstances and differences between the crusading past and the recent past and avoiding both myths and ideology.[45]

Political and cultural history aside, there is yet another aspect of Islam that transcends the problems of Arabization and nationalism—that of the new, religious pan-Islamism generally designated as Salafism.[46] The guarded optimism of Sivan's account of Arab revisionist historians disappears before the utterly ahistorical assertions of such thinkers as the Pakistani Maulana Sayyid Abul-Ala Maududi (1903–1979) and his opposite number in Egypt, Sayyid Qutb (1906–1966) and their growing number of followers. Both professed a foundational Islam that recognizes no national identities and regards the past and present as a continuous conflict between pure Islam and a new Jahiliyya, an age of ignorance and barbarism (the term usually otherwise reserved in Arabic for the pre-Islamic period in Arabia). Between the two there can never be a truce because Salafism professes absolute religious certainty based upon its authentic reading of scripture and its rejection of cultural differences within a global Islamic community. This explains its appeal to groups in the Islamicate diaspora,

---

given probing interviews by Israeli security, either departing for or leaving Israel, being asked such questions as, "Why did you become a crusade historian?"

44. Sivan, "Modern Arab Historiography," *Interpretations*, 3–43. Unfortunately, the perceptive and wide-ranging survey by Michael Brett, "Islamic Historiography of the Crusades, 1951–2001," a paper presented at the Third International Conference: Half a Century of Studies on Crusades and Military Orders, 1951–2001, Teruel, Spain, 19–25 July, 2001, has not been published.

45. Emmanuel Sivan, "Arab Revisionist Historians" in *Interpretations*, 45–72. One solution may be a new Western focus on the Muslim world. The publishing house of Brill has announced a series edited by Suleiman A. Mourad, Paul M. Cobb, and Konrad Hirschler, *The Muslim World in the Age of the Crusades: Studies and Texts*. Forthcoming in that new series is Alex Mallett, ed., *Muslim Historians of the Crusades*, http://www.brill.com/publications/muslim-world-age-crusades.

46. Roel Meijer, ed., *Global Salafism: Islam's New Religious Movement* (New York: Columbia University Press, 2009) and Sivan, *Radical Islam*, 84–107; Antony Black, *The History of Islamic Political Thought from the Prophet to the Present* (New York: Routledge, 2001), 154–59, 219–315.

from Europe to Indonesia, and its characterizations of its opponents as barbarians and crusaders, as occurred in the outburst in the Jakarta courtroom mentioned at the beginning of this essay.

The Crusades Today in Islamic Scholarship

As a number of historians have pointed out, the range of thought in the Islamicate is far broader than both formulaic Arabic nationalist history and Salafism. Liberal Westernizers, residual Marxists, secular nationalists, and professional scholars, some trained in the West, all conceive the past in different ways. Arab students who have studied in the West often return home with the experience of direct access to modern scholarship and can find much of it translated into Arabic at home. There remains, indeed, sufficient room among these groups for nonpolemical history to be done. But the circumstances and facilities for historical research in the Islamicate are usually very different from those in the various parts of the West.

Abbès Zouache has pointed out the extent to which political authority in Middle Eastern states constitutes a formidable presence in history education and research, since it controls the means of support for them, especially funds for research and translation.[47] The location of the study of crusade history is often not in history departments but in faculties of classical Arabic literature and education. Few Muslim historians are actually experts on the subject, and there is often very little communication among them concerning it. Smaller and remote universities often lack the library resources of the great universities like Damascus, Yarmuk (Jordan), Cairo, 'Ain Sams, Alexandria, and d'az-Zaqaziq and often rely on considerably dated Western scholarship, even though Arabic translations of both original Latin sources and more recent Western scholarship regularly appear but often do not seem to circulate beyond the private libraries of a few scholars.[48] Nor is much recent historiography in Arabic (or Turkish or Farsi) translated into Western languages. Much of this holds true for current scholarship on the subject in Turkey, Iran, and the rest of the Islamic world. Any idea of a common historical approach should begin with mutual access to common scholarship.

---

47. Zouache, "Écrire l'histoire des croisades," 121–26.

48. Zouache cites as examples the very frequent use of the 1907 history by William Stevenson and the work of Steven Runciman, René Grousset, and others. One of the authors of this essay was recently asked to provide some biographical information on the career of John La Monte because an Arabic translation of his *Feudal Monarchy in the Latin Kingdom of Jerusalem* (Cambridge, MA: Medieval Academy of America, 1932) was forthcoming from Cairo. A translation of La Monte's work into Arabic for archival purposes is perfectly understandable, but the research and main theses of the book are no longer part of the working scholarship in the West, although a number of La Monte's articles remain useful.

In conclusion, it is also necessary to agree on a working definition of the crusades. Most Muslim historians residing in the Islamic world write on the crusades in Arabic and deal exclusively with the area of the Holy Land crusades, present-day Egypt, Israel, the Palestinian Authority, Syria, Jordan, Lebanon, and Turkey. That is, they focus on their own local crusade history, very much in the line of Hans Eberhard Mayer's "traditionalist" definition of crusade, military expeditions aimed at liberating Jerusalem and preserving it in Christian hands.[49] Other competing definitions, notably the "pluralist" definition associated with Jonathan Riley-Smith and others that sees crusades as all military expeditions charged by the popes with the defense of Christendom and the Church from internal or external enemies, are generally not considered, thus increasing the distance between Western and Islamic approaches to crusade history.[50]

Crusades are a part, but only a part, of the larger history of the Mediterranean world, a history that is not solely one of religious or military conflict but of contacts and exchanges of many kinds. A Mediterranean perspective may prove more useful for scholarship (and ultimately for political and common opinion) than an exclusive and narrow focus on cultural pride and despair, aggression and retaliation, intractable religious differences, imaginary clashes of civilizations, and the unresolvable claims of memory in both the West and the Islamic world.[51]

---

49. Described in the work of Tyerman, *Debate,* and Constable, "Historiography of the Crusades," and wisely discussed in Zouache, "Écrire l'histoire," 141–44.

50. See the Introduction to this book for a discussion of the differing academic definitions of crusading among largely Western crusade specialists.

51. As in the work of Olivia Remie Constable, *Trade and Traders in Muslim Spain: The Commercial Realignment of the Iberian Peninsula, 900–1500* (Cambridge: Cambridge University Press, 1994); *Housing the Stranger in the Mediterranean World: Lodging, Trade, and Travel in Late Antiquity and the Middle Ages* (Cambridge: Cambridge University Press, 2004); and that of Jessica L. Goldberg, *Trade and Institutions in the Medieval Mediterranean: The Geniza Merchants and Their Business World* (Cambridge: Cambridge University Press, 2012).

Epilogue: Putting It All Together

Historical research is fraught with difficulties and pitfalls, and every historian realizes that one must proceed not only with caution but with a humility based on an understanding of the limitations of the evidence. Despite all of this, the historian carries on in an attempt to reconstruct the past in a manner that makes it understandable and relevant to contemporary society but also in a manner that is as true to reality as is possible. Given this twofold mission, the historian must not bend or distort the past in order to provide apparent support for an ideology, theory, or preconception of "how it must have been."

More subtle than willful distortion or selective mining of evidence to "prove" a predetermined conclusion is the temptation to oversimplify complex human realities, to see the past in black and white, to fill the story with stereotypes, and to draw facile lessons or analogies. Put another way, there is the almost universal human tendency to reduce past events to easily digestible bullet points that neatly sum up causation and effect and lay out in a one-two-three sequence the essential qualities of a historical phenomenon or actor. History that is neatly tied up can be seductively satisfying, but it does scant justice to the complexities of the past.

The historians who have contributed to this book understand that they probably do not have the last word on the issues on which they have written, but they also know, with no less humility, that they have presented nuanced studies that draw upon not only their own talents, expertise, and understanding of our medieval past but also the labors and publications of an international body of colleagues, all of whom specialize in crusade studies. As in all areas of human inquiry, collegial communication and dialogue drive further and deeper insight. As noted in our Preface, such interchange also allows historians to winnow out historical judgments that are poorly researched, insufficiently thought out, exaggerated to the point of gross hyperbole, one dimensional, or just plain wrong. In other words, it allows us to separate solid historical work from mythic history.

"Solid historical work," namely the sum of the inferences and interpretations painstakingly drawn by historians, is never static or monolithic. Careful readers of the chapters by James M. Muldoon and Daniel P. Franke will see that there are differences between their respective interpretations of the influence of apocalyptic hopes and fears in the unfolding of the First Crusade. Yet both of their positions are based on careful readings of the evidence and their differences are largely due to their perspectives and the questions they are addressing. Each, in other words, presents us a view of the past based on research conducted along lines of inquiry that accord with the highest professional standards.

This is not to say that history is or should be the exclusive property of the specialists—the trained experts. History is too important to human society and to each of us as involved members of a civil society to simply leave it to the experts. Rather, it is incumbent upon the experts to present a well-researched view of that past that is not only nuanced but coherent and compelling to read, listen to, or see in video format. History that is not clearly presented is poor history, no matter how well researched it might be. It is equally incumbent upon non-specialists to seek out such history and to gain from it a deeper knowledge of the rich varieties of the human experience, thereby understanding more fully who we are as members not just of a specific culture but of the human species. We hope that in taking on the seven myths that are examined in these pages we have lived up to our part of this double duty.

SUGGESTED READING

Several criteria guided our compilation of this list. First, we have, with but few exceptions, included only books that were published within the past thirty years or so. Newer is not always better, but scholarship tends to build on the breakthroughs and insights of the past. Although crusade historians represent many nationalities and publish in a variety of languages, we have directed our little book at a general Anglophone audience and decided that it is best to keep this bibliography fairly short and to limit it to works that are accessible to our intended audience, namely books in English, all of which can be found in libraries, bookstores, and the online sites of vendors.

Likewise, although a large percentage of cutting-edge crusade scholarship initially appears in journal article form, most of these journals are not readily available to our readers. Those who desire more specialized studies of the various issues raised throughout this book should consult the copious, often detailed notes that accompany the Introduction and each chapter. Readers will also notice that we have not included any of the many translated primary sources that are now available, even though several of the contributors to this book are active editors and translators of crusade sources.

The fuller bibliographies supplied in many of the books included here contain lists of such sources, including important sources translated from Arabic and other Eastern Mediterranean languages that have been appearing in ever-increasing numbers. Finally, readers will note that some of the categories that appear here are fuller than others. This in no way indicates relative merit or importance; it is simply a function of the criteria that guide this catalog of suggested readings.

Reference Works

Andrea, Alfred J. *Encyclopedia of the Crusades*. Westport, CT: Greenwood Press, 2003.
Lock, Peter, *The Routledge Companion to the Crusades*. London: Routledge, 2006.
Murray, Alan V., ed. *The Crusades: An Encyclopedia*. 4 vols. Santa Barbara, CA: ABC-CLIO, 2006.
Riley-Smith, Jonathan, ed. *The Atlas of the Crusades*. New York: Facts on File, 1991.

General Crusade Histories

Catlos, Brian A. *Infidel Kings and Unholy Warriors: Faith, Power, and Violence in the Age of Crusade and Jihad*. New York: Farrar, Straus, and Giroux, 2014.
France, John. *The Crusades and the Expansion of Catholic Christendom, 1000–1714*. London: Routledge, 2005.

Jaspert, Nikolas. *The Crusades*. Translated by Phyllis Jestice. Abingdon, UK: Routledge, 2006.

Jotischky, Andrew. *Crusading and the Crusader States*. Harlow, UK: Longman, 2004.

Madden, Thomas F. *The Concise History of the Crusades*. 3rd student ed. Lanham, MD: Rowman and Littlefield, 2013.

————. ed. *Crusades: The Illustrated History*. London: Duncan Baird, 2004.

Mayer, H. E. *The Crusades*. 2nd ed. Translated by John Gillingham. Oxford: Oxford University Press, 1988.

Phillips, Jonathan. *The Crusades, 1095–1197*. London: Pearson, 2002.

Richard, Jean. *The Crusades, c. 1071–c. 1291*. Translated by Jean Birrell. Cambridge, UK: Cambridge University Press, 1999.

Riley-Smith, Jonathan. *The Crusades: A History*. 3rd ed. London: Bloomsbury, 2014.

————, ed. *The Oxford Illustrated History of the Crusades*. Oxford: Oxford University Press, 1995.

Setton, Kenneth M. et al., ed. *A History of the Crusades*. 2nd ed. 6 vols. Madison: University of Wisconsin Press, 1969–1989.

Tyerman, Christopher. *God's War: A New History of the Crusades*. Cambridge, MA: Belknap Press, 2006.

————. *The Crusades: A Very Short Introduction*. Oxford: Oxford University Press, 2004.

The First Crusade

Asbridge, Thomas. *The First Crusade: A New History; The Roots of Conflict between Christianity and Islam*. Oxford: Oxford University Press, 2005.

Edgington, Susan B. and Luis García-Guijarro, eds. *Jerusalem the Golden: The Origins and Impact of the First Crusade*. Turnhout, Belgium: Brepols, 2014.

France, John. *Victory in the East: A Military History of the First Crusade*. Cambridge: Cambridge University Press, 1994.

Frankopan, Peter. *The First Crusade: The Call from the East*. Cambridge, MA: Belknap Press, 2012.

See also Crusaders and Crusader Motivations

Twelfth-Century Crusades to the East

Constable, Giles. *Crusaders and Crusading in the Twelfth Century*. Farnham, UK: Ashgate, 2008.

Gervers, Michael, ed. *The Second Crusade and the Cistercians*. New York: St. Martin's, 1992.

Gillingham, John. *Richard I*. New Haven, CT: Yale University Press, 1999.

Hamilton, Bernard. *The Leper King and His Heirs: Baldwin IV and the Crusader Kingdom of Jerusalem*. Cambridge: Cambridge University Press, 2000.

Nicholson, Helen and David Nicolle. *God's Warriors: Crusaders, Saracens and the Battle for Jerusalem*. Oxford: Osprey, 2005.

Phillips, Jonathan. *The Second Crusade: Extending the Frontiers of Christendom.* New Haven, CT: Yale University Press, 2007.

Phillips, Jonathan and Martin Hoch, eds. *The Second Crusade: Scope and Consequences.* Manchester: Manchester University Press, 2001.

Thirteenth-Century Crusades to the East: 1202–1274

Angold, Michael. *The Fourth Crusade: Event and Context.* Harlow, UK: Longman, 2003.

Gaposchkin, Cecilia. *The Making of Saint Louis: Kingship, Sanctity, and Crusade in the Later Middle Ages.* Ithaca, NY: Cornell University Press, 2008.

Jordan, William Chester. *Louis IX and the Challenge of the Crusade: A Study in Rulership.* Princeton, NJ: Princeton University Press, 1979.

Laiou, Angeliki, ed. *Urbs Capta: The Fourth Crusade and Its Consequences.* Paris: Lethielleux, 2005.

Lower, Michael. *The Barons' Crusade: A Call to Arms and Its Consequences.* Middle Ages Series. Philadelphia: University of Pennsylvania Press, 2005.

Marshall, Christopher J. *Warfare in the Latin East 1192–1291.* Cambridge, UK: Cambridge University Press, 1992.

Perry, David M. *Sacred Plunder: Venice and the Aftermath of the Fourth Crusade.* University Park, PA: The Pennsylvania State University Press, 2015.

Phillips, Jonathan. *The Fourth Crusade and the Sack of Constantinople.* New York: Viking, 2004.

Powell, James M. *Anatomy of a Crusade, 1213–1221.* Philadelphia: University of Pennsylvania, 1986.

Queller, Donald E. and Thomas F. Madden. *The Fourth Crusade: The Conquest of Constantinople.* 2nd ed. Philadelphia: University of Pennsylvania Press, 1997.

Siberry, Elizabeth. *Criticism of Crusading, 1095–1274.* Oxford: Clarendon Press, 1985.

Smith, Caroline. *Crusading in the Age of Joinville.* Aldershot, UK: Ashgate, 2006.

Later Crusades to the East and Beyond

Housley, Norman. *The Avignon Papacy and the Crusades, 1305–1378.* Oxford: Oxford University Press, 1986.

——————. *The Later Crusades, 1274–1580: From Lyons to Alcazar.* Oxford: Oxford University Press, 1992.

Schein, Sylvia. *Fideles Crucis: The Papacy, the West, and the Recovery of the Holy Land, 1274–1314.* Oxford: Clarendon, 1991.

The Iberian and Baltic Crusades

Bysted, Ane, Carsten Selch Jensen, Kurt Villads Jensen, and John H. Lind. *Jerusalem in the North: Denmark and the Baltic Crusades, 1100–1522.* Turnhout, Belgium: Brepols, 2012.

Catlos, Brian, A. *The Victors and the Vanquished: Christians and Muslims of Catalonia and Aragon, 1050–1300.* Cambridge: Cambridge University Press, 2004.

Christiansen, Eric. *The Northern Crusades: The Baltic and the Catholic Frontier, 1100–1525.* Minneapolis: University of Minnesota Press, 1980.

Fletcher, Richard A. *The Quest for El Cid.* New York: Knopf, 1990.

Fonnesberg-Schmidt, Iben. *The Popes and the Baltic Crusades, 1147–1254.* Leiden, The Netherlands: Brill, 2007.

Murray, Alan V., ed. *The Clash of Cultures on the Medieval Baltic Frontier.* Farnham, UK: Ashgate, 2009.

Murray, Alan V., ed. *Crusade and Conversion on the Baltic Frontier: 1150–1500.* Aldershot, UK: Ashgate, 2001.

O'Callaghan, Joseph F. *The Gibraltar Crusade: Castile and the Battle for the Strait.* Pennsylvania: University of Pennsylvania Press, 2011.

—————. *The Last Crusade in the West: Castile and the Conquest of Granada.* Philadelphia: University of Pennsylvania Press, 2014.

—————. *Reconquest and Crusade in Medieval Spain.* Philadelphia: University of Pennsylvania Press, 2003.

Urban, William L. *The Baltic Crusade.* 2nd ed. Chicago: Lithuanian Research and Studies Center, 1994.

—————. *The Teutonic Knights: A Military History.* London: Greenhill Books, 2003.

Crusades at Home against Heretics and Political Enemies of the Papacy

Barber, Malcolm. *The Cathars: Dualist Heretics in Languedoc in the High Middle Ages.* Harlow, UK: Pearson Education, 2000.

Housley, Norman. *The Italian Crusades: The Papal-Angevin Alliance and the Crusades against Christian Lay Powers, 1254–1343.* Oxford: Clarendon, 1982.

—————. *Religious Warfare in Europe, 1400–1536.* Oxford: Oxford University Press, 2002.

Kienzle, Beverly Mayne. *Cistercians, Heresy, and Crusade in Occitania, 1145–1229: Preaching in the Lord's Vineyard.* Rochester, NY: York Medieval Press, 2001.

Marvin, Laurence W. *The Occitan War: A Military and Political History of the Albigensian Crusade, 1209–1218.* Cambridge: Cambridge University Press, 2008.

Pegg, Mark Gregory. *A Most Holy War: The Albigensian Crusade and the Battle for Christendom.* Oxford: Oxford University Press, 2008.

Rist, Rebecca. *The Papacy and Crusading in Europe, 1198–1245.* London: Continuum, 2009.

Crusaders and Crusader Motivations

Bachrach, David Stewart. *Religion and the Conduct of War c. 300–c. 1215.* Woodbridge, UK: Boydell, 2003.

Bull, Marcus. *Knightly Piety and the Lay Response to the First Crusade: The Limousin and Gascony, c. 970–c. 1130.* Oxford: Clarendon Press, 1993.

Constable, Giles. *Crusaders and Crusading in the Twelfth Century.* Burlington, VT: Ashgate, 2008.

Erdmann, Carl. *The Origin of the Idea of Crusade.* Translated by Marshall W. Baldwin and Walter Goffart. Princeton, NJ: Princeton University Press, 1977.

Housley, Norman. *The Crusaders.* Charleston, SC: Tempus, 2002.

——————. *Fighting for the Cross: Crusading to the Holy Land.* New Haven, CT: Yale University Press, 2008.

Kostick, Conor. *The Social Structure of the First Crusade.* Leiden, The Netherlands: Brill, 2008.

Paul, Nicholas. *To Follow in Their Footsteps: The Crusades and Family Memory in the High Middle Ages.* Ithaca, NY: Cornell University Press, 2012.

Phillips, Jonathan P. *Holy Warriors: A Modern History of the Crusades.* London: Bodley Head, 2009.

Prawer, Joshua. *The World of the Crusaders.* New York: Quadrangle Books, 1972.

Purkis, William J. *Crusading Spirituality in the Holy Land and Iberia, c. 1095–c. 1187.* Woodbridge, UK: Boydell Press, 2008.

Riley-Smith, Jonathan. *The First Crusaders, 1095–1131.* Cambridge: Cambridge University Press, 1997.

——————. *The First Crusade and the Idea of Crusading.* 2d ed. London: Continuum, 2009.

Rubenstein, Jay. *Armies of Heaven: The First Crusade and the Quest for Apocalypse.* New York: Basic Books, 2011.

Throop, Susanna. *Crusading as an Act of Vengeance, 1095–1216.* Farnham, UK: Ashgate, 2011.

Muslims, Eastern Christians, Mongols, and the Crusades

Bonner, Michael. *Jihad in Islamic History: Doctrines and Practice.* Princeton, NJ: Princeton University Press, 2006.

Catlos, Brian A. *Muslims of Medieval Christendom, c. 1050–1614.* Cambridge: Cambridge University Press, 2014.

Christie, Niall. *Muslims and Crusaders: Christianity's Wars in the Middle East, 1095–1382, from the Islamic Sources.* London: Routledge, 2014.

Cobb, Paul M. *The Race for Paradise: An Islamic History of the Crusades.* Oxford: Oxford University Press, 2014.

Ghazarian, Jacob G. *The Armenian Kingdom in Cilicia during the Crusades.* Surrey, UK: Curzon Press, 2000.

Harris, Jonathan. *Byzantium and the Crusades.* London: Hambledon and London, 2003.

Hillenbrand, Carole. *The Crusades: Islamic Perspectives.* New York: Routledge, 1999.

Holt, Peter M. *The Age of the Crusades: The Near East from the Eleventh Century to 1517.* London: Longman, 1986.

Jackson, Peter. *The Mongols and the West: 1221–1410.* New York: Longman, 2005.

Laiou, Angeliki E., and Roy Parviz Mottahedeh, eds. *The Crusades from the Perspective of Byzantium and the Muslim World*. Washington, DC: Dumbarton Oaks Research Library, 2001.

Maalouf, Amin. *The Crusades through Arab Eyes*. New York: Schocken, 1984.

MacEvitt, Christopher H. *The Crusades and the Christian World of the East: Rough Tolerance*. Philadelphia: University of Pennsylvania Press, 2008.

Mallett, Alex. *Popular Muslim Reactions to the Franks in the Levant, 1097–1291*. Burlington, VT: Ashgate, 2008.

Nicolle, David. *Crusader Warfare*. Vol. I: *Byzantium, Western Europe and the Battle for the Holy Land, 1050–1300 AD*. London: Hambledon Continuum, 2007.

—————. *Crusader Warfare*. Vol. II: *Muslims, Mongols and the Struggle against the Crusades*. London: Hambledon Continuum, 2007.

Smail, R. C. *Crusading Warfare 1097–1193*. 2nd ed. Updated by Christopher J. Marshall. Cambridge: Cambridge University Press, 1995.

Tolan, John V. *Saracens: Islam in the Medieval Imagination*. New York: Columbia University Press, 2002.

Jews, Anti-Judaism, and the Crusades

Abulafia, Anna Saphir. *Christians and Jews in the Twelfth-Century Renaissance*. London: Routledge, 1995.

Berger, David. *Persecution, Polemic, and Dialog: Essays in Jewish-Christian Relations*. Boston: Academic Studies Press, 2010.

Chazan, Robert. *In the Year 1096: The First Crusade and the Jews*. Philadelphia: Jewish Publication Society, 1996.

—————. *The Jews of Medieval Western Christendom 1000–1500*. Cambridge Medieval Textbooks. Cambridge: Cambridge University Press, 2006.

Cohen, Jeremy. *Sanctifying the Name of God: Jewish Martyrs and Jewish Memories of the First Crusade*. Philadelphia: University of Pennsylvania Press, 2004.

Glick, Leonard B. *Abraham's Heirs: Jews and Christians in Medieval Europe*. Syracuse, NY: Syracuse University Press, 1999.

Rubin, Miri. *Gentile Tales: The Narrative Assault on Late Medieval Jews*. Philadelphia: University of Pennsylvania Press, 2004.

Utterback, Kristine T. and Merrall Llewelyn Price, eds. *Jews in Medieval Christendom: "Slay Them Not."* Leiden: Brill, 2013.

Yuval, Israel Jacob. *Two Nations in Your Womb: Perceptions of Jews and Christians in Late Antiquity and the Middle Ages*. Berkeley: University of California Press, 2006.

Children's Crusade

Dickson, Gary. *The Children's Crusade: Medieval History, Modern Mythistory*. New York: Palgrave Macmillan, 2008.

MacLehose, William. *A Tender Age: Cultural Anxieties over the Child in the Twelfth and Thirteenth Centuries*. New York: Columbia University Press, 2008.

Templars and Freemasons

Barber, Malcolm, *The New Knighthood: A History of the Order of the Temple*. Cambridge: Cambridge University Press, 1994.
——————. *The Trial of the Templars*. Cambridge: Cambridge University Press, 1978.
Baudin, Arnaud, Ghislain Brunel, Nicolas Dohrmann, Archives départementales de l'Aube, and Archives nationales. *The Knights Templar: From the Days of Jerusalem to the Commanderies of Champagne*. Paris: Somogy, 2012.
Crawford, Paul, Jochen Bergtorf, and Helen Nicholson, eds. *The Debate on the Trial of the Templars*. Aldershot, UK: Ashgate Press, 2010.
Martin, Sean. *The Knights Templar: The Histories and Myths of the Legendary Order*. New York: Avalon Publishing, 2004.
Nicholson, Helen. *A Brief History of the Knights Templar*. London: Running Press, 2010.
——————. *The Knights Templar: A New History*. Stroud, UK: History Press, 2001.
Partner, Peter, *The Knights Templar and Their Myth*. Rochester, VT: Destiny Books, 1990.
Riley-Smith, Jonathan. *Templars and Hospitallers as Professed Religious in the Holy Land*. Notre Dame, IN: Notre Dame University Press, 2010.
Roberts, J. M. *The Mythology of Secret Societies*. London: Watkins Publishing, 2008.

Modern Memories and Interpretations of the Crusades

Achcar, Gilbert. *The Arabs and the Holocaust: The Arab-Israeli War of Narratives*. New York: Metropolitan Books, 2010.
Bar-Yosef, Eitan. *The Holy Land in English Culture, 1799–1917: Palestine and the Question of Orientalism*. Oxford: Oxford University Press, 2005.
Housley, Norman. *Contesting the Crusades*. Oxford, UK: Blackwell, 2006.
Irwin, Robert. *Dangerous Knowledge: Orientalism and Its Discontents*. Woodstock, NY: Overlook Press, 2006.
Lassner, Jacob. *Jews, Christians, and the Abode of Islam: Modern Scholarship and Medieval Realities*. Chicago: University of Chicago Press, 2012.
Nicholson, Helen, ed. *Palgrave Advances in the Crusades*. Basingstoke, UK: Palgrave Macmillan, 2005.
Riley-Smith, Jonathan. *The Crusades, Christianity and Islam*. New York: Columbia University Press, 2008.
——————. *What Were the Crusades?* 3rd ed. San Francisco: Ignatius Press, 2002.
Siberry, Elizabeth. *The New Crusaders. Images of the Crusades in the Nineteenth and Early Twentieth Centuries*. Aldershot, UK: Ashgate, 2000.
Sivan, Emmanuel. *Interpretations of Islam, Past and Present*. Princeton, NJ: Darwin Press, 1985.
Tyerman, Christopher. *The Debate on the Crusades*. Manchester: Manchester University Press, 2011.
——————. *Fighting for Christendom: Holy War and the Crusades*. Oxford: Oxford University Press, 2004.

CONTRIBUTOR BIOGRAPHIES

Alfred J. Andrea, emeritus professor of medieval history, the University of Vermont, has published extensively on the sources for the Fourth Crusade and on papal-Byzantine relations in the Age of the Crusades. He is currently exploring the manner in which crusading ideology drove Portuguese and Spanish actions in the Indian Ocean and the Americas during the sixteenth century. In 2014, the World History Association named him a "Pioneer of World History."

Paul F. Crawford, associate professor of medieval history at California University of Pennsylvania, is a specialist in the crusades and the military-religious orders. He has translated the fourteenth-century chronicle known as "The Templar of Tyre," co-edited a volume of essays re-evaluating the trial of the Templars, and published on the Templars and Hospitalers. He is currently working with a team of scholars to produce a biographical volume dealing with Renaud of Châtillon.

Daniel P. Franke, has served as an assistant professor of history at the United States Military Academy at West Point and specializes in military and crusades history, particularly in England and Germany from the tenth to the fourteenth centuries. He is currently studying Frederick Barbarossa's campaign in the Third Crusade.

Mona Hammad, associate professor of medieval history at the University of Jordan, has taught in several American institutions. Most of her published works are about the perceptions of the crusades among Muslims and Latin Christians. Currently, she is working on the Arab popular and academic images of the crusades and chronicling Arabic historiography on the crusades.

Andrew Holt, associate professor of history at Florida State College at Jacksonville, is the co-editor of *Competing Voices from the Crusades* (2008) and the former editor of the crusades section of the Oxford Bibliographies Online project. He is currently co-editing a three-volume encyclopedia covering pivotal events in religious history for ABC-Clio as well as developing a monograph titled *Knights, Crusaders, and Templars: Warrior Masculinity in the Era of the First Crusade*.

James M. Muldoon, a medieval legal and ecclesiastical historian, is a graduate of Iona College (1957), obtained an M.A. at Boston College (1959), and obtained a Ph.D. at Cornell University (1965). He taught at St. Michael's College in Vermont (1965–1970) and at Rutgers University (1970–1998). He is now professor emeritus at Rutgers and an invited research scholar at the John Carter Brown Library. He has written or edited a number of books and articles dealing with the interaction of Christians and non-Christians on the frontiers of Europe.

Edward Peters, Henry Charles Lea Professor Emeritus of History at the University of Pennsylvania, has taught crusade history and published several volumes of annotated crusade sources in English translation. He has also reviewed crusade scholarship in several languages and for twenty-five years edited a series of books at the University of Pennsylvania Press that focused frequently on crusade history.

David L. Sheffler, associate professor of medieval history, the University of North Florida, regularly teaches courses on the history of the crusades. He has published primarily on medieval education and is currently working on a project in which he examines the intellectual and educational networks of the early fifteenth-century Augustinian hermit Berthold Puchhauser.

Corliss Slack, chair of the history department at Whitworth University in Spokane, Washington, is the author of the *Historical Dictionary of the Crusades* (2nd ed., Scarecrow Press, 2013) and an earlier book on charters produced by crusaders as they left for the battlefield. She is currently charting the memorials created by returning crusaders, who often donated relics acquired in the Holy Land to home churches in Europe.

Jace Stuckey, assistant professor of history at Marymount University in Arlington, Virginia, has presented and published work on the crusades and on the history and memory of the legend of Charlemagne. He is currently working on a monograph on the legend of Charlemagne in the High and Later Middle Ages.

crusades, chroniclers of the, xxv, xxviii, xxxii
  n84, xxxiv, lxxvii, 6 n55, 32, 34n27, 35,
  36, 38 n38, 39, 40, 44, 46, 47 n73, 53–61
  passim, 63, 66, 74, 78, 79, 81–85, 89,
  93–94, 100–105
crusades, contemporary criticism of, xxv, xxxi, 45
crusades, numbering of the, xv–xvi.
crusades, organization and financing of, 37–43
  passim, 46, 55, 108. *See also* charters of
  crusaders.
crusades, other myths of the, xv–xvi, xix–xxxv,
  70, 87
crusades, papal authorization of, xiv, xvii, xviii,
  81–84, 85, 99, 149. *See also* Gregory VII;
  Innocent III; Urban II.
Crusades of Louis IX (1248–1254 and 1270).
  See Louis IX.
Crusades, Shepherds' (1251 and 1320), xviii,
  65, 100 n35, 104
crusades, views and memories of, Muslim, xii,
  xxxvi, 90, 127–28, 133–35, 138–149
crusades, views and memories of, Western, xii,
  129–32, 135–38, 141
crusades as colonial enterprises, 3, 42, 70–90,
  131, 137–38, 145–47. *See also* crusader
  states of the Latin East.

DaVinci Code, The, 123, 124
Derschowitz, Alan M., 31, 48, 50, 66, 68
dhimmis, 7–9, 17
Dickson, Gary, xviii n30, 92, 98, 99–100, 101,
  102, 104
Doré, Gustave, xxi, 94
Duby, Georges, 87

Edward I, King, xv–xvi, 64
Ellenblum, Ronnie, 77–78
Emicho of Flonheim, 53–54, 60
Enlightenment, the, xi, xx, 12, 131, 135
Erdmann, Carl, xviii n31
Esposito, John, 1, 28, 127

Fatimids, 17, 19, 20, 76
France, John, xxvi, 37–38, 45–46
France, the French, and the crusades, xx–xxi,
  28, 40, 83, 84, 136–37. *See also* Louis IX;
  Michaud, Joseph François; Normans.
Frederick II, Emperor, xv, 66
Freemasons, xxxvi, 109, 112–26

Gassicourt, Louis Cadet de, 120, 122
genocide, xxiv, xxxiii–xxxv, 50, 51, 68
Gibbon, Edward, xx, xxi, xxiv, 32, 33, 140
Gillingham, John, 51
Godfrey of Bouillon, Duke, xxxv, 3, 42,
  54–55, 56, 60, 136 n19
Gray, George Zabriskie, 95–97
Gregory VII, Pope, 4, 18–19, 36, 37, 39, 57,
  73, 79

Al-Hariri, Sayyid Ali, 140–41
Hay, David, 57
Hillenbrand, Carole, xxvii–xxviii, 7, 8
Holy Sepulcher, Church of the, 11, 17, 55, 56,
  67, 75, 76, 77, 116
Hospitalers, Order of, xxvii, 110, 116, 117, 119
Housley, Norman, xvi–xvii, xxvi, 99
Hund, Karl Gotthelf von, 117–18

indulgence, crusade, xiv, 26 n99, 40–41,
  82–85 passim, 88
Innocent III, Pope, xiii, xx n71, 41, 62, 94,
  96, 99
Italy and Italian islands, Muslim attacks on,
  20–24. *See also* Sicily.

Jerusalem, goal of the crusades, xii, xv, xvii, xix
  n32, 2, 4, 16, 17, 34–37, 42, 60, 73, 78,
  80, 81, 83, 85, 89, 91, 93, 100, 105, 149.
  See also crusade goals/crusading motives.
Jerusalem, holy sites of, 10–11, 75, 83. *See also*
  Holy Sepulcher, Church of the; Jerusalem,
  goal of the crusades.
Jews, attacks on and massacres of, xviii, xxvi,
  xxviii n62, xxxiii, xxxvi, 2 n6, 5, 42, 48–69
  passim, 91. *See also* anti-Judaism/anti-Semitism;
  genocide.
Jews and Islam, 5, 7, 17, 28. *See also* dhimmis.
jihad, xxvii–viii, 5 n15, 6–7, 21, 90, 134 n14,
  142
Jones, Terry, xxiii, xxiv–xxx, xxxv, 47 n73,
  70–72 passim, 88
Jordan, William Chester, 87

Kedar, Benjamin, xxvi
Kingdom of Heaven, xxii, xxiii, xxix, 71–72, 89
knighthood and chivalry, xxvi, xxxii, 38, 46,
  82–84 passim, 86, 88, 112, 115, 116, 117,
  119, 121